THE OPTIMUM POPULATION
FOR
BRITAIN

SYMPOSIA OF THE INSTITUTE OF BIOLOGY No. 19

THE OPTIMUM POPULATION
FOR
BRITAIN

(Proceedings of a Symposium held at the Royal Geographical Society, London, on 25 and 26 September, 1969)

Edited by

L. R. TAYLOR

Rothamsted Experimental Station
Harpenden, Hertfordshire
England

1970

Published for the
INSTITUTE OF BIOLOGY
by
ACADEMIC PRESS
LONDON and NEW YORK

ACADEMIC PRESS INC. (LONDON) LTD.
Berkeley Square House
Berkeley Square
London W1X 6BA

U.S. Edition published by
ACADEMIC PRESS INC.
111 Fifth Avenue
New York, New York 10003

Library of Congress Catalog Card Number: 79-109029
Standard Book Number: 12-684250-7

Printed in Great Britain by
The Whitefriars Press Ltd., London and Tonbridge

Contributors

Session No. 1: CHAIRMAN SIR FREDERICK C. BAWDEN, F.R.S.

MISS JEAN H. THOMPSON   *Chief Statistician, General Register Office, London, England*

DR. G. W. COOKE, F.R.S.   *Deputy Director, Rothamsted Experimental Station, Harpenden, England*

DR. KENNETH MELLANBY   *Director, Monks Wood Experimental Station, Abbots Ripton, England*

Session No. 2: CHAIRMAN MR. R. E. BOOTE

SIR ALAN S. PARKES, F.R.S.   *The Galton Foundation, London, England (Formerly Mary Marshall Professor of Reproductive Physiology at Cambridge)*

MR. GEOFFREY P. HAWTHORN   *Lecturer in Sociology, University of Essex, England*

MR. A. JOHN BOREHAM   *Head of Economic and Statistical Analysis Division, Ministry of Technology, London, England*

Session No. 3: CHAIRMAN PROFESSOR V. C. WYNNE-EDWARDS

DR. T. R. E. SOUTHWOOD   *Professor of Zoology, Imperial College, London, England*

DR. D. E. C. EVERSLEY   *Professor of Population Studies, Sussex University, and Chief Planner (Strategy), Greater London Council, England*

RT. HON. A. L. N. DOUGLAS HOUGHTON, C.H.   *Member of Parliament for Sowerby Division, House of Commons, London, England*

Session No. 4: CHAIRMAN SIR DAVID RENTON, Q.C., M.P.

MRS. MADELEINE SIMMS   *Abortion Law Reform Association, 17 Dunstant Road, London N.W.11, England*

LADY JEAN MEDAWAR   *Family Planning Association, Margaret Pyke House, 24-35 Mortimer Street, London W.1, England*

DR. MILTON M. R. FREEMAN   *Assistant Professor in Anthropology, Memorial University of St. Johns, Newfoundland, Canada*

DR. PAUL R. EHRLICH   *Professor of Biology, Stanford University, California, U.S.A.*

Preface

It is a pleasure to thank the overworked people who contributed to this volume and the Chairmen, discussants and the Institute staff who made the meeting a success. I am also grateful to the Council of the Institute of Biology for making available the opportunity to pursue this topic and especially to Mr. D. J. B. Copp, General Secretary, for organizing the meeting. Dr. Freeman and Dr. Ehrlich wish to thank the Social Science Research Council of Canada and the Royal Society of London respectively for financial support. Professor Eversley wishes the G.L.C. to be dissociated from responsibility for his opinions.

The Introduction to this volume is my personal approach for which the Institute is not responsible. The contributors were chosen to give a wide range of viewpoints, as well as of disciplines, and the reader must use his own judgement to steer between the deliberately provocative extremes of *laissez faire* conservatism on the one hand and radical alarmism on the other.

The audience was mainly of professional biologists with their invited visitors and 90% registered their opinion that:

"The optimum population for Britain has already been exceeded."

This may not represent a general public view, but is that of a responsible group of people, disciplined in the study of living organisms, whose prime concern is the continuation of life processes. *Their opinion is not lightly to be dismissed.*

L. R. TAYLOR
Symposium Convenor

December, 1969

Contents

Introduction

From the original immigration of a few hundred families of modern man into Britain, about 11,000 years ago, the population grew at a rate of about 100 a year to reach one million in 10 thousand years and another thousand years elapsed before numbers reached 10 million; in less than 2% of British history, since 1800 A.D., population has risen a further 44 million, an average of a quarter of a million additional people each year (Thompson, Ch. 1). Briefly and over-simply, the early stages of unstable colonization were followed, during the period 1066 to about 1740, with the establishment of law, politics and economics founded on exploitive agriculture. The number of people was directly dependent on the area of land under cultivation and was so maintained by what appear to be classical ecological restraints; lowered fertility and child mortality were apparently endemic; adults as well as children died during spasmodic famine, wars and plagues of which the Black Death was the most devastating and, displaced from home territory, especially in the 13th and 16th centuries, many outlaws, itinerants and beggars probably failed to reproduce. The minor population cycles that initiated these environmental restraints were themselves the result of the delayed response of population to each expansion in land use, with the ensuing population rebound creating another cycle of land hunger. During this period the net effect was a leisurely growth of population, probably with a moderate amount of endemic misery.

The real explosion of population was initiated by the land enclosures culminating in the 18th century with the change from exploitive to improving agriculture, the agrarian revolution, in which communal exploitation of land gave way to the capital investment and careful nursing that continued to improve both soils and yields of crops throughout the 19th century (Table XI, p. 26).

This, the first of the recent technological revolutions, permitted the increase in numbers and aggregation of population that produced the industrial revolution, insured against famine by the certainty of an adequate, sometimes abundant, food supply. The growth of communications and of commercial and economic skills increasingly dissociated people from their formerly more direct dependence on agriculture. These skills buffered the population from short-term effects of good and bad harvests and introduced a new dependence on capital and natural resources derived from the markets of a world in which 23% of the land surface owed some allegiance to Britain. Along with the growth of industry and commerce, the population of Britain grew at a faster rate, progressively less supported by an immediate food supply and, as the potential of agriculture increased, its contribution to current resources declined. Industrial potential and economic stability became more relevant to urban communities than land systems and climate, but population still had to match the labour market for the system to function well and fear of a slump replaced fear of famine. The 1914-18 war demonstrated Britain's underlying vulnerability when food imports were cut and agriculture was suddenly, but briefly, revived; the ensuing recession redirected attention to economic solutions. The 1939-45 war repeated the warning and demonstrated that, for Britain, loss of imported food would be as unpleasant as a slump, which increased economic understanding and social responsibility now seems able to avoid.

In the interim, economic and commercial expertise had built up a complex network of world trade paid for by industrial enterprise so that, when the claims of Britain on overseas territories were progressively rescinded, no decline in imports of essential resources was obvious in spite of a few anticipatory scares such as the shortage of vegetable oils that led to the groundnut scheme. This engendered confidence in British ability to buy essential resources with technical expertise and justified the belief that diversity of world trade improves overall efficiency. Nevertheless, the increase in population fed by resources from abroad left behind a 50% deficit in food production. In future, the resources ultimately reliable are those derived from the land within the islands. All else, including at present half the food and many industrial raw materials, must be competed for in world markets. And the demands made on resources are rising faster, not only by increase in population which has continued its climb, but because of increasing aspirations of a higher standard of living. Successive Governments in Britain, as elsewhere, have encouraged population growth for political and economic reasons, so that many responsible parents sincerely believe large families are beneficial to the community (Houghton, p. 121). Now, ensnared by their own publicity, which commits them to maintain or improve real living standards however the environment and resources may change, Governments have a tiger by the tail. At the present rate of increase, living standards and with them many resource demands, will double by the end of the century.

Within about the same period of time, if international disasters are avoided, world population will almost double and the aspirations of the world's new generations will increase, as those in Britain, even though they are not satisfied. The pressure on world resources will increase and the effect on British imports remains open to speculation; it will not be negligible; it could be considerable. The problem here is not the unquestioned desirability of international trade from the viewpoint of economics, but the limiting conditions set by absolute shortage of raw materials. For example, the world's forests are inadequate to supply even the present world population with a small daily newspaper.

Food is the ultimate limiting resource and the one to which Britain is currently most exposed. World agriculture is biologically capable of doubling its production; there seems much doubt if it will do so in time to meet demand (F.A.O. 1969). The scale of Britain's increasing exposure to world-wide competition for food is indicated by comparison with India's annual imports of cereals from North America. These increased from 4 to 14 million tons in the five years 1961-66 (Maheshwari, 1966), that is from half to twice Britain's total imports of cereals and, during the next five years, the *increase* in India's population will equal the whole population of Great Britain. Again, the currently essential supply of beef from Argentina depends on unpredictable factors (Barrass, p. 48; Ehrlich, p. 152).

In short, according to Hutchinson's (1966) thesis, Britain, and any other country, is overpopulated when it has too many people to support from the resources of the land available to it. The controversial word here is "available"; just how limited are resources? The other assumption involved is that agriculture, hence land, is the likely main source of food in the near future. There is little reason to doubt this. Pirie (1958), an ardent advocate of novel foodstuffs, recognized that in 1958 "the primary source of our food is likely to continue to be higher plants growing essentially as they grow now"; in 1969 this remains essentially true. Hence agriculture must bear the brunt of the world competition for food in which, even if Britain can continue to acquire food abroad, the ethical dilemma of justification remains. The irony of a country that operates Oxfam on 50% imported food cannot be entirely explained away in economic ratiocination.

Agriculture operates within an economic framework subject to political manipulation and has been the object of political pressure in the past. The insistence that populations should try to live within the limits of their own food resources now comes mainly from biologists and agriculturists and is based in necessity rather than choice. But a tendency to regard this approach as reflecting former nationalism lingers on. Nevertheless the Agricultural Research Council, on the advice of a non-political working party, has accepted the need to plan research on the assumption that Britain will require at least twice its present net production of home-grown food in 30 years' time (Cox, 1969).

This realistic approach to one aspect of resource management poses questions about other resources that are not pursued here. Perhaps a public enquiry into future resources of the commodities listed by Ehrlich (p. 158) would not come amiss?

In attempting to decide how many people British agriculture can support, Cooke (Ch. 2) found less difficulty in assessing the likely productivity than in assessing the necessary requirements. This is not only because there is currently no attempt, or even will, to limit future population increase, thus placing numerical requirements beyond public policy, but also because the available data on individual nutritional requirements have been confused. However, by making a great effort, it seems the production standard set by the A.R.C., i.e. to double agricultural output by the end of the century, might be achieved. This would be equivalent to feeding 60 million people at the present standard on 30 million acres. It should be emphasized that subsistence standards are not relevant to a prospect that also envisages raising standards of living, maximum economic growth rates, and higher material, moral and political standards.

These increases in food production will not come easily. They involve the application of all existing knowledge, plus the expected results of new research and capital investment. They are technologically realistic, not escapist pipe-dreams, but will not be achieved without new agricultural policies. Farming, as all human endeavour, depends on people and economics and the improvement of crops has to be thought to be profitable as well as possible before it happens. British agriculture is already very efficient by world standards and also humane, but factory farming with its ethical problems will almost certainly be a part of this necessary increase. Humanity has reached the point when conversion of other forms of life into human biomass will impinge increasingly on other creatures. Out of this difficulty other problems arise.

If the need to stop the flow of food from less fortunate lands to Britain is the first ethical issue and factory farming is the second, pollution in its widest sense is the third. Pollution means not only the inconvenience of dirty rivers and smoke, but also the destruction of wild life by various concomitants of manufacturing and farming and, especially, pollution means eutrophication. Given the will, we may be able to pay for disposal of wastes, especially when many waste products become increasingly scarce and hence valuable. But Mellanby (Ch. 3) seriously suggests that excess nitrogen may limit agricultural production. Perhaps more carefully controlled fertilizer manufacture and application will mitigate this problem; perhaps not. If not it may be that the limiting factor in man's density is, as with other organisms, the accumulation of waste products.

Britain is fortunate that, comprising small islands, a natural sewage system already exists. Hawthorn's comment in the final Discussion, that North America's much greater problems result from lack of social responsibility, would seem to most ecologists to underestimate the importance of the topographical environment. North America's problem is size, shape and standard of living; with mountains down the edge the wastes collect inland. In Britain, rivers and the wastes they carry rapidly drain away because of the shape of the main island mass. But we are not, as yet, fully responsible in our attitudes, and the cost of properly conducted waste disposal would be considerable. Using the sea as a sewer is no final solution now that the wastes are so great and some so toxic. A large-scale investigation by the Natural Environmental Research Council into the cost of environmental maintenance is apparently overdue.

It is perhaps the encroachment of town on country, with the increased contact between individuals, as much as the increasingly intensive use of agricultural land, that most affects people's aesthetic senses. With the increase in standard of living, the space people actually use increases greatly. Demand for more immediate living space raises the pressure on housing; increased space is needed to produce more food especially if it is all to be produced within these islands. But the space needed for recreation is also real; some people are more space-conscious than others. Some feel the pressure of others on their freedom more directly and deeply. New worlds in which a new population can be started are no longer available to satisfy the incipient migratory drive in this element of the population; the world, as Britain, is filling up with people even as communications diminish isolation.

The British scene is already man-made; the large expanses of parkland are not climax vegetation. They are still beautiful to many people because of their variety and it is a loss to some standard or other when they are replaced by endless uniform fields of purely utilitarian food further restricting public access. The transition from lambs in a flock to lambs in a box is a loss of some quality, however hard to define. The casual response is to blame farmers for commercialism and this complaint is then interpreted by others as naïve longing for the golden past. Neither attitude shows much imagination. Farming practice must change and houses must be built for the present population. But it is legitimate to ask why this process should go on indefinitely. Is the whole country going to become a mass-production factory for human life? If, at the end of the next 30 years when agriculture has done its job and can feed the extra 30 million, agriculturists find they are then faced with the prospect of another ten million to feed in the next 30 years, who has gained? Leyhausen (1969) writes "I have never yet heard or read a reasonable argument as to why ever more and more people should live on the limited space of our Earth". Neither have I, and I suspect that the support given at the meeting (see Preface) to the proposition "Britain is already past its optimum population", was conditioned very much by this unspoken question.

In the present cycle of human society, population has continued to increase for so long that the idea of population control from within society is often denied expression. Nevertheless, even when it is rising, population is controlled by society as well as by extrinsic ecological factors. The evidence of the declining birth-rate during the first half of this century (Chart 2, p. 5) has inclined other people to doubt that extrinsic factors still operate. They seem to believe that man has succeeded in gaining control over his environment and his destiny in the brief moment of time since the industrial revolution. Hutchinson (1966) wrote "The characteristic of our age is the dominance we have achieved over our environment" and Eversley (Ch. 8), "the history of the last few thousand years is the progress of the species toward the more complete subordination of the natural environment". The difference between approaches lies, not in this historical statement, but in its interpretation. Eversley sees in this past achievement evidence that man has succeeded in breaking barriers previously imposed by purely biological relationships. Southwood (p. 99) likens man's current position to a child with a box of matches and claims that man holds his environment in trust for future generations and should behave as a trustee, with caution and concern. The increased sophistication of society does not remove the biological limitations although it makes them operate less directly by interpolating additional economic and social buffers.

The difference between the social scientists and the biologists lies, not in accepting that the gates are open, but in what lies outside. The social scientists seem to say that the environment is not too important because it is so modified by economic and technological expertise. The biologists claim that the rate of adaptation of the environment is limited and not wholly in man's hands; it is an evolved organism, fragile and complex beyond our present understanding, not to be treated lightly and easier to destroy than to control. The physicist would go a step further and argue that more people means more energy consumed and the heat balance will ultimately be upset. Strangely enough, this fact is intellectually respectable, perhaps because the prospect is not immediate and no action is considered necessary—yet. When the biologist says that the biological balance will be upset long before then he is not altogether believed, perhaps because this requires more immediate action.

The most important evidence from history is presented by Freeman (Ch. 11). There have been closed societies in the past living in balance with their environments. It seems they kept their balance using only 20-30% of natural resources. Because they were primitive they tend to be disregarded (Hawthorn, p. 174). Their technology did not compare with ours and because their control over the environment was poor they are regarded as subject to different natural laws, if any such exist. Ecologically this attitude is unacceptable. The evidence from all organisms suggests that they normally remain in balance well below resource limitation. When for some reason this balance is broken and populations explode, they always disastrously decline again (Southwood, Ch. 7). Different populations use different proportions of their resources and, with changes in the environment, settle back at new levels. Man may be able to modify his environment and manipulate his future by conscious effort, but the idea that his population can rise *indefinitely* is irrational as well as arrogant. If indefinite increase is rejected as impossible, the problem of finding a new population balance remains. Having rejected natural population control by war, famine, disease and displacement as unacceptable, man must attempt to find his own acceptable controls; there is no third alternative. The difference between social and biological scientists then becomes one of complete *laissez faire* on the one hand and a conscious attempt to define a goal to be reached by redirecting society's attitudes on the other; direct government legislation on family size would not only be unacceptable (Simms and Medawar, Ch. 10) but also unsuccessful (Freeman, Ch. 11). As Freeman writes (p. 146) "Any reduction in birth-rate that may occur will result from voluntary (cultural) limitation which will be the conscious expression of changed societal goals, or changed strategies adopted by society to achieve those goals".

The arguments against any conscious attempt by a population to direct its size towards an optimum appear to be fourfold in origin, although the overt expression of views varies with the individual rationalization. First there is the Micawber approach, "God never sends mouths without sending meat" or in modern language "other natural resources will no doubt become available". Involved in this may be an unrecognized primitive or religious belief that the function of Man is to fill the Earth with people; "original sin" Southwood calls it (p. 94). Superficially it seems like a conceptual metamorphosis of the "All-provider" into Technology or Government. Over-enthusiastic technologists and even government self-advertising has tended to foster it and it seems to regard man as exempt from natural laws, to deify man. It should diminish with increased ecological understanding but in the meantime biological scientists are brought to reiterating *"Science can do much, but it cannot work miracles; it cannot produce something from nothing and cannot take out of the system more than it puts into it"* (Bawden, 1967); the italics are mine.

Second, there is the very real political argument about the difficulties of procedure. This draws a parallel with the present difficulty in maintaining long-term economic stability with a short-term political system. There is some confusion of thought or terminology here by which the present political system is sometimes denied the ability to deal with long-term problems because it is democratic. Democracy does not demand an ephemeral approach to planning. Present plans to build new cities, for example under the 1965 New Towns Act, that will take decades to complete and that assume a continuous future population to use them, are not rejected because Governments last only five years. British Governments have always had, and still have, long-term population policies that affect legislation, as a Royal Commission pointed out 20 years ago (Houghton, p. 118). The policy in most legislation is that population will rise, and should continue to rise, because some current economics are helped by it. In the words of the present Prime Minister ". . . an expanding population . . . should . . . help to solve our longer term manpower shortages" (Wilson, 1966), although, as Boreham (Ch. 6) points out, the net economic advantage is marginal. What, if anything, may be undemocratic is that this policy is implicit, not explicit, and has never been exposed to public discussion (Parsons, p. 169). Houghton (Ch. 9) suggests that a main reason for this is the major parties' fear of repercussions from strident minorities; the withdrawal of the economic argument might have a surprisingly enlightening effect on this political attitude.

Third, there is the economic argument that a selected optimum may not maximize real output per head. The problem here is to define cultural goals; to equate material with moral, political and aesthetic values. But this problem is not peculiar to a search for an optimum population; it is as old as mankind and is illustrated in the current distress over factory farming. Hutchinson (1966) wisely suggested that economists might profitably direct more attention to the future, to the study of climax conditions, the optima of population cycles, instead of concentrating on the inflexion, which is neither a permanent nor a desirable condition because of its instability and which, for this country at least, is in the past.

Fourth, there are the sociological premises, that choice of family size is an "irrevocable human right"; that the "improvident behaviour of the parent must not be visited on the children" and that the Government's responsibility is to ' provide a good life" for them (U.N., etc., in Houghton, Ch. 9). More succinctly, society is responsible for rearing the next generation, not for deciding its size. Collectively these three premises, if fully instigated in any other than a monastic society, would spiral to disaster; it seems that many real societies must be more responsible than their international representatives. As Freeman makes clear, societies in equilibrium have determined family size by social convention, not by unbridled individual licence. For a society to have effective conventions it must have effective sanctions and these may affect some children unless the convention has appropriate safeguards. Failing this, the improvidence of some parents will ultimately be visited on all the children by overconsumption of available resources at whatever level of population density. The problem for all societies is to find acceptable social determinants on which to base its demographic structure.

Current determinants probably operate mainly through economic channels. Eversley (Ch. 8) argues that it is hard to have a large family on a small income, and this implies economic inhibition. Southwood points out that children may be an economic asset in poverty. Historically in this society, and currently in many others, this asset has been realized by children working or begging and government allowances may functionally replace these undesirable sources of income. Either view is valid when applied to a different individual, depending on his personal and social responsibility, and it is the mean of this variable social characteristic that determines the response by society, collectively, to whatever choice is open to it. The choice is set by convention and is subject to change; but the human variability in response is a biological necessity, not to be removed by ideological approach, social or political pressure. Eversley's figure of 25% child poverty suggests that, whatever each individual's personal reasons for child-bearing may be, people are producing children well beyond their individual capacity to support them at currently acceptable standards, or the standards set are meaningless. If poverty is to some extent inhibiting child-bearing at present, rising standards of living may release this restraint still further and hopes that the currently increasing birth-rate (see Chart 2, p. 5) will reverse its trend in the near future, without economic or social pressure, appear to be wishful thinking.

It seems unlikely that all people accept the United Nations as the final arbiter on "irrevocable human rights" to produce children and there are no biological precedents for rights to reproduce, although it is clearly a desirable objective. In current society there is certainly strong pressure exerted by advertisers and by press attitudes generally, to consider large families as normal. Simms and

Medawar (Ch. 10) emphasize the need to revise attitudes to the intrinsic virtue of childbirth. Parkes (1969) has suggested that society may also require of its members these obligations:

(a) Not to produce unwanted children.

(b) Not to take a substantial risk of begetting a mentally or physically defective child.

(c) Not to produce children because of irresponsibility or religious observance, merely as a by-product of sexual intercourse.

(d) To plan the number and spacing of births in the best interest of mother, child and the rest of the family.

(e) To give the best possible mental and physical environment to the child during its most formative years and to produce children, therefore, only in the course of an affectionate and stable relationship between man and woman.

(f) However convinced the individual may be of his or her superior qualities, not for this reason to produce children in numbers which, if equalled by everyone, would be demographically catastrophic.

When individuals are faced with a clearly stated choice on these topics, especially on item (b) with its agonizing personal decision, they mostly behave responsibly (Simms and Medawar, p. 136). But this particular choice is purely personal, less equivocal than (f) which involves other people's collusion. Here only social attitudes can succeed. At the moment they are otherwise directed.

This raises the issue of how much family planning can contribute to population limitation. As Eversley pointed out in the discussion, more deliberate and effective spacing of children could lead to larger ultimate families, if early pregnancy limits capital accumulation with a lower subsequent standard of living. Here again, the implication is that economics partially determine family size. Again, family planning will not solve an "excess desire for children". However, Houghton (p. 123) points out that the restraint of population growth may eventually become politically acceptable through family planning. It is clear that the present overt social acceptance of what responsible individuals have been secretly practising for so long has been a great social achievement and a necessary step forward. A similar change in social attitude to "excess desire for children" might complete the process; a change in official attitude in recognition of the problem might be enough to tip the balance. Certainly there is no call for "sacrifice". If population limitation is achieved it will only be because society has accepted that small families are desirable, whatever social or economic pressures make them seem so.

Population limitation is perhaps primarily concerned with preserving ethical standards. There seems to be an obvious *a priori* inverse relation between individual freedom and population density; Adam had no problems before Eve. The early hunters retained their freedom to choose their way of life by their responsibility in controlling their populations within wide environmental margins. The agricultural/technological phase of man's evolution is environment destructive and ever-increasing restrictive legislation appears to be the result. As the resource margins are cut closer to the bone by increasing population and increasing demands, the freedom of individual choice to exercise the personal responsibility that maintains ethical standards is further diminished. The fundamental ethic, that seeks to preserve the environment for future generations, has suffered years of neglect which it will now be difficult to recover (Darling, 1969).

Apart from H-bombs and other "discontinuities", in Ehrlich's sardonic terminology, the alternative to reproductive restraint in Britain is not a sudden visible flood of young people that can now be seen in many other countries, but a slow decline in real living standards, irregular and therefore not easily recognized by the innumerate. The repeated attempts to balance payments by increasing taxation are a direct, logical response, by slowing the rate living standards increase, to compensate for rising demand in a resource-limited world. The danger seems to be that social scientists may not accept the collective ecological significance of relevant warning symptoms and may tackle them individually. Whatever the reason, there is an evident tendency for society as a whole, if not social scientists individually, to deal piecemeal with what may possibly be the medical, social and economic symptoms of a single ecological malaise; to blame inadequate medical services for the death of people in London smog or babies in an enteritis epidemic; to blame inadequate social services for the increase in crime; to blame one side or other of industry for the persistent economic difficulties in balancing payments and to blame the family unit for the restrictive pressures of high density living. These may not be symptoms of a common ecological phenomenon, but if they are, the current political solutions of manipulation within society, both of people and resources, may come to be regarded as being as unsatisfactory as the medical, social and economic solutions already mentioned. This is not to say that these piecemeal correctives do not have a valuable immediate social function, but to suggest that they will not permanently solve problems whose roots are in ecological instability due to overpopulation, for there is probably an optimum structure as well as an optimum size to any population, including the human population of Britain.

In cybernetics, multiple pathways for choice and action are reckoned to enhance the stability of the system; Freeman related this to "freedom coupled with responsibility" in human society. The same principle of maximum diversity of characters is recognized as an essential component of stability in ecology, including population stability, and it seems likely that the variability of biological and social characters is a species characteristic; "nature abhors uniformity". If so, narrowing of the frequency distribution of family size, without a corresponding drop in the mean, may not be a healthy sign and a strictly imposed limit might be even worse. Just as the large estates of uniform houses are an unhealthy pattern for the purely ecological reason of lack of diversity, apart from aesthetic and social ones, so migration is a complex phenomenon whose resultant spatial patterns are highly specific even for human populations (Taylor, 1970) and probably not to be easily duplicated by shifting people, *en bloc,* to contrived new towns. Whether or not we accept the genetic mechanisms of Wynne-Edwards' hypothesis in full (see Southwood, p. 91), we may be wise to consider seriously his evidence that effective self-regulation of populations occurs by social adaptation while resources are apparently still adequate, and the interpretation of this evidence for human populations is a task for the human ecologists we so badly need.

The different disciplines tend to see the population problem with different perspectives, biologists considering it to be more urgent than the social scientists, presumably because of the longer time scales the biologists work in. If, after consideration, it is decided to be possible, proper and feasible to discourage further population growth, the process of deceleration is likely to be either slow or painful and therefore a beginning should not be delayed too long. The ideal of a selected optimum may be far in the future if it involves a reduction from the present level, but some suggestions for its requirements were made.

An optimum population should seek to maximize:

1. the vigour and potential of individuals;
2. the currently acceptable pattern of social organization;
3. the realization of cultural goals which were listed as moral, political and aesthetic standards;
4. real output per head.

It should minimize:

1. pollution;
2. nutritional and
3. social stress.

To do this it must be less than the carrying capacity of the environment and hence *capable of being indefinitely maintained.*

The underlying problem remains "the incubus of maximal reproduction" and society may resent this reminder of its animal origins, although it will continue to be the basis of the biological approach. With more information on available resources, pollution costs, etc., discussion across the disciplines could be more productive, but there is no short-term solution even when agreement on objectives is reached, as it must be some day. Biologists have stated the problem in simple unequivocal terms; man lives in a closed system with a limited absolute input and a more severely limited tolerable output, for all resources end as effluent. He must decide sooner or later to stop turning more and more life into human biomass. Accepting this as inevitable, the sooner he begins, the better. But to convince others that man is not outside natural law, ecologists must show that their evidence applies to man. At present it can too easily be dismissed emotionally, if not intellectually, because it derives partly from primitive man and other "lower" animals and the present over-concern with technological and economic mechanisms obscures the parallels. In particular the evidence must be convincing to sociologists before greater progress is made, for they can help by continuing to clarify the criteria by which real modern societies, not the societies of the moral philosophers whose inadequacies are revealed by Hawthorn (Ch. 5), are regarded as exempt from the generalizations derived from fundamental studies of other organisms. Economists might helpfully consider some longer-term economic climate that encourages the recycling of resources, to supplement one apparently committed to maximum immediate consumption and hence maximum rate of pollution.

Many suggestions are made in these pages for immediate action to discourage population growth. Lacking public will, no immediate implementation is likely even of those suggestions that are feasible and socially innocuous. Nevertheless, the present biological, social and demographic evidence at least warrants Government encouragement of attempts to minimize unwanted births. If this moderate and civilized objective cannot be attained fairly soon, the prospects for an equally civilized solution to the more difficult problems of the future are poor. Britain has a tolerant and flexible established religion and a considerate and viable social system; in a country with these advantages, it would be singularly unfortunate if the evolution of population toward a demographically stable maturity should be frustrated by religious pendantry or uninformed bigotry (Parkes p. 53; Houghton p. 118).

Legislators might, therefore, be well advised to reflect more on the long term consequences of their actions for apparent immediate good; it is socially wise, as well as good, to act humanely toward a child already born, but it is unwise to diminish the full load of personal responsibility of prospective parents for bringing children into an already overcrowded world, and it is foolhardy to hinder their demographically sensible efforts to prevent births. Equating these requirements is the dilemma that must be faced and overcome by a society that professes to be both socially and demographically accountable. The education of the next generation in ecological principles of population stability and the conservation of resources is an obvious pre-requisite for the continued maintenance of a civilized community, for some part at least of the present inability to appreciate the problem is rooted in the deification of man by the Western humanities.

In the meantime the question "Why ever more people?" requires a more rational answer than it is receiving at present in a country that some people believe has a responsibility to set standards for the future.

December, 1969   L. R. TAYLOR

REFERENCES

Bawden, F. C. (1967). Trends and prospects from the standpoint of natural scientists. *Int. J. Agrarian Affairs* **5**, 115-129.

Cox, G. (1969). Agricultural research. *Agriculture* **76**, 411-415.

Darling, F. F. (1969). Man's responsibility for the environment. *In* "Biology and Ethics" (E. J. Ebling, ed.), pp. 117-122. Academic Press, London.

F.A.O. (1969). "Indicative World Plan for Agricultural Development" (provisional). Rome.

Hutchinson, J. (1966). Land and human populations. *Adv. Sci.* **23**, 241-254.

Leyhausen, P. (1969). The dilemma of social man. *Sci. J.* **5A**, 60-65.

Maheshwari, P. (1966). Botany and the food problem of India. *Science and Culture* **32**, 104-114.

Parkes, A. S. (1969). The right to reproduce in an overcrowded world. *In* "Biology and Ethics" (F. J. Ebling, ed.), pp. 109-116. Academic Press, London.

Pirie, N. W. (1958). Unconventional production of foodstuffs. *In* "The Biological Productivity of Britain" (W. B. Yapp and D. J. Watson, eds.), pp. 115-123. London.

Taylor, L. R. (1970). Aggregation as a species characteristic. *In* "Statistical Ecology" (Patil, Pielou and Waters, eds.). University Park.

Wilson, H. (1966). Letter to Rt. Hon. Sir David Renton dated December 22, 1966. "The Population Problem", publ. Renton, London.

Wynne-Edwards, V. C. (1962). "Animal Dispersion in Relation to Social Behaviour", p. 653. Edinburgh and London.

CHAPTER 1

The Growth Phenomenon

J. H. THOMPSON

General Register Office

THE BACKGROUND

Within Great Britain today there are 54 million people. Before examining the current projection that they will generate a population of 66 million by the turn of this century, it is first necessary to look back in time, to try to account for the genesis of the 54 million.

A brief survey of the origin of the nucleus that has grown to 54 million is useful for setting the background to our more recent history. The story of population growth is of one generation giving birth to the next, each generation building on the preceding one and in turn passing on an inheritance to the next in terms of the size and structure of the population of the country as a whole. Also, the economic and social organization of the population at any given point in time is a reflection of the history of preceding generations and a formative influence on generations to come. In a sense we can look on the population itself as an organism, and search for its own laws of cohesion, and of growth. To say this does not mean setting a deterministic framework but rather establishing that while the population is in one sense no more than the sum of its individual members, yet the behaviour of its members is in turn moulded by society. When the phenomenon of population growth is considered it is necessary to have constantly in mind the wider background of economic and social development in this country, of which it is one aspect.

It is believed that man colonized the British Isles in the wake of the last Ice Age. There is evidence of the settlement of successive waves of invaders in the Stone Ages; then what must have been numerically the more important settlements of the Iron Age invaders; lastly of the Dark Age invaders, Nordic and Teutonic.

To give numerical scale to our remoter history is very difficult but one broad generalization can be hazarded. That is, that somewhere before the year AD 1000, new settlement—which is another way of describing immigration—ceased to be the major factor in population growth for this country. The population at the beginning of this millennium has been put at between 1 and 2 million. Its subsequent growth has basically been due to its own natural increase—the excess of births over deaths.

Estimates that have been made of population at various points of time established that in historic times it has had an underlying upward trend with the exception of the period of the Black Death, when over a period of a few years perhaps one-third of the population was wiped out. Chart 1 assembles various

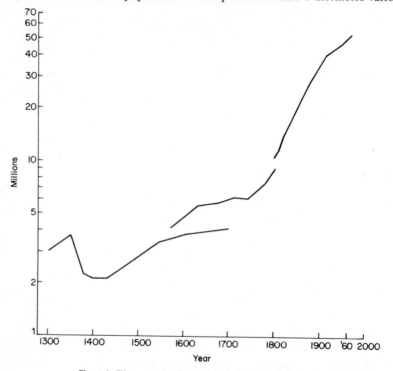

Chart 1. The growth of population in Great Britain.

estimates of the population before the year 1800 and illustrates them, together with the well-documented evidence of the subsequent period. Before 1800 the figures are estimates relating to England and Wales; but the general trends are little affected by the omission of the small population of Scotland. It will be seen that two series are shown for the 17th century which differ to some extent; this is a reflection of the real difficulty of generalizing about the size of the population from the scanty evidence available. Nonetheless there is a clear message in this chart, even allowing for the discontinuities in it.

The chart has been presented on a logarithmic scale to make clear the various phases that population growth has passed through. The fact is that growth in the population has been the norm: it is variations in the pace of growth that form the most interesting phenomenon for study. We see how the Black Death amounted to a catastrophe on a now almost unimaginable scale, killing perhaps one-third of the population. (Some historians suggest as much as 40% of the population died.)

The first general point to make is that after the Black Death, population took some years to resume its growth, but then showed an upward trend that averaged a growth rate of some 0.3% per annum over the three and a half centuries roughly from 1400 to 1750. Secondly, a population explosion of a kind began somewhere the middle of the 18th century and lasted for a century and a half, over which the rate of increase averaged over 1% per annum. Thirdly, population growth has moderated within this century to an average of 0.5% per annum over the years since 1911.

The size of the population of Great Britain (making some allowance for Scotland) can be put at some 4 to 5 million by 1600; 6 to 7 million about 1700; it was 10 million by 1800. Then it increased by 10 million in a half-century, and 17 million in the next, to reach a total of 37 million at 1900. In the first half of this century there was a further increase of 12 million.

This is a bald summary of the phases in the growth of the population. Nonetheless it establishes that there is a growth phenomenon. Clearly we have to turn to the 19th century to try to understand the main factors accounting for the inheritance of 54 million people today, for it was in the last century that the greater part of this aggregate was created. Examination of the successive surges and pauses which underlie the general expansion, particularly those of more recent years, can yield information that is immediately relevant to our attempts today to peer into the future.

POPULATION GROWTH SINCE 1800

In 1801 the first Census of Population was taken, covering Great Britain, and has been taken every decade since (bar 1941). Registration of births, marriages and deaths became compulsory around the middle of the century. From these two sources come data that have been extended and developed as time has passed to give an even more detailed picture of the factors which underlie population growth.

The overall change in population can be broken down into three components: births, deaths and net migration (the balance of immigration less emigration), which between them account for the total. This analysis is a very necessary first step towards understanding the nature of population growth.

For the first half of the 19th century, however, before comprehensive statistics of births and deaths become available, the analysis of population change which can be made is limited in its detail and cannot be precise.

It is known from the aggregate population figures yielded by the Census that over the first half of last century the rate of population growth was, by the historical standards for this country, extremely high, averaging 1.4% per annum.

This growth was primarily the result of the margin by which the birth rate exceeded the death rate. It is however unfortunate that precise measures of the absolute magnitudes of these rates are lacking over a period which can, in retrospect, be seen as having marked the beginning of fundamental demographic change.

Various demographers who have assembled and studied such data as can be gathered about births and deaths before the introduction of registration have debated among themselves as to whether the rate of live births was already falling before the middle of the last century, or whether it was merely fluctuating around a more or less stable level, or even rising slightly.

On the whole, the view of the main authorities on the rapid phase of expansion in population which occurred before 1850 is that it was the consequence of falling death rates in the face of birth rates maintained at a relatively high level. This view is enshrined in the Report of the Royal Commission on Population (published in 1949) which said, of the period of rapid population growth before 1800 (but it applies equally over the next half-century):

> "The causes of this acceleration, beginning in the 18th century, are not known with certainty, but it can be said with some confidence that it was due more to a fall in death rates than to a rise in birth rates . . . It is not unlikely that some rise in the birth rate took place; but it is virtually certain that a considerable reduction in mortality occurred . . . Why mortality declined at this time is not definitely known, but it is possible to point to such changes as the improvement in nutrition and clothing resulting from changes in agriculture and industrial technique, to better sanitation and cleaner water supply and to the expansion and improvement of medical services (e.g. the foundation of hospitals) as probable causes. Even after this reduction mortality rates were high by modern standards."

But starting from the middle of last century an unambiguous picture of population change can be presented, and the various factors can be related to one another in importance. Chart 2 illustrates the magnitudes of the components in the change in the population of Great Britain over successive decades. (The components for the period 1841-61 are estimates based on figures for England and Wales.) The figures have been presented in terms of annual average change in the decades covering inter-censal periods (the most recent period is, however, the average from mid-1961 to mid-1968).

The first point to be observed is that natural increase, the margin by which births exceed deaths, has throughout far outweighed net migration in importance as an element in changing population. Secondly, the considerable fluctuations in the size of the natural increase have been due primarily to fluctuations in numbers of births. The number of births can be seen to have followed over the earlier decades a steady upward trend to reach what was more or less a plateau over the three decades from 1881 to 1911; births subsequently dropped sharply to a trough in the 1930s, but have since recovered to a higher level.

The number of deaths in the population has by contrast fluctuated within relatively narrow limits over most of the period covered. What has happened here is that although true mortality rates, age specific, have been falling over the whole period this has been masked not only by rising numbers of the population at risk but also by changes in the age constitution of the population. The effects of declining mortality are that initially the number of deaths in a population is reduced as the expectation of life is extended; this has an ageing effect on the

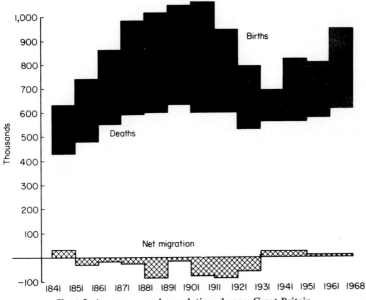

Chart 2. Average annual population change, Great Britain.

population which then in due course experiences a wave of deaths. At this particular point in time a very much damped down and extended wave of deaths is being experienced, the delayed reflection of the wave in births which mounted in the second part of last century.

These elements in population change add together to give overall increases of the order of a quarter of a million persons per annum at 1850, rising to nearly 400,000 per annum at the high point around the turn of the century; the current figure is again of the order of a quarter of a million.

But at the beginning of the period (1850) an increase of a quarter of a million people meant a growth rate of over 1% per annum; nowadays it means a growth rate of less than half a per cent per annum. Or to put this round the other way, although the rate of expansion of the population has dropped by more than one half as compared with a century ago, the absolute increase is the same. This is a point sometimes overlooked, but one eminently worth bearing in mind. For although in dealing with some aspects of population it is the rates of change which may be of importance, in other equally important aspects it is the actual magnitude of the increase in numbers which is significant.

Having observed in Chart 2 the wave pattern in the number of births, and the relatively much smaller fluctuation in the number of deaths, Chart 3 relates these

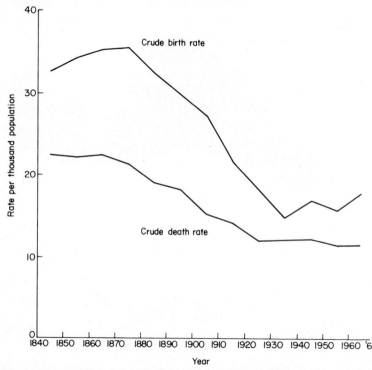

Chart 3. Birth and death rates (England and Wales).

figures to the rising population over the period and shows birth and death rates over the past century expressed as rates per thousand of population, per decade.

The downward trend in the death rate evident since the middle of last century is thought, as has already been said, to be the continuation of a trend that started in the second half of the 18th century if not earlier. It has already been pointed out that the changing age structure of the population has been a factor in the slower decline in the crude death rate of the more recent period.

The more significant factor for analysis of population change lies in births. The trend in the birth rate dropped after 1880 to the 1930s, in one swift and smooth plunge, but has recovered over the three decades since this low point. The crude birth rate moved from 32 to 35 over the four decades up to 1880 down to 15 in the 1930s; the current rate is 17. However, to give an adequate account of this fall and the subsequent recovery, more refined measures of fertility than the crude birth rate are needed.

The number of births occurring in any population has primarily to be related to the number of females of child-bearing age within it; further it is marital fertility that is of most significance. The crude birth rate is distorted by variations from one period to another in the proportion of the whole population accounted for by young married females; for the age distribution of the overall population, the ratio of males to females in it, and the marriage rate have all shifted over time. If the question of illegitimate births is put aside for the moment (this is not to say that they are unimportant of themselves) marital fertility still accounts for well over 90% of all births.

For the purpose of the present study, the course of the major fluctuations in births over the last century can most usefully be summarized and discussed in terms first of the proportion of women in the population who marry, then their family size defined as the number of live births that occur to women within marriage. The child-bearing period can be defined as between the ages of 15 and 44 years; very few births occur outside this age range.

The timing and spacing of births within this 30-year span of life is a further point of importance to the study of fertility. When analysing short-term variations in the number of births it is necessary to discuss age specific fertility in some detail, but for the broader picture the whole course of a woman's fertile life can usefully be summed up in terms of the size of her completed family.

The analysis of fertility in terms of the family size of married women must however be prefaced by a brief examination of marriage patterns. The first point to consider is marriage propensity—the proportion of women who will ever marry in the course of their child-bearing period. This can be adequately measured for our purpose as the proportion of women in the age group 40 to 44 years who are recorded in the Census as married, or having been married.

In the middle of last century some 85% of women married within their child-bearing period. This proportion slid down to 82% in the first three decades of this century, but has risen over recent years to reach 92%. The converse of these figures represents the decline in spinsterdom within the child-bearing period, which has halved, from 15% a century ago rising to 18% in the early decades of this century, to 8% today.

The most striking feature of all however—a feature which will be picked up again later because of its significance for current and prospective fertility—is not just that in recent years there has been a trend towards more marriages in general but that there has been so marked a trend towards younger marriage. Chart 4 (England and Wales data) shows the percentage of women in the age group 20 to 24 who were of married status at Census dates, and how this dropped in the second half of last century but has shot up to unprecedented heights since the second world war. The age group 20 to 24 is of prime importance because it is in these years that age specific fertility reaches its highest levels. This big increase in young marriage over the last three decades has in fact to a large extent been accounted for by marriage before the age of 20.

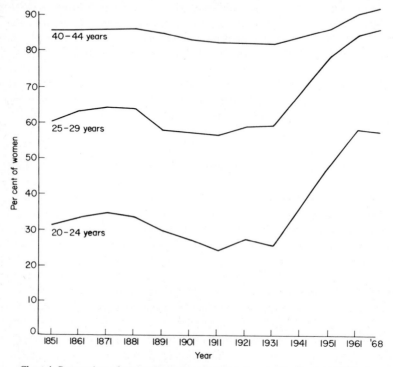

Chart 4. Proportion of women who have married, by age (England and Wales).

The consideration of changing family size over the past century provides a vivid chronicle of the way changes in individual behaviour manifest changes in the whole structure, attitudes, ideals and capabilities of society as a whole. Census data on family size is shown in Chart 5. (These data refer to England and Wales and relate to children of women married once only.) The cohort of women who married in the 1860s had an average of rather over six live-born children. What is not always realized is that as early as a century ago family size had already started on a downward trend. Women married in the first decade of this century had an average of approximately 3½ live-born children. That is, family size dropped by nearly one-half over the second half of last century. The trend continued inexorably downward to average out at fractionally over two for marriages of the later 1920s and the 1930s (in fact the rate fell to two at the end of the 1930s). Since the second world war it has increased again and marriages of around 1960 seem likely to produce over 2.4 children on average.

The progressive limitation in family size up to the second world war has been much studied and commented on. Partly, postponement of marriage can help to explain this, for later age at marriage and smaller average family size have been

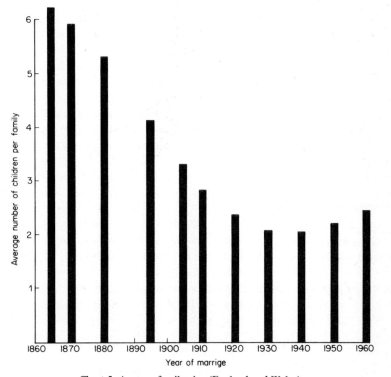

Chart 5. Average family size (England and Wales).

closely connected. But that there was deliberate limitation in family size within marriage is beyond doubt. Women have remained physically capable of bearing larger numbers of children. One particular feature can be picked out for comment: the fact that family limitation on a significant scale can be seen to have started a century ago can be taken as evidence that sophisticated contraceptive techniques are, at least up to a point, not essential to this process.

It is the motivation that lay behind this progressive limitation in family size that is the basic problem to be considered. It might be expected in dealing with a phenomenon which involves questions of the most fundamental significance to human beings, that there is no one simple explanation to be sought. Indeed, commentators are as much to be noted for the divergence of the kinds of reasons they give as for the extent of their agreement.

The general view might be summed up by saying that this decline in family size represented perhaps the most fundamental of responses of people as individuals to the kind of urban civilization that grew out of the Industrial Revolution, and began to be the dominant way of life for the population, reaching one apogee in the early years of this century, before the outbreak of the first world war.

Over this period the aggregate wealth of the nation grew, but the period does not present a picture of uniform economic progress: it must be remembered that there were times of acute economic distress. The postponement of marriage seen in late Victorian times is thought to have been one reflection of the economic trouble of those times, and some of the drop in family size may be argued to have been a response to these stress conditions.

One important feature which must have had some influence on family formation over the longer term has been the decline in the death rate for children. Where women of the middle of last century had on average just over six live-born children, infant and child mortality would have, on average, carried off two before the age of 15. Nowadays, married couples produce their smaller families with a very high degree of confidence that they will survive to adulthood.

First, restrictions on child labour, then the coming of universal schooling and the progressive raising of the school leaving age have been factors in the historic process, increasing the length of time of economic dependency of children on their parents. This has undoubtedly meant that economic forces have increasingly played some part towards encouraging greater limitation of family size. This is not to argue in simplistic fashion that children and consumer goods must be seen crudely as alternative choices in disposing of the family income, but that a concern to realize the increasing standard of living, for their children as well as themselves, must have motivated many parents in limiting their families.

It is in the 1930s when average family size was down to two, that the forecasts of a declining, or at best static, population were first put forward for serious consideration. It was evident that two children per family was well below replacement rate, defining this as below the number needed to maintain the size of the population from one generation into the next: it did not provide the margin to compensate for the unmarried nor to cover mortality in the early years of life. There had seemed to be an inevitability about the preceding downward trend in fertility and in the conditions of the 1930s it was assumed by many that this very low fertility was a characteristic of a highly industrialized, mature economy and furthermore one existing in a country which by comparison with other nations was already relatively densely populated.

The factor which above all has turned the prospect for the future from that of a declining to one of an expanding population has been the post-war recovery in family size. It has already been said that marriages of around 1960 seem likely to produce over 2.4 children on average. While these marriage cohorts are too recent for their pattern of completed family size to be finally established yet, there is already sufficient information about their family formation in the early years of marriage to allow reasonable estimates of the likely out-turn to be made.

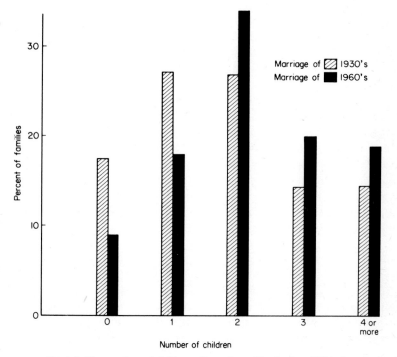

Chart 6. The number of children of marriages (England and Wales).

It is very illuminating at this point therefore to move behind the summary statistic of average family size, to see the considerable shift which has occurred in the span of one generation in the distribution of actual family size. Chart 6 compares this distribution for marriages of early 1930s with the pattern which seems to be emerging as characteristic of marriages of around 1960. (Chart 6 is based on figures for England and Wales relating to women marrying once only before the age of 45.)

The most important change has been the move away from the no-child or one-child marriage. The former has fallen from 17% to under 10% (probably to 9%); the latter from 27% down to an estimated 18%. Taken together the 0 and 1 child categories accounted for 44%—that is, not far short of one-half—of all the 1930s marriages, falling to something like 27% for the more recent period. There has been a distinct swing to the two- and three-child families and also an increase in the families with four children.

The size of the later shift away from small families can be seen as some measure of the degree to which the conditions of the pre-war period constrained family sizes to be held below the levels that married couples would like to have achieved given more settled and prosperous times. The post-war years have seen not only this move away from the very small families, but at the same time a continued decline in the really big families: in other words convergence from both sides towards the two-child family as occupying the central position, but still with more families above than below this modal value of two. (It is of course this asymmetry in the distribution which leads to the average family size of 2.4).

One feature of the post-war years worth particular notice has been the emergence of the professional classes, the highly educated, those who occupy positions of considerable influence in society as being a group of relatively high fertility. These are the kind of people who are, and were previously, those most capable of achieving just the family size they desire. Their behaviour can be quoted as one illustration of the general thesis that the resurgence of fertility in the post-war years has shown many features that lead to the conclusion that it must largely have reflected a change in the size of family people have both desired and felt capable of supporting.

THE PROJECTIONS

The current official population projections (based on a mid-1968 starting point) lead to a figure of 66 million for the population of Great Britain at the end of this century: an increase of a further 12 million people in a span of 32 years. This projection rests on assumptions about future migration, mortality, and fertility which derive from analysis of current trends.

The assumption about mortality is, briefly, that it will continue to the end of the century on the declining path which it has previously shown. That is, that mortality rates up to middle age, although already low in general, will approximately halve over the period; the reduction in mortality assumed for the older ages is progressively smaller and vanishes by the really advanced ages. There is of course nothing that automatically requires that because mortality rates have declined in the past, this must go on indefinitely in the future. The assumptions, however, implictly allow for further benefits to be reaped from existing medical knowledge, and for the effects of further steady advance not only in medical knowledge and technique but in its application.

What the assumptions do not allow for—and in the nature of things cannot allow for—are the specific effects of any dramatic new advances in medicine: for instance, a breakthrough in dealing with the heart diseases which are so important in mortality at middle age, or the cancers which kill prematurely. The assumption of improved mortality seems reasonable as a continuance of previous trends, though in the event it may not be realized, or it may be exceeded. This is a source of one uncertainty therefore in the projections, not only in the total numbers involved but affecting age structure of the population.

To take net migration next, the assumption here is that a relatively small net outflow, which is the current position, will be the underlying pattern. Migration can be from year to year exceedingly volatile, but on the assumption of the present controls on inflow to this country being maintained, and of the well-established pattern of outflow (in which the Commonwealth is of particular importance) persisting, a small net outward flow is the general expectation. Unless some radically new factor enters the picture, net migration is therefore expected to continue to be a minor element in population change in the years immediately ahead and this has been assumed to persist over the projection period.

Fertility remains as the major influence in our prospective growth in population, and indeed the major source of uncertainty in the projections. Essentially the assumption is that the fertility patterns which have characterized recent years, leading to an average family size of approaching 2.5 children, will be maintained over the projection period. This means in particular, that the pattern of early marriage is assumed to persist, and even to be carried a little further in the short term; that average family size is assumed to remain more or less at the current level is not however to say that the distribution of family size will remain unchanged, for a further convergence towards the two- or three child families can be expected.

In a world where fertility control becomes increasingly simple the problem of looking into the future becomes increasingly that of trying to foresee what size of family people want to have. And fertility control has to be seen not solely as a matter of limiting family size, but in controlling the spacing of births, and also enabling those who would like to have more children to achieve their wish. The evidence yielded by surveys is that only a very small proportion of couples marrying wish to limit themselves to having no child or one only. But above all there remains the question of the extent to which people can be expected in practice to achieve their ideal family and no more.

Illegitimacy has previously been referred to in passing, but can be picked up again at this point for it often seems to be assumed that fertility control means that illegitimacy will be wiped out. Without venturing deeply into this exceedingly complex subject, it is perhaps enough to record for the present purpose that although its incidence is assumed in the population projections to reduce over time there is no evidence that illegitimacy will disappear as long as society remains at least recognizably like that of today. For illegitimacy is to no small extent the by-product of our marriage pattern and marriage law.

The evidence of the post-war years has demonstrated that a generation fertility rate of above replacement level is no transient phenomenon, but seems to be a fundamental feature of society as it exists today. There is of course no certainty that it will persist for 30 or more years at the kind of levels that have emerged as characteristic of the 1950s and 1960s, but on the other hand no firm body of evidence at present exists to give a clear alternative, one way or the other, to this assumption.

What the projections therefore exhibit are the expected consequences by the end of the century of the persistence of the fertility characteristic of recent years, slowly declining mortality and net migration remaining relatively small in its effects. If the population at the end of the century differs from what is at present foreseen—whichever way it goes—then it may be in some degree because the consequences of the present trends are seen as unacceptable, and the trends themselves therefore changed. For it must be emphasized that there is nothing deterministic in projections: rather they should be seen as exhibiting the field of choice and decision.

SOURCES

Central Statistics Office (1968). Annual Abstract of Statistics, No. 105, 1968.
    H.M.S.O., London.
Clapham, J. H. (1949). "A Concise Economic History of Britain from the
    Earliest Times to 1750."
    Cambridge University Press, Cambridge.
General Register Office (1969). "Births, Marriages and Deaths. Quarterly Return
    for England and Wales for Quarter ended December, 1968."
    H.M.S.O., London.
General Register Office. "Census of Population." 1841 Report.
    H.M.S.O., London.
General Register Office. "Fertility Tables, 1911, 1951, 1961."
    H.M.S.O., London.
General Register Office. "Population (Marital Condition) Tables, 1851-1961."
    H.M.S.O., London.
General Register Office (1969). Registrar General's Statistical Review of England
    and Wales for the year 1967. Part II. Tables, population.
    H.M.S.O., London.
Glass, D. V. (1945). "Population in History," Chapter 1 (D. V. Glass and
    D. E. C. Eversley, eds).
    Edward Arnold (Publishers), London.
"Royal Commission on Population (1949)". Report.
    H.M.S.O., London.
Royal Commission on Population (1954). Population. Papers of the Royal
    Commission. Vol. VI. Trend and pattern of fertility in Great Britain.
    Report on family census of 1946." (By D. V. Glass and E. Grebenik.)
    H.M.S.O., London.
Russell, J. C. (1948). "British Medieval Population."
    University of New Mexico Press, Albuquerque.

CHAPTER 2

The Carrying Capacity of the Land in the Year 2000

G. W. COOKE

Lawes Agricultural Trust

INTRODUCTION

The "target" assumed in this paper is that of growing enough food for the *present* population. No doubt our population will be larger in 30 years time, but to grow all we need now is a difficult enough task. The first section of this paper states the resources we have for producing food. Present production from British farms is then compared in the second section with the total food we eat, to show where large increases are needed. The third section discusses the possibilities of increasing or re-arranging the areas of crop, and increasing crop yields and animal produce. Estimates are very approximate but attempt to be realistic; precision is pointless when the progress of scientific work, the weather, and agricultural conditions cannot be forecast. The fourth section is speculative and discusses the possibilities for considerable changes in agricultural systems; using novel foods to substitute for traditional foods; and the ultimate possibilities for producing food in these islands. The emphasis throughout the paper is on the kinds of scientific work that are needed to help us feed more people from British farms.

SOURCES OF DATA

Detailed references are not given for the sources of agricultural statistics used. Older information is mostly from "A Century of Agricultural Statistics. Great Britain 1866–1966" published by the Ministry of Agriculture, Fisheries and Food and the Department of Agriculture and Fisheries for Scotland (H.M.S.O., 1968). Most recent information is from "Annual Review and Determination of Guarantees 1969" (Command 3965, H.M.S.O., March 1969), and earlier issues of this "Annual Review". These recent data refer to United Kingdom, older data are for Great Britain only.

RESOURCES FOR PRODUCING FOOD

Table I shows how much British farmers spend; the proportions of the total that are spent on the main means of production are examined in the following sections.

TABLE I

Total expenses of U.K. farmers and the proportions spent on the main means of production

	1938/9 246	1947/8 476	1957/8 1205½	1968/9 1673½
Total expenses £m				
	Percentage contribution			
Feeding stuffs	27.8	7.1	27.2	29.1
Labour	26.8	43.4	25.2	18.7
Machinery	9.5	17.2	17.6	16.8
Rent and interest	17.8	10.4	7.3	10.7
Fertilizers	3.9	6.4	7.8	9.2
Herbicides and insecticides	–	–	–	1.6
Others	14.2	15.5	14.9	13.9

LAND

The land costs about 10% of total farm expenses. Table II gives areas under arable crops and grass now and 10, 30 and 100 years ago. Nearly 400,000 acres were lost to agriculture in the last 10 years and there has been public concern about the amounts of farmland used for roads, factories and towns. For the 30-year period that we are considering we have plenty of land; losing a further million acres (3% of what we have) will be easily made good by quite small advances in agricultural efficiency. While we have many millions of acres, especially of grassland, that produce much less than they could, farmers cannot legitimately complain that land is taken for uses other than farming. However it is regrettable that often very productive land is taken. Further areas of land with limited agricultural potential, and difficult to improve, can be used for forestry or for recreation without greatly affecting food production, because it will always be best to concentrate improved materials and techniques on the better land.

MEN

Diminishing labour on British farms (Table III) should concern us much more than trivial losses of land. We had nearly a million workers in 1947, now fewer than half a million. Early statistics are uncertain but in 1851 there were about 1.5 million workers in England and Wales, by 1951 only about 0.7 million. Farm workers have been becoming fewer for more than a century, but the pace has recently quickened and the figures in Table III for the last 20 years show the recent dramatic losses that have removed 40% of our labour in 10 years. In spite

TABLE II

*Areas of crops and grass in U.K. in 1957/8 and 1967/8 and in
Great Britain in 1866 and 1938*

	Millions of acres			
	1866 (G.B.)	1938 (G.B.)	1957/8 (U.K.)	1967/8 (U.K.)
Wheat	3.4	1.9	2.2	2.4
Barley	2.2	1.0	2.8	5.9
Oats, rye, other cereals	2.8	2.1	2.5	1.1
Potatoes	0.5	0.6	0.8	0.7
Sugar beet	0.0	0.3	0.4	0.5
Other crops	4.0	2.6	2.4	1.8
Temporary grass (including lucerne)	3.7	3.4	6.4	6.0
Permanent grass (excluding rough grazing)	11.1	17.4	13.5	12.3
Total, crops plus grass	28.7	29.3	31.0	30.6

of this, production increased in the period from an "Index" of 107 in 1956/57 to 135 in 1966/67. But there is a limit to the increases in agricultural efficiency that can occur while labour diminishes and urban industry cannot expect a further 300,000 men from agriculture during the *next* 10 years! Production per man has increased because bigger and more powerful machines are used; few jobs are now done by hand if a machine can do them satisfactorily. Other kinds of scientific work have helped, for example the new pre-emergent herbicides used on sugar beet sown by modern spacing drills have nearly eliminated hand hoeing and singling.

TABLE III

Total workers in U.K. agriculture

	Thousands
1947	980
1952	869
1957	750
1962	633
1965	551
1968	450

Further losses of labour will be stopped only by paying the highly-skilled, versatile and competent workers that remain as much (or preferably more) than they could earn as factory and construction workers. Assessments of future food production must take account of the workers we have and recognize that agriculture is unlikely ever again to have a million men. Schemes for reclaiming marginal and remote land that may never be very productive, or that require much hand labour, will be possible only by paying much more for food and attracting some urban workers to work on farms.

MACHINES

Machinery costs farmers (Table I) nearly twice as much as 30 years ago. Machines and men are largely interchangeable; 30 years ago the two together cost 36.3% of total expenses, now they cost 35.8%.

FEEDING STUFFS

Table I shows how animal feeding stuffs were much restricted during the war when more arable crops were used for human food. The proportions of total spending used for animals now and 30 years ago, when markets were not regulated, are surprisingly similar.

FERTILIZERS

Table IV shows changes in the fertilizers used in the United Kingdom during the last century and emphasizes how the technological revolution, which began in the 1940's, has flourished with the relatively stable economic background that

TABLE IV

Amounts of nutrients (as elements) applied as fertilizers,
1874–1968

	N	P	K
	Thousands of tons		
1874	34	30	3
1913	29	79	19
1939	60	75	62
1948	186	173	147
1958	315	169	289
1965	565	211	340
1968	748	205	366

followed the 1947 Agriculture Act. From 1939 the fertilizers used increased rapidly to support the increased areas of food crops (much grown on poor grass that was ploughed). By 1950 enough P was being used to maintain yields and improve poor soils; 10 years later the same had been achieved with K fertilizers, and the amounts of P and K used have been roughly stable during the last few years. The only large potential increase that fertilizers can give now is from using more nitrogen to increase and to regulate yields from grassland. We have enough fertilizers, and enough scientific information to use them efficiently, to ensure that crops are not limited in yield by inadequate nutrition.

OTHER CHEMICALS

Thirty years ago few insect pests and weeds could be killed without harming the crop. Even now so many pests and diseases remain to be controlled that we forget the progress that has been made. Selective weedkillers clean cereals and a few other crops. Insects that used to make root-growing hazardous can now be well controlled, as can the aphis that often destroyed beans and those that transmitted virus diseases in sugar beet and potatoes. Pre-emergent herbicides have eliminated hand work in root crops and made beans a cleaning crop instead of a weed problem. Total herbicides without residues (e.g. the bipyridyls) have made new systems of farming possible.

TABLE V

Costs and amounts of chemicals per acre used for a sugar beet crop

		Cost/acre		
Plant nutrients		£	s.	d.
Nitrogen $\left\{ \begin{array}{l} \text{liquid fertilizer + NaNO}_3 \text{ to} \\ \text{supply a total of 1.36 cwt N/acre} \end{array} \right\}$		4	10	0
6 cwt of basic slag (0.72 cwt P_2O_5/acre)		2	11	6
6 cwt of kainit		3	4	6
Kieserite (5 cwt/acre)		2	13	9
Manganese			13	0
Boron			15	0
	TOTAL	£14	7	9
Herbicides		£	s.	d.
Aminotriazole		5	15	0
Paraquat			14	0
Pyramin		4	9	0
	TOTAL	£10	18	0
Pesticides		£	s.	d.
DDT			6	0
Thimet		1	15	0
	TOTAL	£2	1	0

Seventeen million pounds were spent on herbicides in 1967 (only £5 m. in 1961), and insecticides have cost British farmers £9–10 m. annually for the last 10 years. The advances in weed, pest and disease control during the last 25 years have been spectacular and we may expect them to continue as new materials are discovered and developed. An indication of the way that chemistry may dominate agriculture in future is given in Table V, which shows the chemicals used to grow an acre of sugar beet on the East Anglian Breckland, described recently by Hagen (1968).

SCIENTIFIC HELP TO AGRICULTURE

In addition to the direct means of production shown in Table I, long-term assessments of possible increases in food production must take account of scientific work intended to increase yields and lessen costs. Without this, progress would be slow and uncertain, and limited to the "trial and error" improvements made by progressive farmers. In Britain most research and some development is sponsored by the Agricultural Research Council (ARC) and some development is done by the National Agricultural Advisory Service (NAAS), which also provides much of the advice to farmers. Industries that sell to farmers also do much research in developing new products to aid crop and animal production; they also do some less specialized research of value to agriculture as a whole and advise farmers on how to use their products.

The United Kingdom now spends on research and development about 2.7% of the "Gross National Product" (Royal Institute of Chemistry, 1969). In 1967/68 the Agricultural Research Council spent about £12 m., representing only about 0.7% of the value of agricultural produce (about £1800 m.). To this must be added the amounts spent by the Agricultural Departments in England and Wales and in Scotland, and by industry; I do not have estimates of these. It seems that we spend a much smaller proportion of the value of output from agriculture on research than is spent in other industries. If we intend to produce all our food in these islands, current research will not be sufficient. Hunt (1969) has recently discussed the need for planning of both research on grassland and the use of the results in practice on British farms. He states "A National Programme for Research in Agriculture" has been published in the United States which analyses the needs for research and calculates the workers needed to sustain future farming in America. Hunt suggests a similar plan is needed in Britain. Some existing knowledge is not yet fully applied, for example the use of fertilizers on grassland and newer information on animal feeding. But in other branches (for example, cereal growing) yields are not rising quickly because they are limited by pests and diseases that need more research on their control. Much of the extra food produced by A.D. 2000 will be a result of money spent on research in the next 30 years.

PRESENT AGRICULTURAL PRODUCTION IN RELATION
TO THE FOOD WE EAT

PRODUCE FROM LIVESTOCK

Table VI shows numbers of stock 20 years ago (before the post-war increases) and now.

TABLE VI

Numbers of livestock in U.K.

	Millions	
	1946	1968
Dairy cows	} 3.5	3.3
Beef cows		1.2
Total cattle and calves	9.6	12.2
Sows for breeding	0.2	0.9
Total pigs	2.0	7.4
Ewes	8.3	11.4
Total sheep and lambs	20.4	28.0
Total poultry	67.0	127.0

Meat produced. Table VII shows the striking increases in the meat produced by British farmers, nearly three times as much as 20 years ago; about as much is imported as then. So at present we produce roughly two-thirds of the meat we eat (but we produce much more than the total we had in 1946/47, and just about as much as we had in 1953/54). To replace imports and yet maintain our food we would have to produce here, or replace by other meats about:

　　250 thousand tons of beef and veal

　　330 thousand tons of mutton and lamb

　　400 thousand tons of bacon and ham.

In estimating how much more could be produced we have to look at the past changes in production and examine the food needed by the animals.

Beef and veal. These meats have increased by 60% in 20 years and there is little doubt we could produce the extra beef needed by fertilizing our grassland better and so carrying more stock. (Veal might be difficult because killing a calf for veal means the loss of a potential source of either beef or milk, or both.)

Mutton and lamb. Nearly twice as much is produced as in 1946/47, although numbers of sheep and lambs have increased from 20 to only 28 million. Although increased technical efficiency would help, numbers of sheep would have to be increased greatly to produce all the mutton and lamb we eat;

probably the ewe flock would have to be doubled (to 22 million—Table VI). I think it would be difficult to produce this extra meat. Five million extra ewes need at least a million acres of well-fertilized grass to keep them through most of the year. Sheep need skilled labour at lambing and shearing, and good shepherds are scarce. New methods of feeding and handling lambs in "batteries" may be needed if we have to produce much more.

TABLE VII

Production and imports of meat into United Kingdom

| | | Thousands of tons | | |
| | | 1946/7 | | 1967/8 | |
		Home	Imported	Home	Imported
Beef and veal		550	398	909	248
Mutton and lamb		135	427	251	331
Pork		15	29	555	15
Bacon and ham		87	156	210	402
Poultry meat		70	27	474	9
	TOTAL	857	1037	2399	1005

Pork, bacon and ham. These imports (Table VII) are best considered as total pig meat, of which we produce about 750,000 tons and import 420,000 tons. Total production was only about 100,000 tons in 1946/47. Clearly an industry that increased production 7½ times in 20 years could expand by another 40% during the next 30 years; all that is needed is extra feed (mainly cereals and some extra protein), housing and factories.

Milk products. We produce all the milk we drink. Table VIII shows the products made from milk that are produced and imported. The main imports are 449,000 tons of butter and 174,000 tons of cheese. The total amounts of milk produced in the United Kingdom in 1967/68 and 20 years ago, and the uses made of it were:

| | Millions of gallons | |
Used	1946/7	1967/8
As liquid	1446	1750
For butter	96	243
For cheese	47	278
For cream	–	163
For other products	64	210
	1653	2643

TABLE VIII

Production and imports of dairy products in U.K.

		Thousands of tons			
		1946/7		1967/8	
		Home	Imported	Home	Imported
Butter		18	205	46	449
Cheese		20	191	119	174
Cream { fresh		–	} 161	47	2
Cream { sterilized		–		14	9
Other products		97		426	95
	TOTAL	135	557	652	729

Ignoring the "other products" imported in 1967/68 (Table VIII), I estimate that to replace imports we need 2,500 million gallons of extra milk for butter and 400 million more gallons for cheese. Therefore to become self sufficient in dairy produce means doubling our present production of milk.

Average milk yields have risen from 691 gallons per cow per year in 1955/56 to 808 gallons in 1966/67. Assuming that better stock and better management can give a national average yield of 1000 gallons/cow—which is a reasonable target—about 3 million more cows in milk will be needed to produce all the butter and cheese we eat. Making the extra butter and cheese will need more factories, but the by-products (skimmed milk and whey) will be useful for pig and human food and for industry. The dairy cows culled from the herd would probably provide more meat than we need.

Eggs and poultry meat. Production and imports of eggs 20 years ago and now were:

	Million dozen of eggs	
	1946/7	1967/8
Home supplies	451	1243
Imports	436	47
Total	887	1290

Imports are trivial and, as with poultry meat (Table VII), we produce all we eat.

PRODUCE FROM ARABLE CROPS

Table IX gives the amounts of cereals, potatoes and sugar produced and imported. During 20 years we have doubled the cereals produced and increased sugar by 50%. The large imports in Table IX are 8 million tons of cereals (a third of our total supply) and 2.1 million tons of sugar (two-thirds of what we use).

The *early potatoes* imported could easily be grown here, or replaced by main crop.

TABLE IX

Home produced and imported crops and crop products (U.K.)

	Thousands of tons			
	1946/7		1967/8	
	Home	Imported	Home	Imported
Wheat	1967	4575	3841	4004
Barley	1963	83	9069	107
Oats	2093	166	1364	5
Maize	–	280	–	3741
Sorghum	–	–	–	123
TOTAL GRAIN	7222	5106	14,403	7991
Potatoes				
Earlies	1031	16	584	337
Maincrop	9135	98	6503	12
TOTAL POTATOES	10,166	144	7087	349
Sugar	593	1570	919	2147

Sugar. The sugar now imported would need an extra million acres of beet. This area could be found and farmers on suitable land would welcome the opportunity to grow more beet. Whether it would be worth finding the capital for trebling the factory capacity or risking disturbance with our international trade are matters I shall not discuss. We could also do without these imports of sugar by using chemical sweeteners and replacing the energy of the sugar in our diet by cereals.

Cereals. Roughly half of the 8 million tons of cereals imported is hard wheat used for bread. The other half is maize, which could not be grown here unless early maturing varieties of much greater promise than existing ones are produced. The maize and sorghum could be replaced by barley and wheat products. To replace these imports cereal production would have to be increased by 50%. (Producing an extra 4 million tons of wheat for bread making is not as simple as it seems; using more home-grown wheat introduces problems that are discussed later.) An extra 4 million tons of barley would be needed by the present animal population to replace maize and sorghum; more barley would have to be grown to feed the extra pigs and cattle needed to produce more meat and milk. Altogether twice as much barley as we now produce would be needed so, at one extreme, the area grown would have to be doubled or, at the other extreme, the present yield/acre would need doubling.

IMPORTS IN THE UNITED KINGDOM

Imports of food, beverages and tobacco cost £1765 m. in 1967; food itself totalled £1611 m. and details are shown in Table X. Meat and dairy products

TABLE X

The value of imports of food into U.K. in 1967

	£m.
Meat and meat preparations	372
Dairy products	208
Fish and fish preparations	68
Cereals and cereal preparations	222
Fruit and vegetables	327
Sugar, etc. and honey	103
Coffee, tea, cocoa, spices etc.	171
Animal feed stuff	67
Miscellaneous foods	22
Beverages	64.5
Tobacco	89
Inedible oil seeds, oil nuts, oil kernels	51
Animal and vegetable fats and oils	63

were responsible for over a third of this total, cereals and fruit and vegetables for more than another third. Fish is outside the scope of my paper; we cannot grow coffee, tea, cocoa and spices here. The "targets" set here mean that British farmers must produce additional foods that cost £1300 m. in 1967—over two-thirds as much as our own produce was worth. Imports of animal and vegetable fats and oils are listed in Table X. I do not know whether all of these are used to make butter substitutes and cooking oils, and I have taken no account of them or of the animal feeding stuffs shown in Table X.

SUMMARY

Cereals. Probably about 30 million tons of cereals would be needed. This means doubling present production—a change equal to that achieved during the last 22 years.

Grassland. A rough assessment is that grassland must support twice as many livestock as at present if the dairy herd (plus followers) and the ewe-flock are to be doubled. Because both cereal and grass yields must be doubled there is little room to manoeuvre by ploughing grassland for cereal growing, or vice versa.

Land could be found for growing the temperate fruit and vegetables we import but it might be difficult to treble the sugar beet acreage and certainly it would be difficult to treble sugar factory capacity.

PROSPECTS FOR INCREASED YIELDS FROM CROPS AND ANIMALS

CEREALS

Estimates of cereal yields since A.D. 1200 are in Table XI. Whereas both

TABLE XI

Estimated yields of wheat and barley (approximate)

A.D.	Changes in agriculture that may be relevant	Cwt/acre Wheat	Barley
1200	Open field system	4	—
1650	Enclosure and fallowing	5	—
1750	New methods of drilling	8	—
1800		10	—
1850	Four-course rotations	14	—
1900	Fertilizers and new varieties	17	16
1935		19	16.5
1948	Selective herbicides; more fertilizers used	20	19.5
1958	Varieties with shorter straw	25	23
1962	Nitrogen fertilizers much increased	34	28.5
1963		31.5	28
1964		33.5	29.5
1965		32.5	30
1966		30.5	28
1967		33	30
1968		29	28

wheat and barley yields increased by only about 3 cwt/acre, or 20% from 1900 to 1948, since 1948 they have increased by about 10 cwt/acre, or about 50%. The first part of this increase was no doubt from better varieties, new herbicides and more fertilizers. The large increase in the six years from 1958 to 1964 was mainly because much more N-fertilizer was used. For the last five years yields have not increased. Nevertheless potential yields are much larger than present national averages. Boyd (1968) gives average yields for runs of years from the best treatments in the Rothamsted Ley Arable Experiments exceeding 55 cwt/acre of wheat and nearly 50 cwt/acre of barley—nearly twice the national average. The prospects for larger national yields are discussed below.

Fertilizers. On average, cereals now receive nearly enough fertilizers (Church,

1968). Some crops would benefit from more nitrogen, others receive too much and yield is lost because they lodge. There are no *large* increases in yield to be had from better manuring. Some increase in dressings for cereals grown continuously, plus much more care in adjusting dressings to fit local conditions and the likely supply of N from soil will increase yields, but I estimate the potential gain is only a few cwt/acre. Losses of wheat by lodging caused by excess nitrogen can now be minimized by chemicals (such as CCC) that shorten straw; more use of such chemicals might add 2 cwt to wheat yields, but would not help barley so much.

Diseases. *Root diseases* caused by the fungi *Ophiobolus graminis* and *Cercosporella herpotrichoides* are encouraged when cereals are grown frequently. Slope (1966) showed that soil-borne fungus diseases often caused the loss of a ton/acre of wheat and several cwt/acre of barley in Rothamsted experiments. The only control at present is by using rotations where susceptible crops do not follow each other; because the acreage of suitable non-cereal crops is limited, this remedy cannot be applied to much of our cereal-growing land in south, central and eastern England except by growing much more grass. This means that either high-quality grass must be dried for sale from arable farms, or livestock will have to be kept where there are now few or none. Chemical methods of control by systemic fungicides are needed so that cereals can be grown continuously on the land that suits them best.

Leaf diseases of cereals are common and cause some loss in most seasons, but there are no estimates of the average losses. In some years diseases such as yellow rust have spectacular effects; mildew is often severe and must then diminish yield considerably. If leaf diseases can be controlled by new systemic chemicals (or by breeding varieties that are resistant and remain so) 5 cwt/acre might be added to wheat and barley yields.

Pests. Occasional losses in yield of wheat are caused by wheat bulb fly and by larvae that burrow in stems, and all cereals are sometimes damaged by wire worm. However, these pests occur sporadically rather than generally (their incidence has been discussed by Strickland (1968)). The damage done by cyst-forming and free-living nematodes to cereals grown on light soils is probably more serious. Cereal cyst nematode has been a well recognized pest of oats for many years, but it also damages wheat and barley where these are grown often on light soils. Damage to barley by ectoparasitic nematodes seems common on some of the light soils of Eastern England, but no estimates have been made of average losses.

The problems of controlling leaf and root diseases and parasitic nematodes are difficult and we cannot be sure of complete success, even in 30 years. But it is reasonable to expect new methods of control might raise yields by 10-20 cwt/acre in areas where crops are now often damaged.

Varieties. Cappelle Desprez wheat and Procter barley, both introduced in the early 1950's, were responsible for a considerable increase in national average yields. They had larger potential yields than the varieties they replaced; they were also stiff-strawed and responded well to larger dressings of N-fertilizer without so much risk of loss from lodging. These two varieties are becoming obsolete. The varieties replacing them give slightly more grain and some have special characteristics of disease resistance or are suitable for special purposes such as bread making. In some other countries new varieties of wheat and rice have been bred with much larger potential yields.

New dwarf wheats that do not lodge were developed in Japan and this seed was taken to the United States in 1946 and used in breeding programmes. Gaines wheat, introduced in Washington State in 1961, was one result; it is now much grown in Western states where farmers often harvest "100 bushel crops" (about 3 tons/acre) and more from it. Parallel developments in breeding in Mexico so increased yields that the country changed in a few years from importing to exporting wheat although the population increased considerably. Swaminathan (1968) described how Mexican seed of the dwarf wheats was introduced in 1963 to India where national yields had been about 800 kg/ha for several decades. After testing in 1963–1965, two million hectares were sown in 1967/68 when over 17 million metric tons of wheat were harvested from 13 million hectares, compared with 12 million tons in 1964/65. The older tall varieties had maximum yields of about 3000–4000 kg/ha; the new dwarf wheats have doubled this limit, yielding 7000–8000 kg/ha. Other changes in farming have had to be made to achieve these larger maximum yields. The timing of irrigation was changed, the seed had to be sown more shallowly and more nitrogen fertilizer used.

R. F. Chandler (1969) at the International Rice Research Institute described success in breeding rice with much larger potential yields than the *Indica* varieties commonly grown in south-east Asia which are tall and do not respond to nitrogen. One old variety discussed by Chandler, Peta, yielded 5.1 tons/ha without N in dry season experiments and 5.5 tons/ha with 30 kg N/ha; giving more N lessened yield. Variety IR8, which replaced it, yielded 4.6 tons/ha without N-fertilizer but 8.5 tons with 120 kg N/ha. In the wet season, Peta yielded 2.9 tons/ha and its yield was depressed by N; IR8 gave 4.1 tons without N-fertilizer and 5½ tons with 80 kg N/ha.

With these examples of success elsewhere, I think that there could be substantial gains during the next 30 years from breeding varieties of wheat and barley that yield much more. Assuming the development of chemicals to control root and leaf disease, and better fertilizer practice, it is possible that average cereal yields by A.D. 2000 may be double the present.

Quality. Only yield has been considered in this discussion. For barley this is sufficient because most will be used for animal food; some barley will replace maize and its larger protein percentage will be an advantage, but some of its physical characteristics will be disadvantages. Greater difficulty is likely in replacing the 4 million tons of hard wheat we import each year for bread making. Most British wheats do not have the chemical composition required by millers and bakers. Our baking industry is committed to machine baking and packing of kinds of bread that store well; it is essential that new varieties of wheat intended to replace hard wheat must be suitable for present milling and baking methods and have characteristics that are reliably maintained from year to year. Considerable progress has been made in breeding new British wheats suitable for making bread and this must continue. In addition we must find how cultural conditions and fertilizing alter the grain's composition, for example late dressings of N-fertilizer may give grain with more protein that is better for bread making. Kent (1969) reviewed problems of using more British grown soft wheats in place of imported hard wheats and concludes "the possibility of increasing the usage of home-grown wheat for bread making is thus closely dependent upon finding a solution to the technological problem of milling soft wheat flour with an adequate degree of starch damage". (This change in milling is needed to ensure that the flour from soft wheat takes up as much water as "stronger" flour.)

GRASSLAND

The yield from grassland which has enough lime, P and K and water is proportional to the nitrogen available, which can come from soil, legumes, or fertilizer (Brockman, 1969). Sandy soils and most arable soils supply far too little for grasses grown alone as leys on "arable" land. Traditional permanent grass is usually a mixture of several legumes and many grasses. Most temporary grass is sown with mixtures ranging from one or two grasses with white clover to several grasses with both white and red clovers. The production of mixed swards where legumes are relied on for nitrogen is limited to 50–70 cwt dry matter/acre when pastures are well managed. A legume grown alone in Britain may fix 200–400 lb N/acre in a year; when grown with grasses, clover often fixes only 100 lb N and rarely more than 200 lb N/acre, and only a portion of this becomes available to associated grasses as clover roots die. Results published by Armitage and Templeman (1964) are typical of many. With 133 lb N/acre used in a year an all-grass sward yielded the same as clover-grass sward without N-fertilizer. When more N was used the grass sward yielded more and responded linearly up to about 350 lb N/acre used in the year. Most experiments show that with adequate N British grassland can average five tons of dry matter/acre, more in a wet season and less when dry. With irrigation or in wet climates consistent yields around 6 tons/acre can be had.

In 1966 only 75% of our *temporary grass* received nitrogen and the average on dressed fields was about 75 lb/acre. Only 46% of permanent grass fields had nitrogen at an average rate of about 60 lb/acre. Clearly there are very large gains to be had from using much more N on grass.

Assessing the carrying capacity of our grassland if all received adequate fertilizer is difficult because we do not know current yields. Hay yields recorded by the Ministry of Agriculture are in Table XII. After 75 years in which they did

TABLE XII

Hay yields in Great Britain

	cwt/acre
1885	28.2
1905	23.9
1925	24.2
1935	23.0
1945	25.4
1955	26.7
1960	27.7
1964	32.2
1965	31.6
1966	32.3

not improve, yield increased during the last few years (Table XII), presumably because farmers were beginning to use a little N-fertilizer. Estimating total yield of grassland from hay yields (usually a single cut) is difficult. The long-term (1920–1959) average yield of *two* cuts of hay in Park Grass experiment at Rothamsted from plots with PK fertilizer (averaging limed and unlimed land), but without N, was 32 cwt/acre, equal to the recent national average yields. The total produce from plots receiving only 129 lb N/acre (the largest N tested) was 59 cwt of dry matter/acre. At present British farmers use a little N on about two-thirds of their grassland; although some extra nutrients are provided by excreta from grazing animals, the average total yield from our grass is not likely to be as large as twice the national average hay yield. All experimental work with nitrogen fertilizers suggests we could produce twice as much. Hunt (1969) says that surveys show average utilized starch from grass is only half what it should be.

There are considerable technical problems in using the extra grass grown by large amounts of N-fertilizer efficiently, but I assume that these can be solved in the next 30 years. We may develop systems where most forage is harvested and fed to cattle in enclosures, the extra cost of handling grass being offset by the close control in feeding and by avoiding the waste inevitable in grazing. Enough pioneer farmers are experimenting with large N dressings (9% of fields in leys had more than 190 lb N/acre in 1966, 3% of permanent grass fields had 175 lb or more) and with new methods of handling herbage and stock, to ensure that, with favourable prices, our average grassland could be feeding twice as much stock in A.D. 2000. This assumes the present pattern of feeding continues—mainly grass products with some cereals, imported protein feeds being replaced by the high protein grass that fertilizer—N makes possible.

Table XIII shows changes in areas of grass and in livestock numbers in the last century. Between 1936 and 1966 cattle *increased* by 40% and sheep by 20% while the area of grassland diminished by 20% and proportionately less imported

TABLE XIII

Land and stock in Great Britain, 1866–1966

	Total cattle and calves millions	Total sheep millions	Total permanent grass	Total temporary grass million acres	All grass
1866	4.8	22.0	11.1	3.7	14.8
1896	6.5	26.7	16.7	4.6	21.3
1916	7.4	25.0	17.5	4.1	21.6
1936	7.8	24.2	17.4	3.6	21.0
1946	8.7	19.7	11.1	5.1	16.2
1956	10.0	22.7	12.1	5.6	17.7
1961	10.9	27.8	11.7	6.6	18.3
1966	11.0	28.9	11.2	5.6	16.8

cereals were used for animal feeding. This seems to be the beginning of the technical revolution needed in our grassland farming that will have to be completed in the next 30 years. If enough fertilizer is used to achieve the most yield from grass, and methods of handling stock are developed to use all the grass efficiently, it does not seem unreasonable to expect to double animal produce. Yields may also be increased by research on pests and diseases of grasses, of which little is known, and from breeding more productive strains. Species that are particularly suitable for local conditions need to be developed; for example species that survive by forming rhizomes may have advantages in light soils in dry areas.

POSSIBLE GAINS FROM USING CHEMICALS TO INCREASE PRODUCTIVITY

Herbicides. The "hormone" weedkillers that destroy broadleaved weeds and do not damage cereals were first used by farmers about 25 years ago. Since then selective weedkillers have been developed for use in many crops; these have given new "degrees of freedom" to farming. Selective herbicides are being developed to deal with new problems arising from new farming systems such as continuous cereal growing. Others make it possible to produce larger yields with diminishing labour *and* to keep the crops clean. Other chemicals that can replace cultivations by destroying weeds, or the remains of one crop before sowing another, are discussed later as these give greater freedom in using land. The history of herbicides in the last quarter century suggests that new materials will be developed quickly enough to overcome problems of special cropping systems as they arise.

Chemicals to alter crop growth. Several groups of chemicals are known that can alter the way plants grow. Some, such as the kinins, have not yet been used in agriculture. Gibberellic acid increases the height of plants, and its discovery about 12 years ago suggested there may be ways of adjusting the size and shape of plants to make them suit specified purposes. Early hopes of gains in yield from gibberellic acid were not fulfilled, though gibberellin preparations are used to increase sugar cane yields in Hawaii. The growth regulator best known to British farmers is CCC (chlorocholine chloride), which shortens the distance between nodes of stems of wheat and helps to prevent lodging that occurs when straw is too weak to support the ears of grain. CCC, and another regulator "B9", speeds the growth of potato tubers early in the season.

Chemicals that modify plant characteristics or growth rates may produce larger yields or lessen the farmer's costs of handling crop or soil. Some possibilities were discussed by Humphries (1968).

OBTAINING MORE LAND FOR CROPS

Using existing land more fully. The maximum is produced from land only when plants cover the ground fully and grow whenever temperature and radiation are enough. No annual plant satisfies these conditions. For example sugar beet and potatoes are sown early in spring but grow slowly at first and rarely cover the whole of the soil surface before mid-June. Therefore about 10 weeks of radiation, increasing temperature, and rainfall, are used in simply establishing such crops, which have to begin to synthesize carbohydrate for storage when days are shortening. Ways of establishing annual plants so that they have a full leaf canopy earlier in the season would increase yield and make better use of land. An ideal crop would have no seasonal characteristics in growth except those related to rainfall, radiation and temperature. Grass produces large yields in cool weather during the first five months of the year if it has enough radiation, water and nitrogen fertilizer, but it usually yields less in the second half of the year than in the first. Research in crop physiology and practical experiments on new ways of handling crops will become even more important if, as has been suggested, the climate here is likely to become colder during the rest of this century.

Marginal land. Suggestions are often made for increasing agricultural produce by reclaiming "marginal" land or rough grazings. Much land un-farmed or under-farmed before 1940 was reclaimed by correcting simple nutrient deficiencies that had been unrecognized, or by work such as drainage or clearing scrub that had previously been uneconomic. Most of the lowland that needed reclaiming is now properly used and there is little scope for increasing our farmland in this way. The only large gains that are possible would come from obtaining more water for irrigating the sandy soils common in southern, central and eastern England.

Marginal land usually means hill land above 800 or 1000 feet, some is fenced, some not; the traditional farming is with livestock. These lands have several disadvantages. Most are hilly and inaccessible, which increases costs and lessens the work a man can do. The soils are poor and because of altitude, growing seasons are shorter and potential yields less than on lower ground. The only usual advantage is the doubtful one of large rainfall. Production *could* be increased considerably by fertilizing and liming hill land, but yields would be less and costs greater than for better and lower land. At present milk is the most profitable produce from upland farms, but the milk costs more than lowland milk because more feed has to be bought. When capital and labour are limited, it seems wrong to spend them on marginal land until all the lowland, where costs are less, is producing the maximum. More *could* be produced from the uplands if cost did not matter and some of the urban population transferred to farm work, but at present it is best to concentrate on improving yield on low country that is accessible and yields more reliably.

A survey of soils and potential land use in the uplands is needed, with particular attention to slope, accessibility, annual accumulated temperature, and rainfall. Uplands that are level, or only moderately sloping, and well-drained, could produce grass to be mechanically harvested, dried and exported to other areas as rich protein feed. Much nitrogen, a little phosphate and some lime would be needed, together with machinery to dry the grass. Other upland not needed by existing farmers for their traditional activities should be forested. (We imported £192 m. worth of wood and lumber in 1967 and £126 m. worth of pulp and waste paper.)

Altering land use. Our three main groups of farm crops are grass, cereals and the high-value crops grown in wide rows like sugar beet, potatoes, vegetables, plus a smaller area of less valuable animal feed crops like kale. Producing most of the food for the existing population, while keeping to our existing pattern of feeding, means that yield from grassland and from cereals must be doubled and that some land must be found to produce the temperate-climate vegetables now imported; we also have to decide whether we need the imported sugar that would take a million acres of sugar beet to produce. We have plenty of land suitable for growing more potatoes, vegetables and beet; with mechanization labour should be sufficient. New factories for packing and processing will be needed. These crops will have to be grown on land that suits mechanical planting and harvesting best so they may be grown often on the same soil, and we must be able to control soil-borne pests and diseases by disinfectants—this should become possible in the next 30 years.

The main conflict for land will be between grass and cereals. Cereals are likely to be favoured because their grains are convenient packages of easily handled and stored concentrated food for animals and people and some of our existing grassland may have to be cropped with cereals, either in rotation with the remaining grass or in all-cereal systems. (Urea can be used to substitute a portion of the protein ruminants now get from grass.) Soil-borne pests and diseases of cereals will have to be controlled so that growing can be concentrated on suitable land in drier areas suited to mechanical work. Grass will use the wetter areas, the soils that are difficult physically for arable cultivation and the more hilly land.

We will have to grow more wheat and, unless spring varieties are much improved, most must be winter wheat. At present winter wheat acreage is limited by the area that a man can plough, cultivate and sow in an average season; in a wet autumn even less is sown. Most wheat is taken after "break" crops to obtain the larger yields that freedom from "take-all" gives and sowing is delayed until beans, potatoes or sugar beet are harvested or grass is ploughed. If much more wheat is to be grown most will have to follow other cereals and this will succeed only where the soil-borne pests and diseases of cereals can be controlled and if ploughing or deep cultivating can be avoided on much of the area. Most crops will be "direct-drilled" on cereal stubbles, starting in September. The land that has to be ploughed in winter, as a routine "rotational" practice, because it has carried other crops, or because its structure was damaged by heavy machines used on wet soil, can be sown to spring cereals. Methods of "direct-drilling" suitable for this country would permit larger areas of winter crops to be sown. Herbicides such as those described by Boon (1965) kill vegetation but leave no active residue in the soil, permitting one crop to be sown in the residues of the last, but the machines now used for sowing need to be improved.

As ploughing to destroy weeds is no longer essential, shallow cultivating, followed by killing of surface vegetation by chemicals, may become common practice for crops other than cereals (Hagen, 1968), the cost of the chemical being repaid by saving on tractors and labour. Cultivating light land by traditional methods usually gives a good seedbed quickly. But turning the plough furrows of heavy soil into seedbeds takes longer, costs more, and depends much on suitable weather to assist the cultivating. Minimum cultivation methods, associated with herbicides, may therefore be more useful on heavy than on light soils. G. M. Shear (1968) reviewed "no-tillage" systems in the United States and his hopeful conclusions are worth quoting: "Regardless of its limitations at the present time this method appears to hold great promise for the future. It could markedly improve soil and water conservation on land now being tilled, as well as greatly increasing the acreage of land adaptable for food crop production but now in pasture or forest because of its steep slope. 'No-tillage' systems of husbandry could conceivably facilitate an increase in food production comparable to that made possible by the shift from animal power to machine power in agriculture that occurred in the United States during the last half century."

NEW FARMING SYSTEMS, NEW FOODS, NEW FEEDING STANDARDS

ARABLE CROPS

The changes likely in arable farming will increase the present trend for farmers to specialize in growing crops that suit their soils and climate best; ease of mechanical planting and harvesting will be of first importance. Research must concentrate on removing limitations now caused by the need to rotate crops to control disease, and to plough and cultivate simply to bury old crop residues and kill weeds.

ANIMAL FEEDING

While we eat the kind of food we are now used to, animal farming must (a) produce milk products and eggs and (b) convert nitrogen from fertilizer or legumes into meat protein as cheaply and efficiently as possible. To produce more will need (a) new systems of handling animals, such are now being developed by pioneer farmers, (b) increases in the yields of the crops needed for animal feeding, (c) using the crops more efficiently, and (d) developing mechanical handling so that more food is produced without an increase in workers.

Alternative foods for animals. Dried grass is a protein-rich, highly digestible and easily handled feed, it is costly to dry and both drying plants and machines to pack the grass need more development. Grass drying is more efficient than silage or hay making because more of the crop ends in the product. Grazing grass is less efficient than harvesting it, because grazing always involves wasting the part of the crop that is trodden or soiled by excreta; this waste is an incentive for developing systems where herbage is cut and fed to housed stock, which will increase meat yields from grassland. Alternative sources of part of the protein for ruminants are established; urea is converted to protein by microbial flora in the rumen. Dried poultry manure (rich in N and P) is now being developed as a supplementary feed for other livestock.

Raymond (1966) discussed new ideas on making best use of grass that are being developed from research on animal nutrition and on methods of growing and handling stock; the new systems will depend on improvements in efficiency of conversion by the animal. It is easily recognized that large yields of arable crops diminish the effect of fixed costs such as rent, seed and sprays on cost of unit produce. But it is not always recognized that large growth rates increase the efficiency of converting feed to animal product. Raymond gives these simple figures for a 500 lb bullock to illustrate this:

Rate of gain/day lb	Feed/day (lb of starch equivalent (SE))			S.E. per 1 lb gain
	For maintenance	For weight gain	Total	
0	3.8	0	3.0	∝
1	3.8	1.6	5.4	5.4
2	3.8	3.4	7.2	3.6
3	3.8	5.4	9.2	3.1

Because the proportion of food in the final product increases with large live-weight gains or large milk yields, more expensive foods are justified for productive stock. Raymond states that most grass-fed animals produce too little because they are underfed; either they do not eat enough in a day, or the feed has too small a digestibility, or both. To improve animal feeding both amounts eaten and digestibility of feed must be maximal. Raymond considers the more expensive methods of conserving feed, by drying young grass artificially, by drying hay in barns, and by using sealed silos will be justified because they lessen losses of herbage and give feed of better nutritive value.

Handling systems. To use the high-quality but expensive produce from fertilized grassland, new systems of handling livestock will be needed. Grazing will diminish as more cattle and sheep are housed and fed mechanically. All the lamb and mutton we eat could be produced only by keeping sheep intensively, as pigs are now. If the number of lambs from one birth and the frequency of breeding could be increased, housed lambs separated from their mothers could be fed mechanically, "broiler" fashion. A less extreme example of intensive sheep-keeping was described by Round (1969). In a new system developed at Rosemaund Experimental Husbandry Farm 5.4 ewes/acre were kept through the year on clover-grass leys and 7.2 ewes/acre on grass leys with 1.8 cwt N/acre (silage was made for winter feeding).

RELATIVE EFFICIENCY OF PRODUCING DIFFERENT ANIMAL PROTEINS

K. W. Woolley (1969) showed how the ratio

$$\frac{\text{lb protein in product}}{\text{lb protein in food}}$$

varied (Table XIV) and stated "in terms of millions of calories per acre of land, pig production, as measured in terms of fat and lean meat is probably higher than any other common type of animal production". He considered beef may become a luxury food and that pig meat could supply most of the extra we need; producing lamb is even more wasteful of protein in feed than is beef.

TABLE XIV

Milk, meat and eggs produced from 100 lb of feed and the ratio of protein produced to protein in the feed

Product	Total product lb	lb protein in product / lb protein in feed
Milk	105.0	0.25
Eggs	32.7	0.25
Broiler	44.4	0.22
Turkey	28.7	0.16
Pork	27.7	0.14
Beef	12.5	0.10
Lamb	11.5	0.08

Ruminants produce meat less efficiently than poultry and pigs, but they can use poorer feeds than non-ruminants, also some non-protein nitrogen and less-digestible carbohydrates. These advantages may, of course, be worthless, if such feeds give smaller rates of live-weight gain than do more digestible feeds. In future agricultural systems ruminants are certain to have a place because they use foods that cannot be digested efficiently by man and other non-ruminants. These include the by-products and wastes from crops that would otherwise be used only for compost.

Table XV shows the energy values of several feeds for ruminants, pigs and poultry quoted by Woolley (1969). Any national plan for producing meat must take account of the small efficiency of converting feed into high-quality beef and lamb. Producing extra animal protein by increasing pig and poultry farming, and as a by-product of the dairy industry, instead of increasing sheep and beef cattle, would allow some existing grassland to be used for growing cereals. Pigs compete with poultry for cereals; Table XIV suggests it is better to produce

TABLE XV

Comparison of species with respect to net energy values of different feeds

	Absolute value, kcal energy gained per gram of dry matter			Relative values		
	Ox	Pig	Hen	Ox	Pig	Hen
Maize grain	2.04	3.01	3.05	100	147	150
Earthnut cake	1.77	2.61	2.28	100	147	129
Wheat bran	1.50	1.71	1.06	100	114	71
Wheat chaff	0.63	0.28	—	100	44	—

broilers than pork because broilers give 50% more live-weight and 50% more protein in the product. Converting protein in feed to protein in milk is even more efficient; there is no waste from milk and the system gives cow beef as a by-product. The "protein" in feed for cows can be all from grass (the cheapest source) and can include much non-protein nitrogen. Producing eggs (in which there is no waste) uses protein as efficiently as making milk, and culled hens are by-products.

SUBSTITUTES FOR ANIMAL PRODUCTS

Raymond (1968) states that with present husbandry, grass and forage crops fed to ruminants yield less energy and protein for human food than does wheat grown on the same area of land. If small-yield grassland systems cannot be made to produce meat and dairy products efficiently, they could be replaced by crops that can give substitutes for animal protein already being developed by food technologists. Raymond states that meat made from spun soya-bean protein, and "non-dairy milk and cream", are already widely accepted in the United States, where they are called "analogue" rather than "synthetic" foods.

Soya bean. F. E. Breth (1968) described "textured meat", "filled milk" and high-protein flours, gruels and drinks based on soya bean (which has 40% protein). United States farmers harvested over 1000 million bushels in 1968; the American average yield of 13 cwt/acre is disappointing (45 cwt/acre yields have been reported), but the protein yield/acre is five times that of beef. Breth stated relative costs:

	Per lb s. d.	Protein %	Per lb of protein s. d.
Beef	5 10	15.2	38 4
Pork	4 2	11.6	35 10
Poultry	2 6	20.0	12 6
Non-fat dry milk solids	1 2	35.6	3 5
Soya beans	5	34.9	1 2

Soya proteins are adversely criticised because they have only 60% of the methionine and cysteine in an equal amount of egg protein, but an ounce supplies as much of these essential aminoacids as an adult needs. Soya bean also provides cheap fat; a pound of fat in milk cost 6s 8d, in soya bean 1s 0d.

Field beans. Soya bean can be grown here only in the most favourable seasons, so these are no help to us in producing alternatives to animal protein. Field beans *(Vicia faba. L)* with 24 to 28% of true protein, are our most concentrated source of protein; they are a good source of lysine, rating second to soya bean, but they contain only half as much methionine and cysteine as soya. The acreage of beans has increased lately because they have found a (subsidized) place as a "break" crop between cereals and because pre-emergent herbicides, and systemic insecticides, make them cleaner and more reliable. Nevertheless they do not seem to have been readily accepted by makers of animal feeding stuffs. Research on methods of extracting protein from beans is needed to see if a protein concentrate can be prepared that would replace part of our meat protein and also be useful in pig and poultry feeding.

Leaf protein. The most favourable figures in Table XIV show that even in milk and eggs no more than a quarter of the protein in animal food is converted to protein in human food. For this reason the direct use of leaves as a source of protein in human nutrition has long been advocated and in recent years machinery has been developed at Rothamsted and elsewhere to extract protein on a large scale. Protein can be extracted for human food from leaves that man cannot eat and also from leaves that are by-products of crops grown for other purposes.

Byers and Sturrock (1965) recorded the yield of leaf protein extracted by large-scale processing of several crops grown at Rothamsted. The largest yields of extracted protein per acre were from cereals. By cutting wheat twice and then growing mustard in the second half of the year 900 lb/acre of extracted protein could be obtained in a year. Pirie (1969) reported later work, stating that in 1968 nearly a ton/acre of protein was extracted from winter wheat followed by two crops of fodder radish. Worthwhile yields were obtained from crop wastes, about 300 lb/acre of protein was extracted from waste vines and pods of peas, potato haulm at the end of August gave 225 lb/acre, and sugar beet tops 450 lb/acre. These yields may be compared with the total 10 cwt/acre of protein in a 40 cwt/acre crop of beans or the 6 cwt of protein in a 50 cwt/acre crop of wheat grain—both yields are much more than current farm averages.

The fibrous material remaining after protein is extracted is useful as a food for ruminants and its nitrogen content can be supplemented with urea. Pirie (1969) considers it is likely to be more valuable nutritionally than a "super-hay" with the same % N. The final benefit from such processes is that the liquor remaining after protein is separated from leaf juice is a suitable medium for growing micro-organisms that could provide more edible protein. Woodham (1969) has recently summarized research on separation of protein concentrates from green leaves and seeds and concludes "If good quality protein is the prime requirement, there seems little point in producing ripe seed containing a mixture of good and poor proteins only to be faced with the task of separating them, when more good protein was available much earlier in the leaf, with a useful by-product feed for ruminants as well".

Other sources of protein. Other methods of producing edible protein are being developed such as growing yeasts on hydrocarbon residues from the oil industry, and tank cultures of other organisms. As these do not use agricultural land they are outside the scope of this paper; they may, however, become important sources of concentrated protein for man and livestock.

THE ULTIMATE LIMIT TO FOOD PRODUCTION

Agricultural efficiency. The ultimate limit to producing food is set by the efficiency of photosynthesis, and this is small. In an irrigation experiment at Woburn, Penman (1962) found the best return from grass (growing from March to October) was a little over 1% of incoming radiation converted into plant yield; from the time potatoes and sugar beet covered the rows in June they converted 1.8% and 2.1% respectively. Penman states on theoretical grounds that at most 8 or 10% of incoming radiation might be converted to product and says "this gap is a measure of the challenge facing agricultural science".

Dietary standards. Clark (1968) could not substantiate FAO's assertion that 10-15% of the world's population were hungry and a further 35-40% were "malnourished". He says FAO's "Third World Survey" assumes people were malnourished unless they were eating Western-European diets, and deriving at least 20% of their total calories from animal products, fruit, vegetables and oils. He says no evidence was given for this assumption except "it is generally agreed". Clark suggests that most people in Western Europe, far from being on the borderline of malnutrition, are in considerable danger of being overfed. He considers the calories needed by the whole population range from a "little over 2000 for larger bodied people, or in a cold climate, to as little as 1625 for small bodied people, in a hot climate". He also says it is quite possible for man to live almost entirely on cereals (*not* on roots for these contain too little protein); the 60 grams of protein/person/day required would be more than supplied by wheat and barley products used to provide 2000 calories/day.

Clark calculated that, after allowing for a small amount of animal products, and for land to produce green vegetables and textile fibres, each person needs each year agricultural produce equivalent to 250 kg of grain. So if we grew 20 million acres of cereals in the United Kingdom, and used 10 million acres for vegetables and to provide some animal products, these islands could support more than 100 million people without assuming much increase in current yields. In contrast Clark shows that an American-type diet costs 11 times as much as a subsistence diet and needs several times as much land.

It is difficult to discuss how many people our land could support when the amounts of food needed seem so uncertain. Clark quotes differences such as the FAO standard of 2100 calories for a 7–9 year child and other estimates of 1072 calories for an African child of the same age. Similarly, for a 16–19 year male FAO states 3600 calories are needed, another author estimates 3012 calories are needed in India, and yet another states 1526 calories are enough in Africa. Whatever the "correct" standards may be it seems certain that FAO figures are too large. Clark discusses the diet that seems satisfactory in Japan, mainly cereals with a little fish and animal protein. He says that, even with an allowance for the "wood" needed (supplied by bamboo), a person in an Asian country can be fed and sheltered by the produce from 680 sq. metres of land.

Fanciful calculations that extend such estimates to allow for larger photosynthesis per unit area, and for larger agricultural efficiency, have suggested that much smaller areas could support one person. Presumably difficulties would then arise from the dense populations shading the crops they depended on, and from the vices analogous to feather picking and tail biting that occur in battery farming!

REFERENCES

Armitage, E. R. and Templeman, W. G. (1964). Response of grassland to nitrogenous fertilizer in the west of England.
J. Br. Grassld Soc. **19**, 291-297.
Boon, W. R. (1965). Diquat and paraquat—New agricultural tools.
Chemy Ind. pp. 782-788.
Boyd, D. A. (1968). Experiments with ley and arable farming systems.
Rep. Rothamsted exp. Stn 1967, p. 316.
Breth, F. E. (1968). Ersatz-foods, the dangers ahead.
Fmr Stk Breed., 3 December, p. 49.
Brockman, J. S. (1969). The relationship between total N input and yield of cut grass swards. *J. Br. Grassld Soc.* **24**, 89-97.
Byers, M. and Sturrock, J. W. (1965). The yields of leaf protein extracted by large-scale processing of various crops. *J. Sci. Fd Agric.* **16**, 341-355.
Chandler, R. F. (1969). Improving the rice plant and its culture.
Nature, Lond. **221**, 1007-1010.
Church, B. M. (1968). Fertiliser use on cereals in England and Wales, 1966.
Ceres (J. Home-Grown Cereals Auth.) **3**, 7-14.
Clark, C. (1968). "Population Growth and Land Use", pp. 123-157.
Macmillan, London.
Hagen, R. J. (1968). Beet without ploughing. *Br. Sug. Beet Rev.* **36**, 180.
Humphries, E. C. (1968). CCC and cereals. *Fld Crop Abstr.* **21**, 91-99.
Hunt, I. V. (1969). Presidential address: "The need for action".
J. Br. Grassld Soc. **24**, 1-5.
Kent, N. L. (1969). Bread: the problem of increasing the usage of home-grown wheat. *Ceres (J. Home-Grown Cereals Auth.)* **5**, 3-8.
Penman, H. L. (1962). Woburn irrigation, 1951-59. I. Purpose, design and weather. *J. agric. Sci., Camb.* **58**, 343-379.
Pirie, N. W. (1969). *Rep. Rothamsted exp. Stn 1968, Pt. 1*, pp. 118-121.
Raymond, W. F. (1966). The best use of grassland. *J. Fmrs' Club*, March.
Raymond, W. F. (1968). Grassland research and practice.
Jl R. agric. Soc. **129**, 85-105.
Round, F. J. (1969). An intensive sheep enterprise.
Agriculture, Lond. **76**, 169-172.
Royal Institute of Chemistry (1969). *Chemy Br.* **5** (No. 2), 52.

Shear, G. M. (1968). The development of the no-tillage concept in the United States. *Outl. Agric.* **5**, 247-251.

Slope, D. B. (1966). Getting to grips with disease that cuts back cereal yields. *Arable Fmr,* December, 20-23.

Strickland, A. H. (1968). Some pesticide inputs and crop outputs in wheat. *Ceres (J. Home-Grown Cereals Auth.)* **4**, 18-22.

Swaminathan, M. S. (1968). India's success with dwarf wheats. *Span* **11**, 138-142.

Woodham, A. A. (1969). Society of Chemical Industry Symposium, Lancaster. (In press.)

Woolley, K. W. (1969). Pigs in the future. *J. Fmrs' Club,* April.

CHAPTER 3

The Price of Pollution in the Year 2000

K. MELLANBY

Nature Conservancy

Pollution is essentially the presence of substances in the wrong place. Pollutants may be poisons, by-products of human activities, or they may be otherwise desirable substances transferred by human activities to places where they are not wanted. The greater the number of people, the greater the possibilities of pollution, and the greater the number of people to be adversely affected by that pollution. Man is an animal who often fouls his own nest. Pollution control is the prevention of this process.

The prospects for successful pollution control in Britain, even with a greatly increased population, are good, if we are prepared to pay the cost in money and trouble. During the last hundred years the population has more than doubled, but in many ways our environment, particularly in our cities, has improved. The air of London is far less smoky, the Thames is no longer a stinking sewer. However, any forecast could be widely wrong. Unforeseen changes in industrial practice could produce unexpected pollutants, and present new problems. Improvements in techniques for waste disposal could solve old ones. Also the situation is affected by the economic position of Britain. We may become more and more prosperous, or we may be approaching national bankruptcy. If industry booms, factories will use more energy and will, potentially, produce more pollutants. If there is a substantial recession, safety precautions may be neglected to cut costs and make exports competitive; alternatively industry may stagnate and imports may be cut, with substantial effects on agriculture.

Industrial civilization depends on energy to keep our factories working and to heat (or cool) our dwellings. Energy is derived from fuel. We still mainly use fossil fuels, coal and oil, and when these are burned the air is polluted. We have already reduced smoke output—but open fires in small towns and even in rural areas still present problems. However, by the year 2000 I expect that those who still insist on open fires, as a luxury rather than as a source of heat, will have sufficient supplies of smokeless fuels to meet the demand. Fossil fuels today put over seven million tons of sulphur dioxide into the air, and the amount is still rising. Even natural gas is contributing, for this may have to be purified and the sulphur disposed of. At present the solution is to have very high chimneys, which prevent pollution levels rising in our cities, and there are even signs of improvement. But levels of rural SO_2 are rising, and in countries like Sweden substantial pollution from Britain and Germany is giving rise to alarm. However, we know how to extract sulphur, and this could be done economically if sulphur supplies for industry were a little more expensive. Prices of sulphur will rise, and by the year 2000 I expect that we shall have reduced SO_2 output to negligible amounts.

Atomic power is likely to supply an increasing proportion of our energy. This means that the danger of accidents, which could have global effects, is increased. At present costly precautions in Britain have prevented disastrous radiation pollution in Britain, but with more power stations in more countries, in some of which precautions—particularly in disposal of atomic waste—may be skimped, puts all mankind at risk. The cost may be that we cannot afford a profitable export of equipment to some developing countries where we cannot guarantee safe operation.

At present all power stations produce waste heat which must be dissipated. Thermal pollution, the heating of rivers and even of parts of the sea, already exists. This can be serious, for the hot water is deoxygenated, and fish may be killed. Properly organized this heat could be an asset, for instance for district heating or desalination of seawater, and I expect that by the year 2000 in Britain we shall have modified all systems so that a higher proportion of the heat is usefully used, and so pollution will be reduced, without an additional burden on the economy.

Most industrial pollution today is less serious than a hundred years ago, largely because of the enforcement of legislation. However, accidents still happen, and are costly to both industry and the public. Many industrial effluents are dangerous, and this risk will increase as industry expands. With a rising population stricter laws will have to be more strictly enforced, which will put up the cost of industrial products. At present, after SO_2, fluorine is probably our commonest and most dangerous industrial air pollutant, from brick works, steel works and aluminium plants. In Britain we have instances of fluorine poisoning of cattle and damage to vegetation at present, but the problem is not usually considered very serious. In the Netherlands, where industry and horticulture are adjacent, damage is common. To reduce fluorine emission could increase prices of some products by 10%. Such costs will have to be faced by the year 2000.

Motor cars, using petrol, are a major cause of pollution in the United States, producing "photochemical smog" and carbon monoxide and emitting lead. If by the year 2000 the number of cars is trebled, and they have the type of engine used today, pollution will be serious in Britain. However, other results, such as insoluble traffic problems, will affect the situation. Already the State of California has banned petrol engines from 1975, even with devices to reduce emission of nitrous oxide which, with the sunlight, produces the smog. I believe that by the year 2000 we will have solved, or at least altered, our traffic problems, and that pollution control will be only one reason for this change. The costs will be high, but it will be difficult to assess the proportions due to pollution control.

Sewage pollution today is in general much less serious than it was even 50 years ago, and even with an increasing population this improvement is likely to continue, with no proportional increase in costs to the community. But while raw sewage will be treated, and health risks reduced, sewage effluent rich in nutrient salts will continue the eutrophication of our rivers and may make estuarine barrages, otherwise the logical means of water storage, difficult to operate. The cost of removal of salts from effluents will be high.

Much of the effect of eutrophication is because effluents contain much phosphate from the breakdown of domestic detergents. This may decrease by the year 2000, largely because disposable clothing will not need to be washed. This will leave the increasing problem of waste disposal, including non-returnable bottles, plastic containers and all the debris of civilization. This may be a major cost on the community.

Many pollution problems should, at a cost, be solved by the year 2000, but the greatest difficulties may arise from agriculture. At present persistent pesticides are affecting the ecology of the countryside, and are still being accumulated in the fat of all human beings in small, probably harmless, amounts. If agriculture is intensified, and pest control depends on an increased use of organochlorine pesticides, then really serious effects can be expected. However, I hope that we can solve the problem of pesticide pollution before the year 2000. We may not be able to rely entirely on non-chemical means of pest control, but we will certainly use less persistent substances, even if these are not always so convenient. The cost of this is unlikely to be more than two or three million pounds a year, even with greatly intensified agriculture.

A more intractable problem arising from intensive agriculture is eutrophication. This is a natural process—pure upland water as it flows through lowland areas is enriched by nutrient salts leaching out of the soil. However, sewage effluents and, to an even greater extent, salts in the run-off from agricultural land, produce a degree of uncontrolled eutrophication which has drastic effects. In parts of the United States this has rendered rivers and lakes lifeless. This situation has not yet been reached in Britain, but a great intensification of agriculture could make many water supplies unfit for drinking, and most of our lowland rivers devoid of fish. Research may enable us to avoid these effects, though American experience is not very encouraging. It may therefore, in a crowded island like Britain, be cheaper, in both money and amenity, to continue to import much of our food, and to try to pay for this by industrial processes, the pollution from which may be easier to control.

Discussion

In reply to requests for clarification, Miss Thompson added these remarks.

1. The age structure of the present population, with its relatively large numbers of children and young adults, means that it looks inevitable that (barring natural catastrophes) the size of the population of Great Britain will surpass 60 million even if fertility should from now on drop to replacement level and mortality show no further improvement. Both factors would mean a complete discontinuity with current experience and to that extent hardly seem realistic.

2. Of the three main groups of immigrants resident in this country—those born in Alien countries, in the Republic of Ireland and in the New Commonwealth, each of the same order of magnitude—the 1961 Census showed that those from the Republic of Ireland and the New Commonwealth had age specific fertility rates at that time which were some one-third higher than the average for England and Wales as a whole. The crude birth rate of these groups was affected by their currently young age distribution. This present higher fertility is expected to moderate with the passage of time.

3. There is a clear downward gradient in mortality rates from the north and west of the country to the south and east. The variations in fertility are not consistent, but present a patchy appearance. In making population projections on a regional basis it is assumed that national trends in mortality and fertility are followed but the regional differentials about this are assumed to persist. Net migration can be quite significant in modifying the natural increase in population at a regional level.

J. PARSONS: Dr. Cooke, do you believe the carrying capacity of the land is infinite, and if not, what is the limit?

G. W. COOKE: The carrying capacity of the land is *not* infinite. At present it is set by the efficiency of the plants we grow in converting incoming solar energy into plant material. Given adequate nutrients and water, our present crops can convert no more than 2% of the incident radiation, in a part of the year only, to useful product. Theoretically nearly 10% might be converted and if this was achieved it would represent an upper limit to carrying capacity.

P. WIX: On the Northamptonshire clays mono-culture has caused deterioration in structure and produced drainage problems. Do you envisage restoring stability by the use of a chemical conditioner or by increase in some of the traditional methods?

G. W. COOKE: The Northamptonshire clay country had for long been grass-land until ploughed in the 1939-45 War; much of this remains in arable cropping. Soil under old grass had a much better structure and contains much more organic matter than old arable land on the same kind of soil. When old grass is ploughed and cultivated continuously organic matter is slowly lost, the percentage in the soil diminishing and tending to reach the smaller percentage typical of old arable land. This change is inevitable and does no harm. Old grassland soils are well structured because they are full of roots and for a few years after ploughing this is maintained, but structure tends to become less stable as the grass roots decay; this change is also inevitable but the old arable soil can be cultivated well enough by skilled farmers. Drainage problems are the result of bad farming practices, particularly bad cultivations, and are not an inevitable result of mono-culture.

Where mono-cultures are skilfully done, there is no reason to fear damage to any kind of clay soil and there is no need to use chemical soil conditioners. Traditional organic manures cannot be applied in large enough quantities to make much difference to these soils. If farmers cannot cultivate them well enough for continuous cereal growing, they will have to adopt ley farming systems.

A. H. J. BAINES: It seems a pity that Miss Thompson confined herself largely to the present millennium, which has had only one major demographic catastrophe, the Black Death. It sometimes helps to take a longer view. I should like to have heard her views on the pestilence of the 540s, which seems to have been of the same order of magnitude. If it had not happened, I think we might now be speaking either Welsh or a Romance language, unless indeed the next catastrophe had already overtaken us.

Although the present official projection of the population of the United Kingdom at the end of the millennium is 68 million (66 million in Great Britain), the figure was seen as only 52 million no more than 20 years ago, and has since been as high as 75 million. This is not intended as a criticism; we should be grateful to the demographers for their readiness to revise their projections annually and to set out their assumptions so clearly.

On Dr. Cooke's paper, I would comment that the needs or rather the wants of the population at the end of the century may be materially different from today. For example, there is an underlying weakness in the demand for mutton and lamb—which is, of course, a British habit, not shared either by North America or by the continent of Europe. On the other hand, the demand for pork and for poultry (those efficient converters) is fairly buoyant. I am not however suggesting that the diet will have changed at all radically by the year 2000; in times of peace, changes in the national diet occur over generations rather than decades, because we form our habits in youth and adhere to them very tenaciously. I think a return to a largely cereal diet would be resisted with particular stubbornness.

R. BARRASS: If in the next 30 years we lose 3% of the remaining agricultural land, our total production then, with 3% less land, will be 3% less than it could be. Nor can we justify the taking of land from farmers now on the grounds that they are not using it fully. In the future, if the need is greater, farmers may have to use this same land more effectively.

I am concerned that we may not always be able to exchange industrial products for the food we need. In doing this we compete with other mainly industrial nations for food, from the so-called underdeveloped countries, which these producer nations will increasingly need themselves. We consider South America, for example, as a relatively unexploited market for our goods and yet many countries in South America have been described* as facing biological bankruptcy.

T. A. BENNET-CLARK: Population control in many populations such as those of micro-organisms is partly effected by so-called staling products or pollutants. There may be a similar effect on human populations. Long-term molecules almost certainly will have to be controlled. Another major "staling product" for man consists of cars and habitations. Some census and control of staling might be considered.

T. G. ONIONS: On the same day that I read in Dr. Mellanby's paper and elsewhere that the Thames is no longer an open sewer and that fish may be caught in it at Chelsea, I saw on television that the River Tyne is becoming increasingly polluted.

MRS. P. K. ROBINSON: Very little is known about the capacity of our land, water and air to absorb pollution and what Dr. Cooke said about insufficient expenditure on agricultural research is even more true of pollution research; money needs to be spent on finding out how much pollution we can allow and how we can get rid of the amount in excess of this, otherwise life in A.D. 2000 will be intolerable, at whatever level our population finally settles out.

For instance, increased agriculture, as envisaged by Dr. Cooke, will result in increased use of fertilizers, leading to increased eutrophication of rivers and hence of water in reservoirs. At what level should we attempt to achieve a balance?

* Beltran, E. (1963). Latin America's Prospects. *In* Osborn, F. (Ed.) "Our Crowded Planet", pp. 143-149. Allen and Unwin, London.

CHAPTER 4

The Doctor's Dilemma, 1970

A. S. PARKES

Galton Foundation

INTRODUCTION

Bernard Shaw, in his play *The Doctor's Dilemma,* written more than 60 years ago, presented his fictional medical man with a problem which was highly personal but not of general significance. Today, the practising medical man, whether he realizes it or not, is increasingly faced with two questions which are also highly personal but have very wide implications. First, is it his duty, whatever his private convictions may be, to match his strenuous efforts in the cause of death control with equally strenuous ones in the cause of birth control? Second, has he a duty not only to the individual, but also to the community and to the concept of a population optimal in vigour and potential as well as in size?

THE GROWTH OF POPULATION IN GREAT BRITAIN

The first question arises from the fact that man started to modify his erstwhile low survival rate before interfering effectively with his relatively high reproductive potential. As a result, the population of Great Britain quadrupled in the 19th century.

In the light of Miss Thompson's paper I need elaborate this theme very little. The largest absolute increases in numbers took place towards the end of the 19th and early in the present century. Since then the increase has been much slower, about two and a quarter millions per decade, and relatively, of course, slower still, but obviously even this much decreased rate of growth cannot be maintained indefinitely. The growth of resources might be made to keep up, but we should simply run out of space.

The vastly greater part of the growth has been, and is being, due to natural increase, the excess of births over deaths, latterly around a quarter of a million a year (see Chart 2, p. 5). Between 1870 and World War II there was a continuous and comparatively steady fall in both the birth rate and the death rate. In the year 1940, the crude death rate was fractionally above the crude birth rate, but quinquenially births have always exceeded deaths, though in the 1930s the margin was small enough to arouse gloomy forebodings of a shrinking population. It is indeed intriguing to speculate on the effects of a combination of the death rate of the middle of the last century with the birth rate of the 1930s. In fact, ever since 1915 the birth rate has been below the peak death rate of the 18th century.

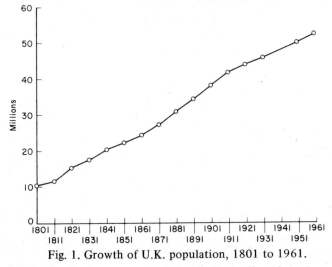

Fig. 1. Growth of U.K. population, 1801 to 1961.

The fall in the death rate must obviously be attributed to the work of the medical practitioner, the medical scientist, the nutritionist, the Public Health and ancillary services concerned with sanitation, water supply, housing, clean air, industrial hazards and the like, and of those involved in ensuring that resources, especially food supply, keep pace with, or outstrip, increases in population. So much for death rate. To what, on the other hand, must we ascribe the decrease in the birth rate between 1880 and 1920? Certainly not to the medical profession, the record of which in this connection is lamentable.

MEDICAL PRACTITIONERS AND BIRTH CONTROL

There is no need to give a detailed account of the long guerilla warfare between the protagonists of birth control, the Church and many members of the medical profession. In her 1963 Galton Lecture, Margaret Pyke recalled that a Leeds physician, Dr. Henry Allbutt, included in his *Wife's Handbook,* a decent popular medical manual published in 1885, price 6d, a chapter entitled "How to avoid pregnancy when advised to do so by the doctor". As a result, he was arraigned by the General Medical Council, and found guilty of "having published and publicly caused to be sold a work entitled the *Wife's Handbook* at so low a price as to bring the work within the reach of the youth of both sexes to the detriment of public morals". This was adjudged to be infamous conduct in a professional respect and Dr. Allbutt was struck off the Medical Register.

Against the background to today's contraceptive publicity and teenage anarchy it is difficult to make an adequate comment on this incident, except to say that, according to the OED, there are three learned professions, medicine, divinity and the law, and to recall Shaw's aphorism that "all professions are conspiracies against the laity". Many years later, in the early 1920s, the first resolute protagonist of family planning in this country, Marie Stopes, a botanist by profession, had almost as much trouble with the medical profession as with the Bishops. The family planning movement was, in fact, a woman's movement aimed at releasing women from the burden of incessant pregnancies, an elementary kindness and consideration which at that time many men were unable or unwilling to give their wives and children. Later again, in the 1930s, the first serious attempt to improve non-appliance methods of contraception was made at some professional hazard to himself by an Oxford zoologist, whose work on spermicides had to be done in a department more enlightened than his own. Finally, in the late 1950s, when the Medical Research Council of political necessity had to stand aloof, the first organization for the systematic testing of contraceptives in this country, the Oliver Bird Trust and thence the Council for the Investigation of Fertility Control, was set up, with the aid of a private benefaction, by two lay women officers of the FPA and a biologist.

Even now the approach to advice on family planning by the medical practitioner is ambivalent and confused with his own emotions, derived from religious or other sources. It is unbelievable to me that clear-cut objective differences of medical opinion should divide along the same lines as the personal religious beliefs of the practitioners concerned, yet that is what purports to happen. Two recent investigations are of interest in this connection: Ward (1969) found that 93% of the GPs in Sheffield would, on occasion, give advice

TABLE I

Methods prescribed by Sheffield G.Ps. according to place of training

Method	Doctors	
	Irish trained (%)	Trained elsewhere in British Isles (%)
Pill	71	98
Condom	12	45
Cap	6	33
Safe Period	65	13
IUD	6	10
Chemical spermicide	0	7

(From Ward, 1969)

on contraception directly, but that the advice offered segregated according to whether the practitioners had been trained in Eire or elsewhere in the British Isles. In this survey, also, there would appear to be evidence of the hypocrisy of prescribing the pill to regulate the cycle to facilitate the use of the so-called rhythm method.

The second survey was carried out by Cartwright (1968) on a random sample of 1954 general practitioners, of whom 1385 provided usable replies. Her results, of which the more relevant are reproduced in Table II, were most illuminating.

TABLE II

Religion and reported practices

	Roman Catholic doctors	Doctors of other religions
Percentage who would introduce subject of family planning with:		
A married woman with mitral stenosis and two children	63	94
A married woman with three children and only one bedroom	32	65
A married woman with three children and no social or health problems	6	23
A married woman of 18 who had just had her first baby	14	41
An unmarried woman who had just had a baby	18	43
A woman just getting married	6	25
Percentage who would not be prepared to discuss family planning if asked by:		
A married woman of 18 who had had her first baby	13	1
An unmarried woman who had had a baby	32	8

(After Cartwright, 1968)

Several highly significant conclusions appear from this table: (a) practitioners, whatever their religion, are more concerned about the possibility of another pregnancy in a married woman with mitral stenosis than in one with three children and only one bedroom, but in both cases a much smaller proportion of Catholic practitioners are willing to raise directly the question of contraception; (b) even now only a small proportion of practitioners are actively concerned about family planning as such, or about population problems, as witness the fact that only a small percentage would take up the subject of contraception directly with a woman with three children and no social or medical problems; (c) a substantial proportion of Roman Catholic doctors have no regard for the obvious interests of very young or unmarried mothers.

The enactment of the 1967 Abortion Act has placed the general public still further at the mercy of the emotions of the medical man. Since April 1968 a woman in this country has a potential legal right to an abortion medically induced for social reasons. However, no medical man is obliged to act against his so-called conscience, and large numbers of them have taken refuge in this funk-hole, and refuse to give women the assistance to which they are legally entitled. As a result, we read of deplorable cases of pregnant women being batted around from one gynaecologist to another until it is too late for a safe termination, and even of a woman who was refused by a Catholic gynaecologist, without examination, a termination of what afterwards proved to be an ectopic pregnancy.

Listening, some months ago, to a parade of medical consciences on television, I got the impression that some medical men still hold the puritanical view that if a woman sins she must suffer for it, and forget that a completely innocent party, the child, is also going to suffer, while an equally or more guilty party, the man, is going to escape comparatively lightly.

In the face of this muddle of medical practice, the two Pregnancy Advisory Centres, in London and Birmingham, must be commended for their excellent work in smoothing the path of a woman seeking a legal abortion.

THE UNWANTED CHILD

This question of whether a medical man is entitled to put his conscience before the interests of a patient—there can be little doubt where lie the interests of a woman frantic with an unwanted pregnancy—goes much further than the interests of the individual. The community is also deeply involved. Few people would say that this country needs a larger population, some would say it needs a smaller one and many would prefer to see it stabilized at its present level. Yet, currently, we have a natural increase of a quarter of a million a year, the excess of births over deaths, and this excess is contributed to per year by more than 60,000 illegitimate births, of which very few can be planned or wanted, by more than 70,000 births occurring less than seven months after marriage, often no doubt shot-gun marriages, and an unknown number of unwanted children conceived in wedlock. A survey by Frazer and Watson (1968) showed that 63% of the maternity patients in St. Mary's Hospital, London, and 42% in the Queen Elizabeth II Hospital, Hertfordshire, stated that their pregnancies were unplanned. Many of the resulting children will, of course, be acceptable even if unplanned, but, to judge from the number of married women currently seeking legal abortion, an appreciable proportion must be categorically unwanted (one-third of the patients at the London Pregnancy Advisory Centre are married). Overall the total number of unwanted children produced must be very large, possibly as great as one-quarter of all births. It is, in fact, virtually certain that (as emphasized by Simms and Medawar, p. 134) the elimination of unwanted children would go far to stabilize the population of this country and enable us to consolidate socially and demographically. In my view, therefore, a medical man (or anyone else) who withholds his skill and knowledge within the law in any way which results in the appearance of an unwanted child does a grave disservice to the woman, the child and the community.

THE TREATMENT OF INFERTILITY

But what about the converse? How far should the medical man go in attempts to remedy infertility and bring about the birth of a wanted child? From the point of view of the community in a demographic climate where fewer not more births are required, the answer could be that he should do nothing—the successful treatment of even one-half of the 8% of involuntarily infertile couples would cause an appreciable increase in the birth rate. From the point of view of the couples concerned, many of whom desperately wish for a child, and leaving aside the question of whether children should ever be planned as psychosomatic agents, the answer could be that any simple treatment, uncomplicated and not making undue calls on medical resources, is justified. The proviso is important because it is said currently that more medical resources in time and money are being expended on attempts to treat infertility than on the limitation of fertility. This is indeed odd, because one would have thought that the misery caused by the production of scores of thousands of unwanted children every year far outweighed the satisfaction caused by the limited success in treating childless couples.

Be that as it may, extreme procedures in attempts to induce fertility seem to me quite out of place at the present time. One of these is the use of gonadotrophin ("fertility drug") to induce ovulation. At present, as is well known, the use of this material may cause a woman to produce a litter of four and five, of which after intensive care one puny survivor may be left in a few months. Is this really in the interests of mother or child or the community, or is it merely in the interests of medical experimentation? In time it should be possible to avoid this hazard in the use of ovulation-inducing treatments, but, if so, extensive medical laboratory facilities will be required and one may well doubt whether, from the point of view of the community, the end will justify the necessary means.

Even more extravagant is the suggestion that certain types of infertility in women might be dealt with by obtaining an ovum from the woman, processing it in the laboratory, effecting its fertilization with spermatozoa from the husband (or some other man) pre-capacitated in the wife (or some other woman) and then re-introducing it into the wife. As a contribution to the study of the biology of human reproduction this is splendid stuff, but as a contribution to the population problem, to the welfare of the community or even to human happiness, it seems to me, in view of the diversion of medical resources which would be required, to verge on therapeutic hysteria. Fortunately, causing women to produce litters, however undesirable, is a minor problem and even partial ectogenesis in man is happily remote. There are more urgent and larger problems in the field of medical ethics.

THE SANCTITY OF HUMAN LIFE

This brings me to the second of the modern doctor's dilemmas: how is he to resolve the confict, which often exists, between his medical ethic based on the sanctity of human life, and the real interests of the indvidual and of the community, which includes the patient's relatives. Specifically, how far ought efforts to be made to keep alive seriously defective babies, especially those that would die naturally without prolonged intensive care? How far is it worth while patching-up adults? And most important of all, what are we to do about the ever-increasing number of old people, especially those in a state of senile decay? In many ways these are different problems, but all three turn on the sanctity of human life and the interests of the individual and the community. To take the first question: in whose interests, apart from that of the medical virtuoso, is it to devote medical skill and resources to keeping alive hopeless and helpless congenital defectives, who can never be anything but a burden to themselves (if they are sufficiently conscious to realize the state of affairs), to their relatives and to the community. Surely better monuments to medical skill and the sanctity of human life could be found than the preservation of catastrophically defective children for a living death. I do not wish to be misunderstood. Anything that can be done to ensure that a mentally or physically defective child becomes a useful and happy member of the community should be done, but where that is manifestly impossible would it not be better to allow nature to take its course?

So much for children. What about the patching-up of adults? Here again the problem is comparatively simple to state. Where an adult, especially a young adult, can be restored to or maintained in health and activity by relatively simple and effective means, the work of the medical profession is to be wholly applauded. Borderline cases must also receive the benefit of any doubt, but what are we to think of the trend towards the spectacular rather than the generally useful? The present international flag-waving competition in organ transplantation is a case in point. Is it really justifiable to squander immense surgical and medical resources on transplantation operations, which at present are very unlikely to produce any lasting results in the case of heart and liver, and which can never be of benefit to more than a tiny minority, when thousands of people wait for months for simple surgery. In the words of a comment by a medical geneticist in a recent issue of the Eugenics Society Bulletin, "Do doctors involved in transplant work lose judgement when exposed to glamorous publicity? Do they compete to a dangerous degree for pre-eminence? How much is it good to be silent and how much to expose in the lay press? Should money be spent on transplant programmes in British Hospitals, already so pathetically financed, housed and staffed for the bread and butter of their work? Can we afford £6000 per patient for a kidney transplant?" The commentator might have added "when 2500 women die every year in the United Kingdom from cervical cancer, the early diagnosis of which by the cervical smear technique is so vitally important and so inadequately provided for.

Again, should medical resources be devoted to the investigation of rare diseases if there is any probability that increased research would expedite the prevention and successful treatment of the common disabling and debilitating diseases, and even of the humble but time-wasting influenza and common cold which afflict so many? Admittedly, the lesson of progress is that the growing points must always be far ahead of the mass of foliage, but equally, it is often necessary to cut them back, at least temporarily, to ensure the maximum crop of fruit, and many might think that currently the medical tree would benefit from some summer pruning. Here, indeed, is a dilemma for the medical scientist and practitioner, and one which should be regarded as a matter of ergonomics rather than of sentiment.

By contrast, the problem presented by old people is heavily weighted with sentiment, but the time may come when we shall have to rationalize our views. Old people are not now living longer—the expectation of life at 70 years of age is no greater than it was before, but owing to decreased mortality at earlier ages many more people are now living to expect it. The tremendous change in the age structure of the population over the last century is shown in Fig. 2, the profile for 1891 being typically that produced by a high death rate, where each age group contains more individuals than the one above it, while that for 1968 is typically the result of a low death rate, where the decrease in numbers is relatively small up to age of 60 years. In this instance, the effect is accentuated by the survival of individuals born in the early years of the century when the birth rate was still comparatively high.

At June 30th, 1968 according to the Registrar-General's estimate, there were about 4.3 million people in the United Kingdom aged 70 years and over, of whom about 2.8 million were women. Few of these can still be producers and we hear a great deal officially of the economic consequences of this top-hamper of old people. We hear, also, but mainly privately, something of the social consequences. Here again, the problem is easy to state and almost impossible to solve. Obviously so long as old people remain healthy and happy; or even comparatively so, every effort must be made to keep them that way, even at the expenditure of time and attention by relatives and the social services. But when they become neither happy nor healthy, and especially when they are overtaken by senile decay of mind and body, what then? Is it really part of the duties of the medical profession to eke out legal life to the last dregs, to use the resources of modern science not to prolong life but to prolong death at whatever cost in distress and frustration to relatives and in resources to the community?

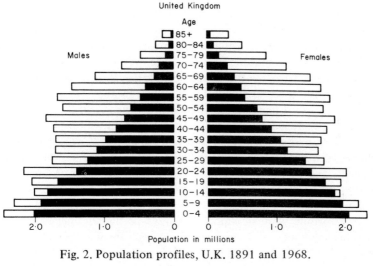

Fig. 2. Population profiles, U.K. 1891 and 1968.

■ = 1891   □ = 1968

Unfortunately the subject is heavily charged with emotion, as was discovered recently by the Medical Officer of Health for Eastbourne who was misrepresented and savaged in the national press for suggestion that after the age of 80 years nature should be allowed to take its course. Provision for voluntary euthanasia would not solve the problem, because those most in need of it are beyond making a decision of any sort, and directed euthanasia is not remotely within sight. The only solution appears to be a new medical ethic, by which treatment in cases of catastrophic defect, illness, injury or senility, in infants, adults or the aged, is related to wider considerations than at present.

BACK TO 30 MILLION

It is not my task to consider what would be, or would have been, the optimal size of population for the United Kingdom, but the various considerations mentioned above are very relevant to any attempt to regulate population size, especially to any attempt to make a substantial reduction quickly, which could be done only by mass emigration. The magic figure of 30 million, sometimes quoted as the carrying capacity of the land, was achieved around 1880 and the less magic but perhaps more realistic figure of 40 million around 1905, and it would have been a brave man who tried to stabilize the population at either of these points. It seems that the greatest number of children ever produced in this country appeared in 1904! To try now to reduce the United Kingdom population to 30 or 40 million by peaceful means in a short time would require an even braver man. But proposals have been put forward. In 1950 a body calling itself the Council for New Era of Emigration set itself up and at its second meeting Sir Frank Whittle, of jet-engine fame, succeeded Norman Angel as Chairman. This Council had the general object of encouraging emigration from Europe to less congested parts of the world, and the special one of considering plans whereby the population of the United Kingdom could be reduced from the then 50 million to 30 million by the mass emigration of 20 million people to Commonwealth countries. The Council produced great quantities of paper, and came to concentrate on the United Kingdom problem as shown by successive changes of name to Migration Council and then to Commonwealth Migration Council. Whether it ever caused anyone to emigrate who would not otherwise have done so is uncertain. Several aspects of the project were discussed in detail, but unfortunately little attention was given to the major difficulty. Differential emigration of a mass of the active producers of the country would place an impossible burden on the remainder in supporting the various categories of dependants. Emigration on the scale of the Whittle project, 40% of the total population, would have to be cross-sectional. And what a cross-section it would be! In present-day terms it would include, in addition to two-fifths of the producers and potential producers (children), two-fifths, say 1.7 million, of the 4.3 million people over 70 years of age, two-fifths of the inmates of mental asylums, two-fifths of the prison population of the country, say 16,000 convicts, as well as 140,000 or so defectives of one kind and another. It seems, therefore, that "back to 30 million quickly" must be counted among the ever-growing number of beautiful big ideas killed by ugly little facts, and if the population of the United Kingdom ever goes back to 30 million it will do so as the result of slow depopulation for whatever reason or of a nuclear holocaust or of mass hysteria caused by overcrowding. In the meantime, conclusions about the optimal population are fascinating but ephemeral.

REFERENCES

Cartwright, A. (1968). General practitioners and family planning.
    Med. Off. No. 3130, 43.
Fraser, A. C. and Watson, P. S. (1968). Family planning—a myth?
    Family Planning 17, 72.
Ward, A. W. M. (1969). General practitioners and family planning in Sheffield.
    J. biosoc. Sci. 1, 15.

CHAPTER 5

Some Social Consequences of Growing Numbers

G. P. HAWTHORN

University of Essex

In the brilliant, idiosyncratic essay that has perhaps had more influence than any other on thinking about man and society since it was written, Rousseau (1755) argues that the factors of population growth, size and density are responsible for the very existence of anything that we would recognize as human society. From the major premise that there once existed a non-social human state of nature, and the minor premise that population had grown, Rousseau deduced that under conditions of rising density men were forced to confront each other for the first time and so enter into social relations. One can, of course, level the alternative accusations of falsity or triviality at this suggestion. If the assumption about the state of nature is correct, it is an interesting theory. But Rousseau himself was quite sure that it was wrong: he was explicit in using it merely as a theoretical device. So, if it is a false assumption, all Rousseau would seem to be saying is that society entails relations between two or more men, and that the number of men is a function of population size and density. However, he said more than this. He went on to draw connections between particular densities, particular forms of society and particular forms of government and degrees of welfare. This is what all general theorists have done, more or less explicitly and in more or less detail, since. It is hardly surprising that, in the hundred and fifty years after 1750 which saw the elaboration of the general sociological theories that we still use, population continued to be given great importance. Up to the beginning of this century North American and European populations were growing in almost all cases at rates in excess of 0.5% per annum (Reinhard and Armengaud, 1961), a fact that any social theorist could hardly ignore. What is unfortunate is that since the first decade of this century, as the rate of increase in the advanced industrial societies (the source of social theorizing) has declined, population growth seems to have become progressively ignored. The result of this is that we have relatively little reliable empirical information on the causes and effects of particular population sizes and densities.

Traditional sociological accounts of the social consequences of particular population sizes and densities are not only scientifically interesting. They are most directly relevant to considerations of optimal levels, since most theorists have followed Rousseau in going on to evaluate the consequences. As on most issues in which there is more heat than light, there are relatively few men who have remained morally neutral about population density. The topic is peopled with vigorous optimists and gloomy pessimists, and the indifferent or cautiously reserved are scarce.

The optimistic argument is as follows. A rising quantitative density implies what has been called a greater "dynamic" density, a greater amount of social interaction. At the beginning of this process, men will confront each other who have been used to performing the relatively general social roles characteristic of smaller societies. On greater acquaintance in conditions of greater density, they will realize the advantages of greater specialization and the corollary of greater co-operation. The case is neatly made by Halbwachs (1923):

> " . . . the division of labour results from the expansion of human groups and from the increase in their density. These are necessary conditions, (1) for the appearance and development . . . of a great variety of aptitudes and also of needs; (2) for bringing aptitudes and needs together in reciprocal stimulation . . . and (3) for establishing increasingly precise adaptation between the techniques of the more and more specialized producers and the needs of the more and more diversified consumers."

Ideally, as this process develops each man will be able to concentrate more and more upon those activities and pursuits for which he has a talent and a liking, and it would thus seem to follow that the division of labour is conducive to greater liberty. It would also appear to be the case that the net increase in the wealth of the society is in excess of the rate of population growth, and to those who believe that liberty is a function of economic well-being this is an added advantage. Since this argument has been framed very largely in economic language, and indeed rests on an equation between the classical market and liberty, it is not surprising that modern proponents of the optimistic case are largely to be found among the ranks of economists (Clark, 1967). The most aware of those who have argued in this way, Durkheim among them, have been aware that the centrifugal process of social differentiation gives rise to problems of social and political control. They have suggested that the implementation of means to effect this control may well result in the elimination of the very liberty that the differentiation originally produced (Wolin, 1965). But as I understand the drift of most sociological thinking in this vein, these qualifications receive scant attention, or are phrased in such recondite ways that their moral and political implications are quite obscured (Smelser, 1963).

Much the most interesting and powerful pessimistic case is put by Rousseau in the *Discourse*. In addition to the two assumptions of his that I describe above, there is a third. This is that of a tendency to evaluation in men, an assumption that seems glaringly obvious until one remembers that Kant overturned much 18th-century philosophy with it and that Chomsky is putting the cat among the pigeons by re-introducing a version of it into modern psychology through his theories of linguistic competence. Adding this premise to his argument, Rousseau concluded that the greater the variety of man's social contacts, the more finely differentiated will his evaluation of other men be. Hence the origin of social inequality. This inequality he saw as an evil. It introduced envy, conflict and disharmony. A second consequence of larger units of population was larger societies, and Rousseau saw this as directly inimical to democracy. True democracy, in which all members of the *demos* can be fully aware of the needs and wants of the others, can only operate under conditions of limited information input. Too many needs and too many wants, a function of too many people, cannot be coped with by the human powers of assimilation and judgement, and democracy is thus likely to be perverted. It is a case that has yet to be answered, and indeed receives some support from modern psychology (Miller, 1967a).

Another pessimistic voice was that of Karl Marx. Although he did say that each kind of society, tribal, feudal and so on, had its particular population dynamics, he never went into the question in any detail or even made any general speculations as to the general character of these dynamics. His main concern was with 19th-century industrial capitalism, and he took rapidly rising populations as a given fact of that form of social and economic organization. Together with his assumption, from elsewhere in his work, that capitalists would gradually replace labour with other factors of production, thus causing unemployment, and that population would nevertheless go on rising, he predicted the creation of a great mass of impoverished men, the so-called "industrial reserve army". Were it the case, on the other hand, that population regulated itself in accordance with the replacement of labour in capitalist economies, no such army would emerge, and there would be no miserization. Without miserization, there would be no revolution. The Marxist theory thus rests squarely on certain conditions of population growth (Petersen, 1965).

There is one further pessimist who deserves attention, particularly in view of the kind of analogies that have been made for human populations from recent findings in ethology. This is Georg Simmel. This quiet, persecuted, elliptical, obscure thinker, in an essay on the effect of the metropolis on mental life, suggested that severe psychological stresses and strains would follow increasing population densities in the cities (Wolff, 1950). For Durkheim, the disadvantage of the progressive concentration of people was that their rapidly diversifying activities would present difficulties of political control; for Simmel, quite apart from the problems of control, it was doubtful that the independence and liberty characteristic of the division of labour would ever be realized at all. They would be countered by crippling disabilities beyond the individual's control.

Such, in general, is the array of arguments. Is population growth, if accompanied by an increase in density, a good thing or not? Is it, perhaps, a good thing up to a certain point and a bad one after that? Can we put a figure to an optimum level, or at least to an optimum rate of growth? And, if the answers to these questions are unclear, uncertain or partial, do we absolve ourselves from any responsibility for recommending certain ameliorating social policies, or must we still act "as if" we knew the facts? These are the questions I wish to ask, and shall do so by taking the evidence for the optimistic and the pessimistic arguments in turn.

It will be seen that we need evidence pointing to an unambiguous causal mechanism linking population size and density with other social factors. It will not do, therefore, to simply point to the correlation between growth and economic development in the West and assert a beneficial causal connection; or to point to an equally impressive association between high density and infant mortality, crime, and so on and infer a malignant connection. We must be satisfied that the observed "effect" is not in fact due to quite different causes. However, as soon as we impose these minimal analytic standards, most of the evidence that has been adduced for and against the effects of population size and density appears to be hopelessly unsatisfactory. Rousseau, Durkheim and Simmel all write from positions of more or less, and usually less, informed speculation. Clark appears to think that quantity of statistics is a substitute for quality of logic. Ironically, it is Marx who, of the traditional protagonists, best illustrates his theories, and who can most easily be shown to have mistaken a temporary state of affairs for a general law.

Nowhere is the promise of evidence, and its manifest absence, more prominent than in the optimistic case. This case rests upon the argument that intervening between population growth and social benefits is economic growth, and that the latter is causally dependent on the first. John Boreham deals with this particular argument (p. 71), and I shall content myself with pointing out that the connection is nowhere near as simple, if it exists at all, as has been made out (Ohlin, 1967). Demographers and economists have traditionally worked on the assumption that populations and economies are closed systems. However analytically useful such an assumption may be, it is empirically fatal for this particular argument, for it leads one to forget that international economic transactions are of crucial importance. Despite what some economists and even the Prime Minister may say (Wilson, 1966), it is almost certainly true that our economic development over the next decades will owe little or nothing to demographic factors. Suggestions, like Wilson's, that a rising population will help alleviate our shortage of labour rest upon the assumption that little or nothing can be done to improve the rate of investment and modernization in the British economy. This is a tired, unimaginative and restrictive assumption derived from an unduly myopic view of economic dynamics.

If there is no clear, straightforward connection between demographic and economic factors in Western economies, then any discussion of optimum populations or optimum rates of population growth can afford to neglect economic arguments for or against demographic expansion. We may thus concentrate upon the non-economic, social and psychological effects of population growth. The first and most prominent of these in the eyes of the optimists is the increase in liberty. However, in the traditional version of this argument, it was maintained that liberty increased with population density through the intervening variable of economic development. But if the latter cannot be shown to bear any dependent relation with population growth, then the case must rest at best not proven. It may well be that the extent to which we value liberty, as distinct from liberty itself, increases with density, but this is another argument, and one to which I shall return presently.

To disentangle population growth from economic development, and to cast doubt on any straightforward causal connections between the two, is to remove the main and virtually only plank of the optimists. But I must insist that I have not shown them to be wrong; merely not proven. What, then, of the pessimists? Do their arguments receive any more firm support?

Consider first Durkheim's reservations about social control and Rousseau's firm denial that democracy could be achieved in large societies. Rousseau nowhere specified exactly how many people made too large a society, but in *The Social Contract* he did suggest that Corsica was the right kind of size for a democratic experiment. This, means, in effect, a society of perhaps 15,000 at the very most. One society that combines the consistently fastest rate of natural increase with true Rousseauistic democracy, and is therefore directly relevant to this discussion, is the Hutterites. This Anabaptist sect, presently resident in the north-western central United States and in Saskatchewan, arrived in North America in the 1870's after three hundred and fifty years of persecution and proceeded to grow without external recruitment from 200 to the present figure of about 15,000 (Bennett, 1968; Eaton and Mayer, 1953). To cope socially with this astonishing growth, they divide periodically into groups of about 150 persons. These groups are politically and (almost) economically self-sufficient, and can fairly be said to be organized on a communistic basis. I am not, of course, implying that we can literally learn from the Hutterites. That would entail unlearning several hundred years of our own cultural evolution. What is interesting is that 150 appears to be a viable unit within which to practice participatory democracy. In large, complex societies, there is the further problem of adequately representing the decisions of these basic cells on more comprehensive bodies. To meet this, many political theorists, Durkheim included, have defended the necessity of a hierarchy of intermediate groups so as to ensure the greatest continuity from bottom to top and back again. The problem can most clearly be seen in large industrial and educational organizations (Ingham, 1967), but its logic applies also to total societies. Much present social dispute can be traced to discontinuities in such structures. To spend time arguing for a return to Rousseauistic prescriptions for the politics of total societies is obviously fruitless. However, the insight that some participation is desirable in the extra-familial politics in which every man and many women are involved is an important one, and at first sight more difficult to resolve in larger structures, themselves a function of population size and density. How this might be done is beyond my scope, but I feel that it should be considered in any analysis of the effects of population increase. It does not, however, follow from what I have said that less participation is a necessary corollory of such increase; on the contrary, it has become more common at the same time as population is growing. All I wish to emphasize is that more effort should be devoted to considering and solving the problems that large intra-societal units present.* Left to their own development, they can destroy freedoms.

A related argument, implied by Rousseau and elaborated by George Miller among others (Miller, 1967a), is that there comes a degree of social complexity in which radically new methods of coping with the greater amounts of information must be developed. Perhaps the most exciting contemporary research of all on human capacity and performance is that currently being done into the psychology of communication and the structure of language (Miller, 1967b; Chomsky, 1968). The promise of this research is ultimately an empirical theory of the mind; more nearly, it is to be able to discover the nature of the mechanisms of human comprehension and intellectual performance in particular spheres, and to construct teaching and learning systems which will be able to utilize these machines more efficiently than our present methods can. The language in which I describe this promise is vague; the research itself, although progressing, is still some way from the desired empirical precision. But its practical promise is as I have suggested, and it seems likely to give rise to practical possibilities of countering and absorbing the effects of larger and more complex social structures. There is as yet no evidence to suggest that we have reached a population size in excess of anything that we could not, potentially, cope with. Grounds for such pessimism thus appear unfounded.

The final strictly empirical case is that outlined by Simmel: namely, that above a certain density human beings cannot function properly, that they suffer stresses and strains conducive to breakdown. This has become a fashionable speculation with the publication of research into the dynamics of animal populations, in which it has been shown that there is a critical population density above which fecundity drops, mortality increases, "deviance" explodes and so forth (Calhoun, 1962; Christian and Davis, 1964; Stott, 1962; Russell and Russell, 1968). At once it must be said that there is no evidence for the kind of alarmist analogies that have been drawn for human societies by, for instance, the Russells, or even by Calhoun himself. Stott's examples are from extremely primitive societies, like certain Aboriginal tribes, operating within a fixed

* The Paymaster-General has been taking sociological advice on the possibilities of increasing participation in political affairs.

resource base, or from more modern populations subjected to extraordinary conditions such as bombing or internment in concentration camps. Familiar correlations between urban density and crime, ill health and so forth are all open to the obvious objection that it has traditionally been the poor and deprived who have settled in city centres. Adverse conditions are more cause than effect of central urban residence.

Two studies, however, deserve mention (Platt, 1937; Winsborough, 1960). Platt studied children who came into care in Newark, N.J. He found that crowding affected their self-sufficiency, that they had less capacity for living within illusions and were more cynical about human motives, that they had what he regarded as an unhealthily strong awareness of the purely physical aspects of sex at the expense of its emotional significance, and that their extreme lack of isolation induced a certain strain which he ascribed to what he called "incomplete ego-building". On the other hand, he found them unusually aware of the needs of others. The research appears to be sensitive and honest, but cannot ultimately stand as incontrovertible evidence, since the concepts and measurements are imprecise and the controls insufficient. It is, nevertheless, interesting, and it is curious that it has not been repeated. Winsborough looked at the human equivalents of the distress Calhoun reported for his rats in central Chicago, and found that, once socio-economic characteristics, race, and dwelling conditions were held constant, the only positive partial correlates of gross population density were infant mortality (0.33) and the amount of public assistance going to young people under 18 (0.14). Adult mortality (−0.62), T.B. cases per 1000 persons aged 15 and more (−0.67) and age standardized public assistance per 1000 persons (−0.39) were all negatively associated with density. The public assistance figures are clearly open to the objection that the Chicago system may operate in ways quite different from those in other cities, but the others are interesting. He concludes, sceptically and wisely, that no firm conclusions can be drawn from such data.

If we nevertheless assume, despite the absence of evidence, that density is adversely related to factors conventionally regarded as beneficial in Britain, there is little cause for alarm. A glance, for example, at the dwelling densities recorded in 1961 and 1966 by the Registrar General (Census, 1961; Sample Census, 1966) shows that high ones are statistically rare, and becoming rarer: in 1961 the census showed about 2.6% of families were living at densities of 1½ persons per room or more; in 1966 the figure was nearer 1.5%. As one might expect, the areas of high density are in places like Kensington and Chelsea, Hackney, Lambeth, Westminster, Liverpool, Manchester and Birmingham, where other factors are likely to interfere in the causal chain that might exist between crowding and adversity. To identify the problems of central city zones as problems of over-population would seem, if analogies from Winsborough's study of Chicago are correct, to be over-simple to the point of distortion. We do have severe problems of poverty, educational backwardness, juvenile delinquency and so forth, as well as a still unacceptable rate of infant mortality in these places. But the solution to these lies in improved social services.

It is clear from the evidence I have reviewed, such as it is, that there is no conclusive case either way on the effects of large populations and high densities. Specific arguments, like Marx's, are easily refuted, but the more general ones remain not proven. Thus, since a calculation of an optimum population size or an optimum rate of population growth involves both a decision on the ranking of the values to be optimized and factual knowledge of the implications of optimizing them, and since we do not have enough facts, we cannot reach a satisfactory calculation. It would seem that many of the environmental factors, in the very widest sense, that may appear to be likely to be pressured by higher densities or larger numbers are highly flexible, and can adapt to the demographic changes. It is not only the case that "living standards measured by an economic yardstick have ceased to be a density-dependent phenomenon" (Wrigley, 1969); other living standards have also ceased to be so dependent.

There is one environmental factor, and one alone, the supply of which can, however, be said to be density-dependent: space. Biologists and conservationists are, as a result of their inclinations and their work, naturally predisposed to consider this as a vital resource, and in principle I would not disagree with them. But we cannot calculate optima on the basis of our own preferences alone. What of others' tastes? These can be inferred to some extent from patterns of internal migration in Britain (Friedlander and Roshier, 1966-67).

Friedlander and Roshier found a net emigration from villages to towns before marriage; after marriage, there was a net immigration *to* villages and a much larger immigration into towns. Sixty-four per cent of those who moved from urban areas to villages were non-manual workers; 64% of those who moved from cities to towns were manual ones. This difference presumably reflects the greater financial flexibility of the middle class: they are less hampered by living some way from their workplace. One might go on to infer from these figures that there exists a much larger taste for escape from living in settlements of 10,000 or more people, a taste that cannot be realized because of the lack of resources. Planners in Britain are faced with a dilemma. It is not at all clear that the New Towns, which represent the most imaginative attempt to date to combine the supposed virtues of village life with those of urban residence, are successful, with the exception of Cumbernauld in Scotland. But what else can they do to satisfy the desire for metropolitan emigration? Perhaps the kind of re-settlement policy that the GLC, for example, is executing in Hampshire and Suffolk will prove to be a satisfactory answer. We still know relatively little about the relative satisfactions of different groups in different areas. Until we do, planners and architects are going to indulge their fancies as they have in the past with the dimmest of notions of how they are meeting needs and preferences.

Recreational space, and the need for conservation, present less of a problem. Even with a population increase of a magnitude as yet unforeseen, there will be large tracts of land almost completely free from dwellings and industry. The case for preserving farmland in Britain is an artificial one, resting upon the supposed virtues of an indigenous agricultural economy, virtues that would not appear to have much relevance to modern conditions. Much present farmland could be left to revert to natural ecosystems, presenting the opportunity for a restoration of a rich fauna and flora in the countryside. Really wild areas could be left as inaccessible as they are, and vehicular access to former farmland would be easy in view of the relatively good road system that we now have in rural areas. It would therefore seem that, once we abandon the silly primitive nationalism that propels the farming lobby, we can make recreational space compatible with a rising population.

Such arguments may seem upsetting. They may also appear to represent an effort that could be avoided if we were to try to limit our population instead. The two are not alternatives. The surplus of births over deaths in Britain is of the order of 300,000. Sixty-seven thousand of these are illegitimate. A further 40,000 or so brides aged 20 or less are pregnant at marriage. Many more births are in some sense accidental; one estimate puts it as high as 65 to 75% (Morris, 1968), which I could not support from my own work, but say that it is more nearly 25%. Assuming that all, or almost all, the illegitimate births are unwanted, that half of the young shot-gun marriages would not have occurred when they did, and that 180,000 marital pregnancies might have been avoided without dissatisfaction to the parents, we would, from these alone, be able to reduce our annual birth rate by 270,000 or so. Our rate of natural increase would drop to a very shallow curve indeed. As yet, we still have to wait for the final results from the study being carried out by the Population Investigation Committee to see how pervasive is the adoption of the contraceptive pill, but it seems very likely that an effect of this chemical will be to eliminate many unwanted births (Langford, 1969; Ryder and Westoff, 1967). Together with greater advocacy of techniques such as male sterilization, which is being vigorously and responsibly promoted by the Simon Population Trust, and with better advice to the young and unmarried on birth control, so that they may realize themselves sexually without any fear for the consequences, we should be able to achieve this. The difficulty comes not from overpopulation, but from uninformed and selfish moral reaction together with nervous legislators, local authorities, and educationists.

I do not consider that we have either enough facts or enough knowledge on the price future parents are going to be willing to pay to advocate more drastic measures. As is clear from Douglas Houghton's contribution, governments are not going to tackle the question with any conviction in any case. Our problem is not so much one of rising population as one of lack of imagination in coping with the consequences and an unwillingness to break out of traditional intellectual shackles so that we can adjust to the future. I do not, however, wish to imply that because we have neither reason nor capacity to calculate an optimum population for Britain as a whole, we cannot consider optimal distributions of the population within the society, geographically and socially (Duncan, 1957). But that is another question.

REFERENCES

Bennett, J. W. (1968). "Hutterian brethren: the Agricultural Economy and Social Organisation of a Communal People."
    Stanford University Press, Stanford. 298 pp.
Calhoun, J. B. (1962). Population density and social pathology.
    Scient. Am. **206**, 139-148.
Chomsky, N. (1968). "Language and Mind."
    Harcourt, Brace and World, New York. 88 pp.
Christian, J. J. and Davis, D. E. (1964). Endocrines, behaviour and population.
    Science, N.Y. **146**, 1550-1560.
Clark, C. (1967). "Population Growth and Land Use."
    Macmillan, London. 406 pp.
Duncan, O. D. (1957). Optimum size of cities. *In* "Cities and Society" (P. K. Hatt and A. J. Reiss, eds).
    Free Press, New York.
Eaton, J. W. and Mayer, A. J. (1953). The social biology of very high fertility among the Hutterites. The demography of a unique population.
    Hum. Biol. **25**, 206-264.
Friedlander, D. J. and Roshier, R. J. (1967). A study of internal migration in England and Wales. Part II: Recent internal migrants: their movements and characteristics.
    Popul. Stud. **20**, 45-59.
General Register Office (1966). Census 1961. England and Wales. "Household Composition Tables." Table 4.
    H.M.S.O., London, (70-906).
Halbwachs, M. (1960). "Population and Society." Translated from 1923 French edition by O. D. Duncan and H. W. Pfautz.
    Free Press, New York. 207 pp.
Ingham, G. K. (1967). Organisational size, orientation to work and industrial behaviour.
    Sociology **1**, 239-258.
Langford, C. M. (1969). Birth control practice in Britain.
    Family Planning **17**, 89-92.
Miller, G. A. (1967a). Some psychological perspectives on the year 2000.
    Proc. Am. Acad. Arts Sci. **96**, 883-896.
Miller, G. A. (1967b). "The Psychology of Communication."
    Basic Books, New York. 197 pp.
Morris, N. (1968). Family planning in Britain.
    Family Planning **15**, 31-34.

Ohlin, G. (1967). "Population Control and Economic Development."
O.E.C.D., Paris.

Petersen, W. (1965). "The Politics of Population."
Doubleday, New York. 350 pp.

Platt, J. S. (1937). "Personality and the Cultural Pattern."
Commonwealth Fund, New York.

Reinhard, M. R. and Armengaud, A. (1961). "Histoire Générale de la Population Mondiale."
Montchrestian, Paris.

Rousseau, J.-J. (1755). "Discours sur l'Origine et les Fondements de l'Inégalité Parmi les Hommes."
Lyon.

Russell, W. M. S. and C. (1968). "Violence, Monkeys and Man."
Macmillan, London.

Ryder, N. B. and Westoff, C. F. (1967). Oral contraception and American birth rates. *In* "Family and Fertility" (W. T. Liu, ed.).
University of Notre Dame Press, Notre Dame, U.S.A.

Simmel, G. (1950). "The Sociology of Georg Simmel." Translated and edited and with an Introduction by K. H. Wolff.
Free Press, Glencoe. 445 pp.

Smelser, N. J. (1963). Mechanisms of change and adjustment to change. *In* "Conference on Social Implications of Industrialization and Technical Change. 1960. Industrialization and Society" (B. F. Hoselitz, ed.).
Mouton, Paris.

Stott, D. H. (1962). Cultural and natural checks on population growth. *In* "Culture and the Evolution of Man" (A. Montagu, ed.).
Oxford University Press, New York. 376 pp.

Wilson, H. (1966). Letter to Rt. Hon. Sir D. Renton.
Published by Sir D. Renton, London.

Winsborough, H. H. (1960). The social consequences of high population density.
Law and Contemporary Problems 25, 120-126.

Wolin, S. S. (1965). "Politics and Vision."
Allen and Unwin, London.

Wrigley, E. A. (1969). "Population and History."
Weidenfeld and Nicolson, London.

CHAPTER 6

Economics and Population in Britain

A. J. BOREHAM

Ministry of Technology

INTRODUCTION

Optima are not absolute but are related to the objectives that we set and to the constraints within which we are obliged to operate in the time-scale within which we operate; and population is so basic that the objectives it is relevant to set cover the whole realm of human activities. In this symposium we have contributions from biologists, agriculturists, economists, sociologists, each considering a limited range of objectives, but even within each range there are conflicts between objectives. The problem of conflicting objectives is manageable so long as there is a system of valuation, not necessarily in terms of money, by means of which the differing objectives can be traded off against each other. I hope to explain how this is possible in the realm of the economic objectives, though even in that limited field there is plenty of scope for argument; for example, what is the "proper" rate of trade-off between price stability on the one hand and rate of growth on the other? When it comes to trading-off one form of social stress against another, however, the difficulties are probably more severe. How, for example, ought we to balance the advantages of high density populations (in the form of schools able to offer tuition in a wide range of specialities) against the disadvantages (in the form of congestion and psychological stress)? It is, of course, true that technology may in time be able to ease the constraints within which we operate, for example by the development of teaching programmes available at terminals widely dispersed from a central control, but in the short term the problem of trading-off cannot be avoided so easily.

We do have an institution intended to solve, pragmatically, the problems of conflicting objectives; it is called democracy. It has defects, but works in a rough and ready way so long as the time-scales are right. We are already in trouble with so basic a matter as the control of public spending; here the time-span of decisions for some programmes is far longer than five years so that decisions taken by one administration commit the succeeding one. However, population changes take even longer to work through—a lifetime in fact—so that if we did have a referendum on the question of the optimum population for Britain and if we could set about producing the size of population that the majority voted for, most of them would be dead before it came about. The people who ought to be asked are the children whose conception is in question.

In summary, then, I believe this a non-question because:

There is no system of valuation by means of which we can trade-off one form of cost or benefit against another in order to arrive at a balanced view.

Democratic processes have the wrong time-span for a population policy.

I do not believe that we yet have acceptable mechanisms for putting a population policy into effect.

However, I agreed to write this paper because I think there are a few things worth saying about the connections between economic objectives and the level and rate of change of population. In the next section I shall present four basic economic objectives and the inter-connections between them.

SOME ECONOMIC OBJECTIVES

In discussing economic objectives I shall take a national point of view. I am not going to speak as if the world were a single economy, ignoring international trade. But I also want to try to climb above taking a short-term United Kingdom view in which the balance of payments almost blots everything else from view. I am for that reason putting the balance of payments last of the four objectives I select. They are:

Given the resources available, achieving the highest possible level of income per head.

Given the resources available, achieving the highest possible rate of growth of income per head.

Price stability.

A balance of payments.

I have left out the objective of achieving an equitable distribution of income, not because I do not think it is an important economic objective, but because I am obliged to limit the length of this paper and because I believe that the connections between population levels and rates of growth and income distribution are of secondary importance in a demographically and industrially advanced society.

I shall discuss each of the four objectives I have selected—what they mean and why they are objectives—and then a little about the inter-connections between them. I shall start by explaining a basic concept in economics; that income, output and expenditure are all equal. I do so because in what follows I shall sometimes use one word, sometimes another, and because in everyday life they are so obviously not equal to each other. The trick is that in everyday life we think about ourselves; we see things from our own point of view, whereas in science—and economics is a science—we look at things from outside and take, or try to take, everthing into account. A system of economic activity, for example a firm, consists of a group of people engaged in production of perhaps something you can touch and see, like a computer, or a service, like retail distribution. For this purpose they work, use tools and equipment, and use materials. Their output can only be measured by the value placed on what they sell by the people who buy it, less the value of the materials bought for production. In economist's language their *gross* output is the value of what they sell and their *net* output (which is what I propose to call output) is the value they, with the aid of their tools and equipment, have added to the materials bought. This output, or value added, is what is available for rewarding them for their work and for rewarding their shareholders for making the tools and equipment available and for replacing the tools and equipment. It is, in other words, the total income becoming available from the economic activity. Output, therefore, equals income. The question whether the output of an individual employee is equal to his income or whether, on the other hand, part of his output is used to provide income for another employee, or even for a shareholder, who has provided (the money for) the tools and equipment the employee has used, is the question of income distribution which I have been careful to avoid. The *total* income and the total output arising from the economic activity are equal to each other.

The equality between expenditure and output is a little more difficult to explain. The total expenditure on the product of the firm is the same as its *gross* output, i.e. it includes the value of the materials bought by the firm as well as the value the firm added to those materials, so that as far as the firm's economic activity is concerned the part of the expenditure on its product, which is the purchase of materials, should be set aside. When we come to add up all the firms in the country, these pieces of expenditure that we have set aside cancel out the purchases of materials for use in economic activity, except those materials purchased from abroad (i.e. imports). These do not have pieces of expenditure with which to cancel out and so have to be subtracted from the total expenditure of the whole country before arriving at output. This can be set out in a highly simplified national expenditure and output table:

	Expenditure for consumption (including by government)		
plus	Expenditure by enterprises	(i)	Materials for further processing (Set aside)
		(ii)	Tools and equipment for use
plus	Expenditure by foreigners		
Equals	Total expenditure		
less	Purchases of materials	(i)	From other U.K. enterprises (Set aside above)
		(ii)	From foreigners
Equals	Output		

As explained earlier, output for the firm, and therefore for the whole country, equals income.

The first of the four objectives that I have selected is the highest possible level of income per head, given the resources available. I do not think it necessary to say much about why this is an economic objective, but it is important to remember that economic objectives are not the only ones. There are also social and cultural objectives which conflict with economic objectives both in general and in particular cases. The social and cultural price of a higher level of income can also be too high. This idea lies behind most conservation movements, behind much legislation limiting the use of land for economic activities and even behind many economic policies. The support of declining industries like agriculture, textiles and coal, is only partly justified by keeping men in employment who would otherwise be unemployed or by the effect on the balance of payments; it is partly justified by the unacceptability of the social and cultural costs of a too rapid rate of industrial change. I suspect that we would not nowadays accept the degree of social misery caused by the rate of change in the first Industrial Revolution.

However, as an economic objective (to be striven for according to its price in terms of non-economic objectives) the highest possible level of income per head can be accepted. It breaks down into two parts; first the highest possible level of employment—or the lowest possible level of unemployment—and second such a distribution of employment between industries as will produce the highest average level of income per head. Both of these should be considered against the background of a given level of resources. Since for all practical economic purposes there are only two resources—manpower and capital—and since one of them (manpower) is what we are seeking an optimum for, this proviso comes down to a given level of available capital.

I want to hurry on to the second of my four related economic objectives, the highest possible rate of growth, because it is logically almost indistinguishable from the first. The same reservation, about the need to consider the social and cultural price of this economic objective, applies to this as to the level of income. Equally I do not think the validity of growth as an economic objective can be questioned.

There are two points to note in defining the rate of growth of income per head. The first is that income—or more sensibly output—must be measured at constant prices. An increase in (the value of) output that results solely from the fact that people are prepared to pay a higher price for each item is in a sense not "real". So it is a growth of income, or output, per head at constant prices that we are after. The second point is that the level of utilization of resources should be the same at the beginning and end of the period over which the growth is measured. It is possible for a time to achieve a high rate of growth of income per head by employing a growing proportion of the nation's resources, by reducing unemployment in other words. That was done in the United States in the first half of the 1960's, when unemployment as measured fell from 5½% in 1962 to 4½% in 1965 and output per head at constant prices rose at 3½% a year. In the preceding period unemployment changed little and the rate of growth was only 1½% a year.

Defined in this way the constraints on the rate of growth are the increase of capital and those improvements in organization and technique which are not embodied in increases of capital.

The third objective I selected was price stability. This is a different point from the need to define the rate of growth at constant prices as that was not an objection to price rises but merely an observation that price rises do not constitute a "real" increase in the value of output. The case for price stability as an economic objective needs to be carefully argued. A headlong inflation, such as the Germans experienced in the 1920's, which by making money literally incredible destroys the whole basis of an advanced economy, is obviously disastrous, although a more modest rate of increase in the average level of prices—say 3% a year—is not so obviously to be avoided. It really has only two undesirable features. The first is that of itself it penalizes people whose incomes are fixed or exceptionally sticky in money terms. To counteract this, special measures are needed to make the money incomes of those people more flexible; this may be difficult but should not be beyond our powers. The second undesirable feature appears if the rate of increase in the average level of our prices is greater than in countries which are our economic competitors. If that happens our products will be less price competitive than theirs and our balance of payments will move towards, into, or deeper into, deficit, so why have I made a balance of payments (i.e. neither deficit nor surplus) my fourth economic objective?

There is a habit of likening Britain to a great industrial corporation which must balance its books if it is to stay in business. The analogy, on the whole deplorable, is useful, however, as long as it is dropped at the right point of the exposition. If a firm does not balance its books it loses money. Its bank balance declines until the point is reached when its cheques are unacceptable and eventually it goes out of business. On the way down it will do all it can to borrow money while it puts its business in order and hopes to make money again.

The early stages of this process are valid analogues for the British economy. If we have a balance of payments deficit we lose money, but money is an even trickier thing to define in the international context than it is in the national context. There is sterling—pound notes if you like, which we can print easily enough—there is gold, there are balances at the International Monetary Fund and soon there may be Special Drawing Rights at the I.M.F. too. So if we continue to run a balance of payments deficit for several years we make use of as many of these forms of international money as we can lay our hands on. There is not really a danger that at some stage Britain will go out of business; the island will not sink. But there will be mounting pressure, from all the providers of the various forms of international money, for us to put our business in order and start once more to make money—or at least to balance our books. At this point the analogy breaks down completely because whereas the management of the firm can, more or less, control its business operations the government of Britain does not control the business operations of the British economy. Three-quarters of national output is produced in the private sector not managed by the government. The question of what sort of actions the government can take to improve the balance of payments is the same question as how my four economic objectives are inter-connected.

RELATIONSHIPS BETWEEN OBJECTIVES

Thus, if Britain continues to run a deficit on its balance of payments, there will be mounting pressures from the providers of the various forms of international money for us so to alter the forces at work in the economy that our international payments move back into balance. What actions are available to the government to do that?

Firstly it can reduce the level of expenditure; it can do this in three ways; by reducing its own consumption (the "government" part of the first line of the simplified expenditure and output table); secondly, it can, by taxation or by monetary policy, reduce the rest of consumption; thirdly, it can, even more indirectly, influence the level of expenditure by enterprises on tools and equipment for their own use. All of these will act to reduce imports because a proportion of the expenditure is met from imports, so if the expenditure is reduced so also will be imports. On the other hand, if expenditure is reduced so *ipso facto* is output and income which limits the extent to which we achieve the first two of my four objectives. There is also controversy about whether for certain products (e.g. motor cars) the reduction of imports brought about by reducing expenditure is not equalled or exceeded by a reduction of exports caused by higher unit costs of home production which is, it is claimed, itself caused by reducing home expenditure. I do not intend to go into that, but merely to state that I do not accept it as a total objection to the government attempting to operate on the balance of payments by operating on expenditure at home.

A second type of action available to the government for operating on the balance of payments is to influence the level or the rate of increase of money incomes and prices. If effective, this would lower the prices of British goods and services in relation to those of our competitors and should therefore enable us to sell more. Although that action would therefore assist in achieving price stability (the third of my four selected economic objectives) this cannot be claimed as a bonus because part of the justification for price stability as an objective is that it will strengthen the balance of payments. The remaining justification for price stability as an objective was that it protected people whose money incomes are relatively slow to change and it is not necessarily true that an effective incomes policy will not discriminate against some of these people.

A third type of action available to the government for influencing the balance of payments is to intervene in the industrial market place so as to favour types of activity which particularly benefit the balance of payments. Examples of this are support for agriculture, the aircraft industry, aluminium smelters. Again there are arguments that these actions are ineffective because the activities *from* which the government diverts resources would benefit the balance of payments as much as those *to* which it diverts resources. Whatever the force of these arguments (and I do not believe they are very powerful) this method of operation almost certainly works to limit our achievement of the highest possible level and rate of growth of income per head. I believe this because I believe that on the whole these actions will divert resources from uses in which total output per head is relatively high (but where the foreign exchange output per head is relatively low) to uses in which total output per head is relatively low (but where the foreign exhange output per head is relatively high).

There is also a whole range of government activities which are aimed at influencing the balance of payments and which can be covered by the phrase of "export promotion". These are similar in intention to the preceding set but are confined to exhortation and influence, not involving the spending of money except for the direct cost of the people employed in the persuading. To the extent that they are effective they will operate in the same way as the preceding set, namely benefiting the balance of payments at some expense of the level and rate of growth of income per head.

Finally, the government can and does try to improve the balance of payments by what can be called missionary work for higher productivity. If effective this will not only improve the balance of payments but also the level and rate of growth of incomes per head. For that reason it is strange, at first sight, that there is any need for the government to act as a missionary because raising the level of income per head might be thought to be the prime objective of all economic enterprises.

I have tried to explain, by listing and describing the actions open to government for influencing the balance of payments, how the four economic objectives that I selected are interrelated, now I shall discuss the ways in which population bears on the objectives.

RELATIONSHIPS BETWEEN POPULATION LEVEL AND RATE OF CHANGE AND THE ECONOMIC OBJECTIVES

Five aspects of the array of relationships are:

Foreign trade requirements	$\propto$	Population density
Flexibility of labour supply	$\propto$	Population change
Investment requirements for a given growth rate	$\propto$	Population change
Availability of savings at a given income level	$\propto$	(Population change)$^{-1}$
	or	(Family size)$^{-1}$
Inactive/Active ratio	$\propto$	Population change.

The first of these looks like an obvious economic argument for a lower population. The land and natural resources available to us are fixed so that a higher population must mean that we shall need to import more food and raw materials; if we need to import more we shall have to export more so that this increased dependence on foreign trade increases the vulnerability of our basic economic objectives to the balance of payments. I do not believe that this argument stands up to examination, because firstly it is not true that the natural resources available to us are fixed. The natural resources actually *there* are fixed, in the sense that coal always lay in Wales, but their availability to us is all the time being increased by technology. North Sea gas, which was always there, has just become available to us, and other natural resources (minerals from the Continental Shelf? Fusion power from sea water?) will no doubt become available in future.

Second, this same vulnerability to external trade applies just as powerfully to each separate economic enterprise as to a whole country. The firm has to buy in a large part of its raw materials and components and it is not this which limits its ability to prosper but the extent to which it fails to exploit the available scientific, technological and managerial techniques and skills.

I can illustrate the weakness of this argument, or the strength of my objections to it, by three observations.

First, the United States, which has a level of income per head one and a half to two times as high as that of Britain, and about the same rate of growth of income per head, has a population density (persons per square kilometre) only one-eleventh of Britain. The higher American level of income per head, however, owes very little to their higher level of natural resources per head because only 3½% of their national income is derived from "natural resource" industries of agriculture, forestry, fishing, mining and quarrying. All the rest comes from manufacturing and services, for the individual enterprises of which the possession of an indigenous United States source of supply of raw materials is not a very great economic advantage.

Second, although United Kingdom imports increased twenty-fold in volume terms during the 19th century, when population was increasing most rapidly, the increase in population alone can explain only a small part of the increase in imports. The population increased to two and a half times its size but imports per head multiplied nine times. The causes of the great increase in imports per head are complex, including a major reduction of tariffs and other statutory barriers to trade as well as technological changes in transport (railways and steam ships) and other technological changes leading to much higher levels of income and expenditure per head. Greater population leading to greater vulnerability to foreign trade was swamped in importance by technological changes making it possible to welcome a much greater openness to foreign trade.

Third, although Britain's population density is high (221 persons per square kilometre) it is not the highest. The Dutch, who manage to survive their vulnerability to foreign trade, have a population density of 356 persons per square kilometre which, at our present rate of increase, we shall not reach for another 70 years.

The second aspect of the relationship between the economic objectives and population is the link between the flexibility of labour supply and the rate of change of population. I have used the word "flexibility" rather than rate of growth not because the alternative of saying the "rate of growth" of the labour supply would almost reduce the point to a tautology, but because in an advanced industrial economy flexibility of the labour supply is the difficult and important objective. In our position of exposure to foreign trade, strength can only be based on ability to respond to changes in the products demanded in world markets by changing the products that we make and sell, and we cannot do that solely by changing the products that are made in each factory; some will have to contract or close down, others to grow. That in turn calls for the movement of men and women from one job, and one skill, to another. Our growing awareness of this has led to extensions of further education and training, and government training centres, but shifts in the distribution of labour between products can be achieved either by transfers of existing workers from one job to another (which these schemes are designed to speed) or by the replacement in the whole working population of older workers retiring from jobs in one product by young workers taking their first jobs in a new product. This second source of "transfers" is larger if the number of young workers taking their first jobs is larger and that means a growing population.

In Britain in the past, and still today in the United States, France and Germany, a great deal of flexibility in the industrial labour supply was gained at the expense of a decline in agriculture and migration from country to town. That process has little further to go in Britain, though textiles, coal and possibly the other energy industries may take the place of agriculture.

The third aspect of the relationships between the economic objectives and population is the link between investment requirements for a given growth rate and population change. I do not intend to discuss the relationships between growth and investment but merely to assert again that the level of available capital is the effective constraint, and to add that a higher level of capital per head means a higher level of output (= income) per head. If this is accepted it follows that with a static population all investment will increase capital per head and will help to increase income per head but that if population is increasing some investment will be needed merely to maintain the existing level of capital per head and the amount available to increase that level will be less. This, together with the next aspect, is a point of major significance for developing countries with rapid rates of population increase but it is also relevant for Britain. In the early 1960's in Britain, when gross investment was £4000–5000 million per year, just under 20% of national output, very roughly £2000–2500 million served to replace existing assets as they wore out, £400 million served to maintain the existing level of capital per head against working population growing by 200,000 a year, and £1600-2100 million (40% of total investment) served to raise the level of capital per head.

The relationship between savings and population change acts to intensify the squeeze imposed by that between investment and population change.

A rising population needs more investment for a given rate of growth of income per head than does a static population, but a rising population is likely to demand that a large proportion of total output will be used for current spending, leaving less for investment, and it will make this demand felt by spending a larger proportion (and saving a smaller proportion) of its income than a static population. This is most easily demonstrated by considering families of different sizes. At present British mortality rates, the population would eventually stabilize if the average married couple had 2¼ children. The present level is probably about 2½, which means a growing population. There are no facts on saving levels for different sizes of family but the Family Expenditure survey does give figures of total spending for different sizes of family and this, with the added assumption that family size does not cause income to change (except for tax allowances and social security payments which do not count for this purpose as they are not part of the output generating the income), sheds some light on savings. In 1967 households with incomes from £20–30 a week spent very roughly 10s. a week (2½%) more for each extra child they had. Since the average proportion of personal income that is saved is less than 10%, this difference of 2½% per child is not insignificant. Even the difference between the "static population" family size of 2¼ children and the present level of 2½ children could possibly reduce personal savings by as much as 6% (from say 8% to say 7½% of income), and savings in the whole economy (of which personal savings make about one quarter) by about 1½%.

The last of the aspects of the relationship between the economic objectives and population which I shall look at is the link between the Inactive/Active ratio in the population and population change. The link is extremely complex; it works itself out over a lifetime because the inactive includes the old as well as the young and those people (mainly mothers) who, though of working age, are not, economically, active.

Changes in the proportion of the old in the population depend on birth rates of 60 years or more ago and on current mortality rates, both of which I propose to consider as not subject to influence, the first because they have already happened and the second because I do not regard it as sensible or respectable to assume anything other than that efforts will be directed to lowering mortality rates as rapidly as possible. This approach reduces a complicated link to a simple one, that a rising population means, for the next few decades a rising proportion of economically inactive young people. Since young people consume, in the form of education and health services as well as other consumer goods, not much less than adults, this means a growing claim on national output from those who do not contribute to it.

This purely demographic phenomenon will be strengthened if, as seems certain, the proportion of children over the statutory age who continue their education continues to increase. That will, it is hoped, lead to higher income (= output) per head when the children do start work but in the meantime it involves a larger claim on current resources. It has been forecast that the proportion of children under school age, schoolchildren, and university students in the population will rise from about 25% in 1968 to about 30% in 1985.

I am not leading here to any hard and unequivocal conclusion. I have said that the level of population is not now, and need not be for perhaps 70 years, any constraint on achieving the economic objectives that I selected, and also that a growing population scores as an economic plus in that it aids the flexibility of labour supply but scores as an economic minus in that it calls for more investment to achieve a given rate of growth of output per head, and makes available less savings at a given level of income per head and imposes a large burden of inactive young people on the working population. What I have not done is to attempt to assess the relative sizes of these pluses and minuses in order to conclude firmly that, from an economic point of view the optimum for Britain would be a population growing at a rate progressing from p_1' to p_2' and stabilizing (if $p_2' = 0$) at P_3.

A PERSONAL VIEW OF ECONOMIC POPULATION POLICY FOR BRITAIN

It is important to repeat that our present position is that population density in Britain is 11 times that of the United States but 60% lower than that of Holland; that the rate of growth of population in Britain is just over ½% per annum and that if the average family were 2¼ instead of 2½ children the population would eventually stop increasing. Thus, we have not a population problem of any gravity and if we attempted to have a population policy it would have to concern itself with very small changes from the present position which would take a long time to make themselves known.

In these circumstances, and since the economic arguments for and against population changes of the sort of size that seem at all likely in Britain are finely balanced, I conclude that it would be misguided to attempt a policy aimed deliberately at influencing population changes. Economic and social policies all have effects on demography and it is right that demographers should examine them and try to predict what their consequences for population change will be. But I am quite sure that in Britain now and for the next 50 years or so economics and sociology are the dog and demography is the tail they wag.

Specifically, the present prospects are that Britain's population will grow from 55 million now to 66 million at the end of the century. Given all the uncertainties of predicting so small a rate of change (we are talking about a quarter of a child) I see in this no case for an active population policy.

Discussion

E. B. WORTHINGTON: Sir Alan Parkes, you have spoken a good deal about contraception through the female, but very little about contraception through the male. Could you indicate how research on that subject is proceeding and whether a reliable "male pill" could be expected before the end of the century?

A. J. PARKES: Work on the biological control of male fertility has been building up for a decade or so, and large grants for such research have recently been made by the Ford Foundation. So far nothing effective and acceptable is available, and when something does come along the greatest problem of all will remain—that of persuading the human male to use it.

J. PARSONS: Sir Alan Parkes, what do you think of the rationale underlying the present arrangements in the Health Service as a result of which a man wanting to be sterilized has to pay for it to be done privately, whereas if he subsequently comes to feel he has made a mistake—or his circumstances change—and he wants to be "de"-sterilized, he can have it on the National Health?

A. J. PARKES: I was not aware of the arrangement but I suppose the N.H.S. takes the view that its job is to treat infertility however caused. Vasectomy is not easily reversed, unless done with that possibility in mind.

P. R. EHRLICH: In many parts of the United States surgeons have been afraid to perform vasectomies because they could not get insurance to protect them against malpractice suits. I was on one call-in television programme when a woman phoned and said that her husband had had a vasectomy and that it had been checked in two different hospitals. She then declared that she was pregnant, and pointed out that this meant "that the operation didn't work". One obviously can develop another hypothesis to cover that state of affairs but the point is that even where the legal situation has changed doctors tend to be afraid of the repercussions of doing vasectomies.

A. S. CHEKE: Dr. Hawthorn, in your paper and in various comments made so far at this conference it has been assumed that the abolition of unwanted babies would cause a substantial reduction in the birth-rate. While this is no doubt true for extra babies *within* marriage, it surely does not follow that if a girl is spared from having an illegitimate child she will not in fact have that child later when married; i.e. the effect of prevention of illegitimate and "legitimized" births is only likely to delay for a few years the appearance of the child, rather than to eliminate it and it is thus demographically dangerous to assume that contraception in this field would have a substantial effect on the birth-rate.

J. PARSONS: Mr. Hawthorn, do you agree that although it may well be impossible to give a precise and universally acceptable definition of the term "unwanted child" this doesn't mean it is either meaningless or useless. A woman casting about for an abortion is carrying an "unwanted child", as is a young woman who has become pregnant through having been refused contraceptive advice by her doctor on the grounds that she is unmarried. Surely the term has a hard common-sense meaning in those contexts and one which is valid for at least some scientific purposes—a sort of operational definition. Any woman carrying a foetus whose conception she tried to prevent by contraceptive means, or which she has tried to get rid of by abortion subsequent to that unwanted conception, can surely be said to be having an 'unwanted" child without doing violence to fact, language or logic.

G. P. HAWTHORN: Yes. I did say *almost* meaningless. Your first example would provide one operational definition of an "unwanted" pregnancy. But one still has no idea whether or not the *child,* had it been born, would also have been unwanted. Your second example could be carrying either a wanted or an unwanted pregnancy: there is no evidence either way. My point is that making inferences from existing data about the proportion of births that are unwanted is a dangerous exercise. I did this in my paper, but they were only guesses. The only really reliable evidence apart from that provided by the reported resort to abortion and adoption, is people's own statements. Even here, however, as Dr. William James has pointed out to me, the following situation could obtain:

    i.   a girl knows that sexual intercourse can lead to pregnancy, and

    ii.   she knows that means exist to reduce this possibility, but

    iii. she voluntarily does not use these means, yet

    iv. she describes the pregnancy as "unwanted".

If such a motivational muddle exists, and I am quite sure that it does, how can we know whether or not the pregnancies are "really" unwanted? Any simple definition will distort reality.

J. C. ANDERSON: I do not think that number of people per room is a good measure of population density. It would be perfectly possible to cover the whole surface of the country with little boxes and then say that the population density was not high because there was only one person per room. But this would hardly be an acceptable situation.

A. S. CHEKE: Mr. Boreham, I wonder if you could tell us something about the economics of certain factors that increase, if not exponentially, then at least more than linearly with population increase, e.g. the cost of combating pollution and providing welfare services, transport facilities, the cost of coping with delays due to crowding—queues, traffic jams, etc.

A. J. BOREHAM: It is true that these and other costs increase more than linearly with population but, in the likely circumstances foreseeable for Britain, I do not believe that they will place unmanageable burdens on our resources.

J. PARSONS: Mr. Boreham, I have always understood the definition of "economics" to be "the study of the processes of the exploitation and distribution of scarce resources". Do you accept this definition? If so what, do you think, is the status of an economic argument—touching on this question of an optimum population which starts off, as you do, ". . given the resources . . ."? Given infinite resources an infinitely expanding population is possible; the whole point is that resources are not "given" and therefore your arguments are void.

A. J. BOREHAM: Of course I accept the definition. As my argument does not start off "given the resources" I can hardly answer the second point. Those words introduce the economic objectives that I suggested because without these there are no constraints. I explained the effect of population on those objectives later in my talk, considering population as one resource and, essentially, capital as the other.

D. MALAN: While I accept that Dr. Cooke's and Mr. Boreham's arguments are probably correct taken in isolation, I am greatly troubled by the fact that no one, except our Chairman, mentions the effect on the *quality of life* of an uncontrolled increase in population. This is surely the main factor on which arguments for a control of population should be based.

Mr. Hawthorn has said that he knows of no tangible evidence to link deleterious effects with over-crowding in itself. There is some work that links such effects not with over-crowding, but with *lack of space*. John Rowan Wilson, writing in the *New Statesman* of 1st December 1967, quotes a study by Wing-Commander D. M. Fanning in which a detailed comparison was made of the health patterns of families living (a) in houses and (b) in flats. His results showed that the incidence of ill health was 57% greater in flat-dwellers than in those who lived in houses, a highly statistically significant finding. Not only this, but the incidence of ill health increased with the height of the flat occupied.

Our Chairman of this morning said that no one here seemed to be prepared to name an actual figure for the optimum population for Britain. It is a pity that Sir Joseph Hutchinson was not able to take part in this Symposium, as he has done this. I quote from his Presidential address to the British Association for the Advancement of Science (1966)

> "But do we really believe that a population twice the present size—as it may well be a century hence—can live and work and enjoy adequate leisure and recreation within the confines of this island? And if we do not, now is the time to set about ensuring that our numbers are stabilized.
> "We need first a target figure. I would like to set about 40,000,000 though I believe that, short of catastrophe, it would take two centuries to achieve it . . .
> "For, make no mistake, this country already carries a population as great as the environment can support without degeneration, and it will call for all the knowledge and skill we can command to prevent irreparable damage before we achieve a stable population, even if we set about stabilization without delay."

R. E. BOOTE: It is clear that more research is required into all aspects—economic, social, environmental—of the population question. It might be that from this research will emerge a series of optima, related to changing circumstances and expectations. Above all, education and information are required to dispel the apathy and ignorance of most people about the significance to them of population numbers, especially if they are to develop the relatively sophisticated approach that would enable variation of total population numbers to be made in time, according to needs and conditions in any given era. And new forms of participation are required, if this is to be achieved on a democratic basis, reflecting the wishes of the people in this ultimately, most personal and fundamental of issues.

CHAPTER 7

The Natural and Manipulated Control of Animal Populations

T. R. E. SOUTHWOOD

Imperial College

None of us would deny that man is an animal, a product of evolution and hence, for all his social sophistication, he still carries attributes that have been forged in Evolution's furnace. Evolution works on the individual and, basically, evolutionary success is the survival of the individual's genes and the long-term maximization of descendants. The individual therefore strives to reproduce. For many species of animal it is possible to calculate its rate of increase if all the progeny survived and bred. Such an approach, originally pioneered by Malthus and others, shows that we should soon become "knee-deep" in mice, moths or maggots! As we are not, some processes must act against this increase. Many of these processes are unrelated to the density of the population, for example most of the direct and indirect effects of climate, but others act more severely the higher the density of the population. These are often called regulatory processes and they are what I imply by the term "control".

Control is a word that has led to a great deal of controversy in ecology (Solomon, 1964; Ehrlich and Birch, 1967). In using it I am not implying a steady state; the system is continually subject to disturbance due to climatic fluctuations and environmental change. Furthermore each particular interaction is most appropriately described by a stochastic model: for example, at given densities of predator and prey a precise forecast of the outcome cannot be determined, for even in identical conditions a predator may by chance encounter more prey on some occasions than others. It is not surprising that the variance around any density-dependent relationship may be considerable (Southwood, 1967a). Nevertheless in many, but probably not all, animal populations, controlling (or regulating) factors occur (Richards and Southwood, 1968).

The purpose of this paper is to outline the processes of control in animal populations. These are relevant to our present symposium because:

1. Man is an animal, unique only in that he has currently been able to free himself to a large extent from normal ecological control, from the processes of natural selection, but not from his evolved characters or their consequences (Morris, 1967).

2. By studying animal populations we can discover some of the normal ecological processes from which man has escaped and perhaps forecast the consequences of this escape.

3. We have some experience of manipulating the populations of other animals: the approaches and models used may be of relevance if we are to attempt to manage our own population.

NATURAL CONTROL

There have been many theories emphasizing various aspects of the mechanisms of population control. They have all made useful contributions to

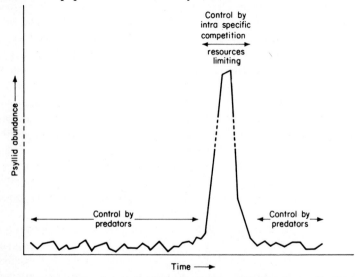

Fig. 1. The two levels of control of the population of the Eucalyptus Psyllid (modified from Clark *et al.*, 1967).

our progress, but I do not propose at this point to dwell on their differences in terminology and concepts. Nowadays more emphasis is placed on the synoptic or holistic (and I believe realistic) approach, in which the whole life system of the population is considered (Clark *et al.*, 1967; Southwood, 1969).

It seems that the populations of many animals, particularly plant feeders, can be considered to exist at two levels, the endemic and the epidemic: the factors of their control are different at these two levels. Some theoretical aspects of these levels have been elucidated by Takahashi (1964). An excellent example from a natural population is provided by Clark's (1964a,b,c) work on an Australian Eucalyptus Psyllid *(Cardiaspina albitextura)*. In several localities and for many years the population remained relatively low—endemic (Fig. 1). This level was maintained by the action of various predators, especially birds, and parasites that attacked the adults and young stages, the intensity of attack often being greater at greater densities. Many other factors, particularly the climate, acted either directly or indirectly to cause fluctuations in the populations. From time to time, however, these fluctuations are so violent that the population "breaks through" the level of control maintained by the predators and rises to the epidemic level. At this level the eucalyptus leaves, the food supply, are severely damaged and may be shed. Many larvae die of starvation and the numbers dying are proportional to the density of the population. Not surprisingly, the population soon falls: at the epidemic level its further increase has been halted, i.e. it has been controlled, by a shortage of resource, principally its food. This is the type of situation envisaged by Milne (1957) when he said that "the environment rules".

In this psyllid therefore the population is largely controlled by mortality factors, by death from being eaten or by death from starvation. Changes in population can, however, occur through the other two pathways, namely natality (or births) and dispersal; in the course of evolution these have also come to play a role in population control. Indeed in the Eucalyptus psyllid studied by Clark, discussed above, some of the control at the epidemic level is brought about by a reduction in the number of eggs laid by the females (Clark, 1963). There have been many studies on the role of changes in the birth rate in bird and mammal populations: much of the evidence has been collected by Wynne-Edwards (1962) and Lack (1966). These authors differ in their interpretations and indeed, although the effect can be measured, the identification of the cause (and mechanism) is much more difficult. As an illustration of these difficulties, reference can be made to some recent work on an animal that exhibits great variations in its population density, the brown lemming *(Lemmus tri-mucronatus)*. It has been studied in Canada by Krebs (1964) and in Alaska by Mullen (1968). Krebs believed that the reductions in the reproductive rate were primarily associated with changes in the density of the population and the resultant mutual interference at high density. Mullen showed, over a longer period of years, that such reductions could also occur when the population was relatively low. He concluded that reproductive activity and the length of the breeding season were dependent on spring temperatures. As the temperatures also influence the food eventually available, the mechanism is still one that relates the increase in population to the potential of the habitat.

Food and space are the two components of a population system that have been shown to be particularly significant in providing the framework in which mechanisms for population control by reductions in recruitment are achieved. The animal may be influenced by the availability of these components through:

1. The available food—its quantity and quality.
2. The number of encounters with other individuals—stress.

3. The level of the pollution of the space by the products or artifacts of other individuals.

4. The accessibility of sites for reproduction (e.g. nesting sites).

These "signals" can bring into play a variety of mechanisms that result in the lowering of natality. Studies in a wide range of animals have revealed the following principal mechanisms.

EXCLUSION FROM BREEDING POPULATION

This may be brought about by a prolongation of immaturity; many examples are given by Wynne-Edwards (1962) and Sadleir (1969). Alternatively, although adult, the animal may be unable to obtain or hold a territory or breeding site. Carrick's (1963) work on the Australian magpie is a good example of this: he found in most years that there was a non-breeding population of adults that lived peripherally to the main habitat of the local population (Andrewartha, 1959).

REDUCTION IN FECUNDITY

It has been found in numerous insects that the fecundity of the female is proportional to her weight (Waloff and Richards, 1958; Klomp, 1966; Southwood, 1966; Watt, 1968): under conditions of food shortage, individuals will get less food as larvae and hence become smaller and less fecund adults. Also, as Andersen (1957) pointed out, under crowded conditions, the frequent disturbances arising from individual encounters will direct some of the female's energy reserves from reproduction to locomotion. Indeed energy resources can be switched from reproduction to prolonged locomotor activity (i.e. to migration): in his comprehensive work on insect migration Johnson (1969) has emphasized this switch and referred to it as the "oogenesis-flight syndrome". The fecundity of a population may also fall because there has been a change in the qualitative make-up of the population and a less fecund or viable strain has become more abundant (Wellington, 1960; Chitty, 1967; Murdie, 1969a,b).

REDUCTION IN FERTILITY

The number of living progeny produced by a female has been shown to be lowered in dense populations. Particularly good examples have been found in work on small mammals, discussed by Wynne-Edwards (1962). Mechanisms involved include intra-uterine resorption, abortion and, under exceptionally crowded conditions, a lowering of the fertilization rate through the disturbance of, and interference with, copulation.

MORTALITY OF NEWLY-BORN YOUNG

Strictly speaking this is part of the mortality, rather than the natality pathway of population change. There are many examples among mammals and birds. In some game-birds pre-hatching factors have been shown to influence subsequent survival of the chicks (Jenkins *et al.*, 1967; Southwood 1967b). Under conditions of stress parents may neglect to tend the young which die as a result, or they may actually kill and devour their own progeny ("cronism") or those of their neighbours (cannibalism). In some insects the larvae that are most advanced in development may devour their siblings or associates (Banks, 1956; Corbet and Griffiths, 1963; Brian, 1965; Pienkowski, 1965).

These complex mechanisms for the reduction of recruitment are summarized in Table I. It is interesting and perhaps not unprofitable to query which of these mechanisms may have operated in primitive populations of man when, prior to the development of agriculture and technology, the carrying capacity of the environment was much less. Are there signs of any of these signals recurring in our crowded conurbations?

The last pathway of population change is migration. Although the prime evolutionary advantage of this habit lies in enabling a species to keep pace with its ever changing environment (Southwood, 1962), there are several instances where an increasing proportion of the population become migrants as population density rises (Dempster, 1968; Way, 1968; Johnson, 1969).

In conclusion, therefore, in natural populations of animals where control occurs, it acts by the animals being killed (either by a predator or a disease), being starved, moving away, or by the lowering of the recruitment rate of the population. To "control" the population these factors must act with increasing severity as population density rises. Animals also die from other causes, e.g. cold, heat, crushing, but the extent of these hazards is not normally related to the density of the population. One cannot assume that these controlling (or regulating) factors occur in every local population and certainly, if they do, they are often unsuccessful in their action, as evidence for the extinction of local populations has often been recorded (Barnes, 1953; Neilsen, 1961; Ehrlich, 1965; Southwood, 1969). It is clear that such factors require time in which to operate and, given the ever fluctuating and changing environment, together with the stochastic nature of much mortality (referred to above) control cannot always be successful in the prevention of over-population and/or extinction.

Evolution will work in favour of the characters of those individuals whose lines of progeny do not become extinct and hence they will develop "early warning systems" with regard to over-population.When we come to consider whether these systems act just within the "family" or whether they act at the population level, and thus possibly at an earlier stage, we plunge into a very controversial area of animal ecology, but one that is extremely relevant to this symposium. Wynne-Edwards (1962) has put forward the view that the dispersion

TABLE I

The principal mechanisms for reduction of recruitment in animal populations in response to intra-specific effects

Components	Signals	Mechanisms	Effects
Space	Number of encounters with other animals, aggressive interactions—"stress"	Prolonged immaturity Failure to obtain a territory or breeding site	Prevention from breeding
	Concentration of products or artifacts of other individuals—"pollution"	Nutrients unavailable or diverted to other purposes Less fecund strain	Reduction in fecundity
	Number of available sites for breeding	Interference with copulation	Reduction in fertility
Food	Nutritional level	Embryos aborted or resorbed	
		Congenital weakness Inadequate care by parents Cronism Cannibalism	Mortality of newly-born young

of an animal population provides this "early-warning system" and that once the optimum has been exceeded the population as an entity responds by retarding recruitment, even though there may be adequate resources for the immediate needs of the population. That individual populations should be provident in this way is extremely logical. The difficulty arises, however, that evolutionary pressure acts on the individual, and the individual that retards its reproduction, when its neighbours do not, will be at an evolutionary disadvantage. Wynne-Edwards has suggested that evolution may also act on the group, favouring those groups (i.e. populations), that keep their numbers at the optimum. However, Hamilton (1964) has shown that altruism can only evolve when there is close genetic similarity between the individuals involved, as in social Hymenoptera and parthenogenetically reproducing aphid colonies. It is difficult, but perhaps not impossible, to envisage local populations of other animals (that lack the unusual genetic and reproductive mechanisms of these groups), in which the individuals would be sufficiently closely related to permit the evolution of extensive altruism by a genetic mechanism (Hamilton, 1969).

Another view, and one I hold, is that Darwinian evolution has insured that every animal will strive to produce the maximum number of potentially reproducing descendants its environment allows (see also Lack, 1966). At times when resources become short it may invoke some of the mechanisms listed in Table I to prevent its neighbours reproducing, e.g. territorial exclusion. The stress resulting from such encounters, the shortage of resources, etc., may lower its own reproductive fitness or lead to the neglect or destruction of some, often weaker, members in the family, ensuring the survival of the remainder (e.g. cronism in storks). Thus a population can be self-regulatory (Andrewartha, 1959; Milne, 1962), but at a level well above Wynne-Edwards' optimum and where the individuals within it suffer in various ways.

Group selection cannot be postulated for wild ape populations; their characters are too varied and mating too promiscuous (van Lawick-Goodall, 1968). Apes and man have been largely subject to normal Darwinian selection and thus each man and woman will have inherited from past evolution the trait to maximize reproductive fitness. One could claim that this view is supported by the Freudian school of psychology's emphasis on the basic nature of the desire to assert sexual virility. As soon as language, and hence group memory, allowed man to free himself from strict natural selection, when Mather's (1964) exosomatic evolution became possible, then the conflict commenced between this trait and the desire and need of each society to conform more to the Wynne-Edwards' model, i.e. to keep the population at the optimum. Many taboos and religious customs have played a role in this battle (Malthus, 1798; Carr-Saunders, 1922; Wynne-Edwards, 1962). The very fact that this symposium is being held is evidence that the battle is by no means over; it is now more critical because the role of natural mortality is now so reduced. We are still struggling against the incubus of maximum reproduction, fixed on us in the course of evolution. Perhaps this incubus represents, biologically, "original sin"! If we were the product of a significant measure of group selection, as ants or aphids may be, the problem would be much less acute.

MANIPULATED CONTROL

It is desirable that man's recent freedom from many agents of natural control (predators, diseases, starvation) should be maintained. However, our studies of animals outlined above show that as man's population continues to rise the ultimate intra-specific factors will come into play, probably following the signals of stress and pollution, although eventually world-wide food shortage is not impossible. To an ecologist it seems obvious that man must endeavour to manipulate his own population; in doing this we should take cognizance of the principles and methods derived for the manipulation of animal populations. Since the dawn of history man has either intentionally or unintentionally modified the populations of other animals: he has endeavoured to increase those that are beneficial and reduce those that are harmful (Southwood, 1969). The population levels that have been aimed for have been the optimum from the anthropocentric point of view. For pests this has commonly been supposed to be the minimal obtainable; for prey (i.e. fish, game, cattle) the highest level that can be continuously supported (and sometimes, regrettably, a level much higher than can be supported, so leading to disasters like overgrazing).

It is appropriate to attempt, from this ecological view point, to define the concept of optimum human population as used in the title of this symposium. Rejecting the view of the misanthrope, I would suggest:

"The optimum population of man is the maximum that can be maintained indefinitely without detriment to the health of the individuals from pollution or from social or nutritional stress".

The measurement of the health of the population is a medical problem and the assessment of social stress, under which we must include the quality of life, is particularly difficult. The present discussions on the optimum density in intensive farming bear witness to this difficulty. One point that the animal ecologist demands to make is that, because a population of a certain magnitude can exist today in an environment, this is not proof that a similar population will be able to maintain itself indefinitely. There are many examples from laboratory experiments with animals which show that a rapid population increase to a very high level leads to a period of stress followed by a decline to a lower population density (Park, 1948; Slobodkin, 1954).

In considering man's management of beneficial animal populations, it is useful to distinguish between the situation in sea fishing and that in farming and ranching. Hitherto in fishing man can only influence the system through the pathway of mortality, by controlling his own predation on the population. In ranching, additional factors that may be controlled are other predators, migration, the birth-rate (natality) and above all the environment itself. The optimum rate for the exploitation in fisheries will be that which provides the highest yield compatible with stability of production. In the case of whales and some seals there is abundant evidence that the initial rate of harvesting was too high, the population collapsed and in the long-term the industry will be ruined. Once again the optimum can only be determined when the time factor is taken

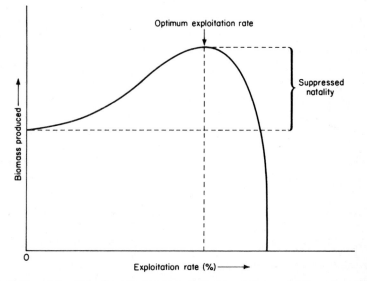

Fig. 2. The relationship of production to exploitation rate in a population where there is intra-specific competition.

into account and from knowledge of the growth of populations it is often possible to determine the optimum fishing levels if sufficient biological data is available (Beverton and Holt, 1957; Ricker, 1958; Silliman and Gutsell, 1958).

It was shown above that the rate of recruitment to a population may be suppressed through various "signals" (Table I). It could therefore be, that by catching some of the individuals the breeding rate would be increased rather than lowered; if the breeding rate is increased then so is the potential productivity—the biomass produced per unit of time—although the actual density of the population may be lessened. Such a situation is represented in Fig. 2 as the percentage of the population culled continues to rise so will the biomass until the culling has "taken up" all the suppressed natality. This percentage represents the optimum rate of exploitation. If even more individuals are removed, the productivity will quickly fall and, in the long run, the population may become extinct. Watt (1968) has determined the optimum exploitation rate, to give maximum biomass production, for various animals (from the data of earlier workers); the percentage of the population culled each day varied from 99% of the adults for blowflies *(Lucillia)* to 2% of the total population for guppies *(Lebistes)*.

The ecological basis for this type of management is the replacement of intra-specific competition effects by harvesting; this may necessitate selecting a particular age or sex. This selection can be made by devices such as fishing nets of a particular mesh, closed seasons or limited hunting bags.

There are, however, many populations in which such intra-specific suppression of natality does not occur; in these, exploitation by man will depend on replacing this natural mortality (Watt, 1968). Man can either aim to harvest in competition with natural mortality factors or he can attempt to eliminate or reduce their effects, as when predators or other herbivores that compete for vegetation are killed or when protection is provided against climatic extremes.

In terrestrial and many freshwater situations, i.e. on farms, ranches, small ponds and streams, man may also modify the habitat so as to increase the resources available to the animal; this will raise the level of population that can be carried and so increase the yield for the same percentage cull.

These changes in the environment, in the carrying capacity of the land, parallel exactly the increases in the limits of settlement by man achieved through his technological advances (Eversley, p. 103).

Summarizing, in problems of the management of the populations of beneficial animals, the basic aim is to achieve the optimum harvest and this involves avoiding the opposing disasters, poised like Scylla and Charybdis, of:

1. an excessive mortality rate—i.e. overfishing;
2. an excessive natality rate, leading to a population level that is too high—i.e. overgrazing.

Recent work in animal ecology has shown that there is no need to "wait and see"—a course between these disasters can be plotted: with careful studies and measurements of the correct ecological parameters and the application of systems analysis and computers the outcome of a particular regime can be forecast (Watt, 1966, 1968). Not only are computers able to cope with the complexity of pathways in a population system (Southwood, 1969), but they are able to take account of the time element or lags and feedbacks which we have seen are so important in the control and management of populations. Pioneering this approach, Holling (1964, 1965, 1968) has made brilliant investigations of predation, and an example of a practical simulation model for the management of North American salmon fisheries is given by Paulik and Greenough (1966).

An outline of the steps in the use of these techniques is:

1. Recognize the basic components and pathways in the system.

2. Determine experimentally, or from field data, the quantitative relationships between the various variables.
3. Construct a model, initially as a flow chart and then as a computer programme.
4. Test the realism of the model by certain computing tests (Watt, 1968) and against independent field data.
5. Use the model to simulate Nature; for example to determine the effects of various changes in the components or to determine the optimum strategy for the maximization or minimization of a particular variable.

An outline flow chart for a simple systems simulation model is shown in Fig. 3. Such a model would provide a method of determining the optimum exploitation rate (% cull) from, for example, a fish pond or a small herd. As in all simulation studies a large amount of ecological data is needed to set up the programme (Watt, 1968). In order to keep this diagram relatively straightforward a number of gross over-simplifications have been made in the underlying biological assumptions and data which are taken as:

1. Effects of pressure on space operate only during breeding season.
2. Mortality is independent of sex and density.
3. Adults breed only once and then die.
4. Generation time = one cycle = one year.
5. Sex ratio is 50:50.
6. Animals must be harvested before breeding.

The other ecological parameters of the population, which are theoretically obtained from field and laboratory experiments, are given in the input trapezoids in the chart. The programme starts with an initial population of 100 individuals introduced into the habitat; these will multiply during each cycle (i.e. each year). When the pressure on space starts to become significant (here the value of $ taken is that when $N = 0.5K$), the programme commences harvesting 5% of the animals just prior to breeding and will continue for a total of 50 cycles (i.e. 50 years) after the original introduction of 100 animals. The programme will then start again, from the original introduction, but when pressure on space reaches 2, harvesting will commence at the level of 10% and continue for a total of 50 cycles. Exploitation rates of every 5% up to 95% will be tested for 50 years. If during any cycle the population falls below the original 100 or exceeds 1000, the cycle for any harvesting régime is stopped, as it is considered too violent. An examination of the print-out of the numbers harvested over these simulated 900 years (obtained in a few seconds on the computer) will quickly indicate the most promising exploitation régime. If necessary the programme can be re-run to test an array of values for h between those used (e.g. 36, 37, 38 and 39%) so as to get a more precise optimum.

Carrying capacity could be treated as a variable for, as other contributors have pointed out, the carrying capacity of man's environment has, through technological progress, continued to increase. One problem is to prophesy the rate of this increase in the future; can we assume that it will always be increasing? The role of pollution could be overwhelming (Mellanby, p. 45); also

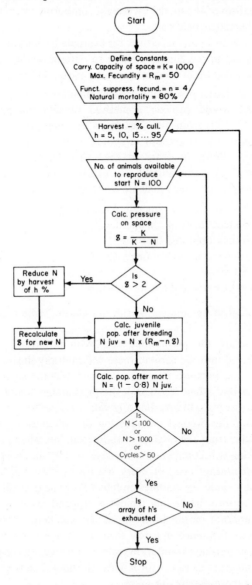

Fig. 3. An outline flow chart for a simple systems simulation model to investigate the effects, over 50 years, of various rates of exploitation (Read and write-in formats omitted).

with economic progress each individual may demand more space for living and leisure (see discussion, p. 127). I consider that the tool of systems analysis as being used by the animal ecologist and his approaches to population manipulation should be utilized for man (see Staff, 1969).

CONCLUSIONS

The approach of the animal ecologist is thus of value in a consideration of the optimum level of man's population. Experimental and analytical studies have identified the range of ecological processes that bring about the natural control of animal populations—the ultimate process is intra-specific stress. Because of man's technological achievements he has been able to remove or reduce some of the environmental factors, e.g. shortage of food and breeding sites (= homes), that might have provided early-warning signals and lead to mechanisms for self-regulation. Man's technology has undoubtedly also greatly increased the carrying capacity of his environment, but studies on manipulated populations, where environmental capacity has likewise been increased, have shown that overpopulation can easily occur. Studies on animals also emphasize the time lag between the rise of the population and the onset of many of the natural controlling factors, especially the ultimate effects of stress. Let us not dismiss these and assume that man can be a law unto himself. We must beware of being like the little boy with the box of matches, of being able to make our technology work, but neither foresee its consequences nor control its outcome. We must think, not in terms of decades, but as biologists, in terms of generations: we hold our genes and our environment, both affected by reproductive pattern and rate, in trust for future generations. As trustees it behoves us, when in doubt, to err on the side of caution and be provident.

With these strictures in mind, it seems likely that the population of Britain (and the world) should be stabilized now. A more precise verdict should be obtained by bringing together the best data that we have, forecasting population growth and determining the carrying capacity of the environment in terms of its limited resources of space, food and energy. Then, by using the methods outlined above, the optimum population can be determined, taking account of the many and varied social effects of population (and economic) growth.

The results of such studies must be heeded; we must turn our back on the original sin of maximal reproduction, with its corollary that the rate of population growth will be determined at the family level and in relation only to the immediate resources of the family. For the very poor, children may even be an economic asset and hence families can be large, whatever contraceptive advice is available. With greater prosperity parents hope and expect to provide certain resources and they will limit their offspring in relation to what is available. Thus in times of economic stress (e.g. Britain in the 1930s) or extreme political uncertainty (e.g. parts of Eastern Europe now) the birth rate may drop. But when the income per family is rising, unless the whole rise is absorbed by parental demands for an increased standard of living, the birth-rate could also rise. There is evidence (Thomson, p. 13) that this is happening in Britain now and therefore it would not seem as if we can completely rely on the elimination of the "unwanted" child to stabilize population.

We must demonstrate our difference from other animals by replacing evolution's weapon of intra-specific stress with a new group-selected, socially imposed, reproductive control. What happens within the "territory" of the family is no longer its sole concern; the environment of its neighbours must also be protected. It is only by positive action that we can continue to remain free from the undoubtedly painful pressures of natural ecological control. That is, we must accept some significant social control now, to preserve some freedom for future generations.

REFERENCES

Andersen, F. S. (1957). The effect of density on the birth and death rate. *Ann. Rep. Pest Infest. Lab., Springforti 1954–1955.* 27pp.

Andrewartha, H. G. (1959). Self-regulatory mechanisms in animal populations. *Aust. J. Sci.* **22**, 200–205.

Banks, C. J. (1956). Observations on the behaviour and mortality in Coccinellidae before dispersal from the egg-shells. *Proc. R. ent. Soc. Lond.* A **31**, 56–60.

Barnes, H. F. (1953). The absence of slugs in a garden and an experiment in re-stocking. *Proc. zool. Soc. Lond.* **123**, 49–58.

Beverton, R. J. H. and Holt, S. J. (1957). On the dynamics of exploited fish populations. *Fishery investigations.* ser. 2, **19**, 533 pp. London.

Brian, M. V. (1965). "Social Insect Populations". London.

Carrick, R. (1963). Ecological significance of territory in the Australian Magpie *Gymnorhina ribicen. Proc. int. Orn. Congr.* **13**, 740–753.

Carr-Saunders, A. M. (1922). "The Population Problem: A Study in Human Evolution". Oxford.

Chitty, D. (1967). The natural selection of self-regulatory behaviour in animal populations. *Proc. ecol. Soc. Aust.* **2**, 51–78.

Clark, L. R. (1963). The influence of population density on the number of eggs laid by females of *Cardiaspina albitextura* (Psyllidae). *Aust. J. Zool.* **11**, 190–201.

Clark, L. R. (1964a). The intensity of parasite attack in relation to the abundance of *Cardiaspina albitextura* (Psyllidae). *Aust. J. Zool.* **12**, 150–173.

Clark, L. R. (1964b). Predation by birds in relation to the population density of *Cardiaspina albitextura* (Psyllidae). *Aust. J. Zool.* **12**, 349–361.

Clark, L. R. (1964c). The population dynamics of *Cardiaspina albitextura* (Psyllidae). *Aust. J. Zool.* **12**, 362–380.

Clark, L. R., Geier, P. W., Hughes, R. D. and Morris, R. F. (1967). "The Ecology of Insect Populations in Theory and Practice". London.

Corbet, P. S. and Griffiths, A. (1963). Observations on the aquatic stages of two species of *Toxorhynchites* (Diptera) in Uganda. *Proc. R. ent. Soc. Lond.* A 38, 125–135.

Dempster, J. P. (1968). Intra-specific competition and dispersal: as exemplified by a Psyllid and its anthocorid predator. *In* "Insect Abundance", pp. 8–17. (T. R. E. Southwood, ed.)

Ehrlich, P. R. (1965). The population biology of the butterfly, *Euphydryas editha*. II. The structure of the Jasper Ridge Colony. *Evolution* 19, 327–336.

Ehrlich, P. R. and Birch, L. C. (1967). "The Balance of Nature" and "Population Control". *Am. Nat.* 101, 97–107.

Hamilton, W. D. (1964). The genetical evolution of social behaviour. I, II. *J. theoret. Biol.* 7, 1–52.

Hamilton, W. D. (1969). Selection of selfish and altruistic behaviour in some extreme models. *Smithsonian Inst. 3rd Int. Symp. Comp. Social Behav.* (in press).

Holling, C. S. (1964). The analysis of complex population processes. *Can. Ent.* 96, 335–347.

Holling, C. S. (1965). The functional response of predators to prey density and its role in mimicry and population regulation. *Mem. ent. Soc. Can.* 45, 5–60.

Holling, C. S. (1968). The tactics of a predator. *In* "Insect Abundance", pp. 47–58. (T. R. E. Southwood, ed.)

Jenkins, D., Watson, A. and Miller, G. R. (1967). Population fluctuations in the red grouse *Lagopus lagopus scoticus* (Lath.). *J. Anim. Ecol.* 36, 97–122.

Johnson, C. G. (1969). "Migration and Dispersal of Insects by Flight". London.

Klomp, H. (1966). The dynamics of a field population of the pine looper *Bupalus piniarius* L. *Adv. ecol. Res.* 3, 207–305.

Krebs, C. J. (1964). The lemming cycle at Baker Lake, Northwest Territories, during 1959–62. *Arctic Inst. N. Amer. Tech. Paper* 15, 7–104.

Lack, D. (1966). "Population studies of Birds". Oxford.

Lawick-Goodall, J. van (1968). The behaviour of free-living chimpanzees in the Gombe Stream Reserve. *Anim. Behav. Monogr.* 1 (3), 161–311.

Malthus, T. (1798). "An Essay on the Principle of Population". London.

Mather, K. (1964). "Human Diversity". Edinburgh and London.

Milne, A. (1957). The natural control of insect populations. *Can. Ent.* 89, 193–213.

Milne, A. (1962). On a theory of natural control of insect population. *J. theoret. Biol.* 3, 19–50.

Mullen, D. A. (1968). Reproduction in brown lemmings *(Lemmus trimucronatus)* and its relevance to their cycle of abundance. *Univ. Calif. Pub. Zool.* 85, 1–24.

Murdie, G. (1969a). Some causes of size variation in the pea aphid, *Acyrthosiphon pisum* Harris (Hemiptera: Aphidae). *Trans. R. ent. Soc. Lond.* (in press).

Murdie, G. (1969b). The effect of size variation on the biology of the pea aphid, *Acyrthosiphon pisum* Harris (Hemiptera: Aphidae). *Trans. R. ent. Soc. Lond.* (in press).

Morris, D. (1967). "The Naked Ape". London.

Neilsen, E. T. (1961). On the habits of the migratory butterfly *Ascia monuste* C. *Biol. Med. Kb.* 23 (II), 1–81.

Park, T. (1948). Experimental studies of interspecies competition. I.
Ecol. Monogr. 18, 265–308.

Paulik, G. J. and Greenough, J. W. (1966). Management analysis for a salmon resource system.
In "Systems Analysis in Ecology", pp. 215–252. (K. E. F. Watt, ed.).

Pienkowski, R. L. (1965). The incidence and effect of egg cannibalism in first-instar *Coleomegilla maculata lengi* (Coleoptera: Coccinellidae).
Ann. ent. Soc. Amer. 58, 150–153.

Richards, O. W. and Southwood, T. R. E. (1968). The abundance of insects: introduction. *In* "Insect Abundance", pp. 1–7. (T. R. E. Southwood, ed.).

Ricker, W. E. (1958). Handbook of computations for biological statistics of fish populations. *Fisheries Res. Board Can. Bull.* 119, 1–300.

Sadleir, R. M. F. S. (1969). "The Ecology of Reproduction in Wild and Domestic Mammals". London.

Silliman, R. P. and Gutsell, J. S. (1958). Experimental exploitation of fish populations. *U.S. Fish Wildlife Ser. Fish. Bull.* 58, 214–252.

Slobodkin, L. B. (1954). Population dynamics in *Daphnia obtusa* Kurz.
Ecol. Monogr. 24, 69–88.

Solomon, M. E. (1964). Analysis of processes involved in the natural control of insects. *Adv. Ecol. Res.* 2, 1–58.

Southwood, T. R. E. (1962). Migration of terrestrial arthropods in relation to habitat. *Biol. Rev.* 37, 171–214.

Southwood, T. R. E. (1966). "Ecological Methods". London.

Southwood, T. R. E. (1967a). The interpretation of population change.
J. Anim. Ecol. 36, 519–529.

Southwood, T. R. E. (1967b). The ecology of the partridge. II. The role of prehatching influences. *J. Anim. Ecol.* 36, 557–562.

Southwood, T. R. E. (1969). The abundance of animals.
Inaug. Lect. Imp. Coll. Sci. Technol. 8, 1–16.

Staff, The (1969). *A Model of Society*. Mimeograph report by Environmental Systems Group, Institute of Ecology, University of California. Davis, 76 pp.

Takahashi, F. (1964). Reproduction curve with two equilibrium points: a consideration of the fluctuation of insect population.
Res. Popul. Ecol. 6, 28–36.

Waloff, N. and Richards, O. W. (1958). The biology of the Chrysomelid beetle, *Phytodecta olivacea* (Forster) (Coleoptera: Chrysomelidae).
Trans. R. ent. Soc. Lond. 110, 99–116.

Watt, K. E. F. (ed.) (1966). "Systems Analysis in Ecology". New York and London.

Watt, K. E. F. (1968). "Ecology and Resource Management". New York.

Way, M. J. (1968). Intra-specific mechanisms with special reference to aphid populations.
In "Insect Abundance", pp. 18–36. (T. R. E. Southwood, ed.).

Wellington, W. G. (1960). Qualitative changes in natural populations during changes in abundance. *Can. J. Zool.* 38, 289–314.

Wynne-Edwards, V. C. (1962). "Animal Dispersion in Relation to Social Behaviour". Edinburgh and London.

CHAPTER 8

The Special Case—Managing Human Population Growth

D. E. C. EVERSLEY

University of Sussex

WHAT OPTIMUM?

This paper starts from the assumption that there is no such thing as a fixed optimum population for Britain, or for any other country. The only categories which have any sort of meaning in the context of social studies of human populations are those concerned with the prevailing relationship, at any one period, between the size of population, the availability of natural resources, the state of technology, and the direction and quantity of foreign trade. We can also recognize the speed of growth of any given population in relation to the speed of change in the other variables—technology and trade in particular.

These relationships are chiefly concerned with the relative sizes of the workforce, the body of non-working people dependent on this workforce, and the rate at which the proportion (dependency ratio) changes. If, therefore, one were to make the observation that "the population of Great Britain is too large", and derived from this the demand that the birth-rate should be cut, one would neglect this relationship in the long run. Thus, if the birth-rate were to fall in the next decade, this would improve the dependency ratio in the short run (because the ratio of workers to non-workers would rise), but in 20 years the situation would be reversed: fewer workers would be available in relation to dependents (these of course include the old people whose number would not be diminished by a fall in the birth-rate, at least not for another 70 years). If, therefore, technology or trade had changed in these 20 years, a remedy applied to the supposed disequilibrium today might produce a serious aggravation of the situation in the next generation (Boreham, Chapter 6).

This "lag" is one of the most important characteristics of human populations. It is especially notable in an advanced industrial society where the delay between the conception of a child and its point of maximum contribution to production is approaching 20 years. In this respect parallels with animal populations are misleading.

It is necessary to enlarge a little on the nature of the relationships briefly stated at the beginning of this paper. We must distinguish between those aspects of the condition of a human society which are primarily functions of the size of that population and the amount of actual land at its disposal, and on the other hand, those aspects which are primarily functions of technology and the state of economic organization.

In the minds of natural scientists, the former relationship looms largest, because in the case of molluscs or rabbits it is of primary importance—so long as they are in the natural state. But what applies to these populations, in respect of their food supply, the space required for reproduction and survival, does not apply, let us say, to battery hens, or fish in a tank. This is due to man's ability to use technology and economic organization to break through the barriers previously imposed by a purely biological relationship.

Human societies have not existed under conditions subject to such barriers for a very long time (though there are probably still a few isolated groups). The history of the last few thousand years is the progress of the species towards the more complete subordination of the natural environment. Not only "advanced" societies such as our own, but even comparatively undeveloped ones in Asia, Africa and South America possess the means of breaking the limits of settlement involved in the primitive relationship between the land and the population it carries.

In the modern world economy, then, settlement density has very little to do with modes of agricultural production. There are many large countries which carry far fewer people than they could support on their own agricultural output—Argentina, Canada, the United States, Soviet Russia, Australia. At the other end of the scale, there are territories which would starve in a matter of weeks or months if they had to rely on what food they can produce within their own limits—with Hong Kong as an extreme case. Britain occupies an intermediate position. If an autarchic economic regime were imposed on this country, it could probably survive with its present or even a larger population. With about half an acre of agricultural land for each person, we could produce enough potatoes, cabbages, milk, pork and poultry to survive—on a low diet, at the expense of our present system of industrial production (which depends heavily on the import of raw materials) and, in a word, at an altogether lower standard of living.

Great Britain, however, shows steady progress towards an ever more complex system of foreign trade, coupled with the introduction of more advanced technology into our everyday life. In real terms, we both import and export more per head of the population today than our ancestors consumed 200 years ago. In 1750, more than half the population was engaged in efforts to feed themselves, and the other half, on a poor diet. Today, with an agricultural labour force considerably smaller than that of 1750, British agriculture produces more than half the food required by 55 million people with a much better diet (Economic Trends, 1969).

The rate of technical and organizational changes, which have brought about the ability of human populations to live at high densities, has never been steady. Despite the rather confident predictions emanating from North American sources, e.g. those of Mr. Herman Kahn (1969), we are not able to project into the future the past rates at which productivity has risen in industry or agriculture. Forecasters in Britain today are fond of predicting fairly simple series, such as those relating the ownership of private motor cars (G.L.C., 1969b). This kind of crystal gazing is of very little help in determining total human environment and function.

It is extremely difficult to forecast agricultural productivity, or changes in the food tastes of a high-income society, or Britain's ability to sell her exports in competition with other countries. We do not know for five years ahead what our labour force requirements will be. On one hand, there is steadily increasing productivity in some branches of industry, so that the same or higher output could be achieved with the same or a smaller labour force. On the other hand, the working week is getting shorter, and holidays longer. Union pressures sometimes prevent the reduction of the labour force to its technological minimum. Management, equally, for fear of being caught short-handed at some future stage, retains a labour force in excess of that which is actually required.

Against the increases in industrial productivity we have to set the expansion of administration and of the personal service sector where, by definition, high consumption means a labour force which grows *pro rata*. For example, if we eat out more in restaurants with table service, as opposed to eating more at home or in self-service cafeterias, we need more employees per unit of food consumed. If we have less of the thrifty "do it yourself" movement, and call in tradesmen more often, we need more workers. More education means fewer young people available in the labour force, and more teachers employed. If we reduce the size of classes, their "productivity" apparently falls.

The tourist trade increases, so do retailing, research and motoring. We buy more expensive clothes and go to the hairdressers more often. We may sell more hand-made pottery and textiles abroad and fewer cheap cottons.

On the other hand, trends may go into reverse. But in general, we are quite unable to forecast the level of economic activity, or the amount of labour any given size of the national product requires, for 10, let alone 20 years ahead. On this score alone, we cannot now calculate an optimum population for the end of the century—the time when the children who would be the result of our "planned population" policy in the next few years would enter the labour force (Boreham, Chapter 6).

Economists working in the 1930s realized the great disadvantages of a declining and ageing population, but accepted the extrapolations of the statisticians (Reddaway, 1939). Thus it was supposed that the United Kingdom would have less than 44 million inhabitants by 1970, of whom over 15% would be over 65 years old—a higher percentage pensionable than of school age. In fact there will be more than 55 million people by 1970, and more than twice as many will be under 15 as over 65 (Cole, 1947). The economists of that time accepted this decline as more or less inevitable, and though they deplored the effect on investment, did at least take comfort from the fact that the declining labour force might ease the problem of unemployment. Had these projections been correct, there would have been just over 30 million people of working age in 1970, corresponding, on present activity rates, to an active labour force of little over 21 million, instead of the 25 million we have. We cannot say how we should have adjusted—whether by becoming more like Sweden, or more like Portugal. In other words, mere numbers are irrelevant to living standards.

Malthus would have found 20 million an intolerably large population for Britain in 1920. Keynes would have been frightened by 60 million in 1930. Similarly there are a number of contributors to this symposium who are appalled by the prospect of 70 or even 80 millions. Why is this? Clearly not, on the basis of the experience of the last few years, because they forecast the inability of the economy to feed, clothe and house so many people. Not, on present showing, because of any fear of unemployment. The arguments therefore have to be reduced to two classes: (a) that we should have higher *per capita* incomes if there were fewer of us, because we are subject to diminishing returns; (b) that the consequences of living at the higher densities involved are detrimental to health and enjoyment of life.

THE OBJECTS OF MANAGEMENT

It is important to identify the objects of any reduction in population size, or growth rates, before we can discuss the methods we can use to adjust them. Taking the arguments just outlined, we can illustrate this point. If we wish to increase *per capita* incomes, we have to ensure that the size of the work-force rises relative to the size of dependent population. This can be achieved both by moving more people into the working group, and by diminishing those who cannot work. The first method consists of reducing unemployment, lowering the average school leaving age, postponing retirement, and bringing in married women, or by encouraging working-age immigrants. The second method consists of reducing the birth-rate (though this inevitably lowers the size of the work-force later), not encouraging people to live longer than they need or at least persuading them to emigrate after they have finished work.

In the second case, where we are concerned with densities, we need either to reduce the total of the population, or to encourage them to spread themselves more equally over the available land of the British Isles.

It will be seen that all these methods are open to some objections, apart from doubts as to their efficacy. It is presumably part of the object of raising *per capita* incomes to increase the enjoyment of life. To reduce the number of people undergoing education, to lengthen working life, or to persuade housewives to forsake their domestic duties for the workbench or office, are all methods of doubtful value. Clearly we could raise output by all going back to pre-1900 working weeks. To encourage immigrants may aggravate other aspects of life. Conversely, the shortening of life, or the encouragement of emigration, for the elderly, scarcely seem humane methods. This is why the reduction of the short term birth-rate is the only practicable method open to us—with its concomitant possibility of a future labour shortage.

At this point we have to introduce a more important economic factor. What matters is not the size of the work-force, but its productivity. The rise in the standard of living of the people of this country since the war is much more due to the fact that each individual produces more, rather than to an increase in the number of individuals in the labour force. Its size has now scarcely changed for many years. In fact what small increases there are are mostly due to an increase in women working (many part-time). But consumers' expenditure (at constant prices) has risen by some 4% per annum over these years. This is due to increases in efficiency in industry, and more favourable terms of trade (i.e. the rate at which we exchange our own products for those, especially food and raw materials, produced by other countries). Our continued prosperity depends on the continued movement in these trends, in our favour. But productivity depends on capital investment and this is where the economy lags. Clearly, the more goods we produce at lower cost (largely in terms of labour content), the more we can all consume, and the greater the profitability of exports (Boreham, Chapter 6).

The question is now changed. It is not a matter of how many people we have at work by, say, 1990, but how much capital investment there is at the back of the labour force: machines, power supplies, roads and means of transport. Clearly, there is much more room for variability there. By changes in the birth-rate and emigration, we can, on the evidence of the last few years, produce changes in the rate of increase within a total range of growth rates from about 0.4% p.a. to a maximum of 1%. But productivity changes can affect *per capita* consumption by at least 4% p.a. and do so in many other countries by 10% or more. We are therefore really saying that we ought to see whether size and growth rates of the present population have any effect on investment, and, at one remove, on savings. Clearly, if a smaller population, and smaller rates of increase, lead to increased savings and increased investment then the double effect would be highly favourable.

Unfortunately, there is no clear relationship. Experts on the developing countries tend to make two main points: (a) that a high rate of increase means a large diversion of investment from the productive sector into unproductive social services and minimum subsistence sectors, such as housing and food and water supplies; (b) that savings are minimal if all available income has to be spent on basic necessities. (And as a corollary to that, if there is no spending on consumer goods there is no incentive to investors.) (Ohlin, 1967).

These arguments do not apply in a developed society in exactly the same way. Firstly, the level of investment in our social infra-structure is not a function of the size or growth rate of our population, but of income. To give just a few examples: our need for houses does not spring mainly from the increase in total population, but from "household fission" (i.e. the propensities of individuals to form separate households, which is derived from real income levels), and from the demand of ever-larger sections of the population for decent and more spacious accommodation. (This is reinforced by a national policy of providing such housing even for those who cannot pay for it themselves.) Had we preserved the household sizes and the standards of 1948, the housing problem would by now have been solved long ago.

Fewer people, given our present social policies, would not mean less investment in social provision, but higher standards. If there were fewer children, we should have smaller classes and more children staying on for secondary and higher education. We should not build fewer hospitals, but reduce overcrowding in wards, look after the mentally ill, and increase preventive care. Fewer families would not mean fewer cars, but more cars per head, and we should step up road expenditure. In other words, the level of this sort of investment is determined politically and economically, not demographically.

The same applies to savings. Savings are held to be a function of incomes, but the propensity to consume is higher if there are more dependents to a given level of income. It is therefore assumed that if there are fewer children, the level of savings will rise. But it is equally possible that if there is no need for future provision for children, parents will spend more on current enjoyments. The higher the level of personal incomes, the higher the rate of savings, but also the higher the total amounts spent on consumption.

Both savings and investment depend on prospects. At present, the demand for investible funds is very high, largely because of the apparent long-term profitability of building of all kinds, whether for residence, retailing, recreation, production or administration. This high profitability is of course itself a reflection of the factors already outlined: the constant increases in total demand for house room and consumer goods, and the level of public services. If there were any danger of these upward trends tailing off, the demand for investment would also fall. This was the main complaint of the economists of the 1930s. The basis of future demand lies not in today's adults, but today's children. They are the free-spending teenagers of tomorrow, and the nest-builders of the day after. The prospect of continued inflation leads to increased demand for investible funds, but to a reduction of savings (countered by rising interest rates). Prospects of reduced rates of price increases lead to less investment, and a

higher supply of savings, even if interest rates fall. The rationality behind the
3-4% cumulative annual growth rates envisaged in the National Plan (1965) was
that this was the sort of level which could be sustained by gross investment of
the order of 15% (allowing for depreciation) and the capital/output ratios then
supposed to operate, and that the savings required to finance this investment
were available, in the public and private sector, given the interest and taxation
rates then in force. Every model of growth depends on this sort of assumption.

THE GROWTH DETERMINANTS DEFINED

The trouble with short-term alterations in population growth rates is that
they have hardly any effect on this sort of national balance sheet–not at any
rate when we are talking about reducing an 0.6% p.a. growth rate to one of 0.3%
p.a. or even zero.

In the long run, of course, a stable but smaller rate of increase of the
population could be achieved which might lead to a slight levelling out of social
investment. However, given the very unequal sizes of the generations dying this
is difficult to achieve. (In 1951, the male 50–54 age group was about 14% smaller
than the 45–49 group, in 1966 it was 4% larger.) The size of the moribund
generation fluctuates fairly sharply vis-a-vis the size of the fertile generation, and
stability involves very frequent revision of the "fertility target" for each group
of parents. Leaving aside the complications of setting, or enforcing, such a
target, it is much easier to think in terms of long-term average growth rates.

We have to remind ourselves that the number of births per married couple is
not the only determinant of growth rates. Apart from the fluctuations in the size
of the oldest generation, there is the question of net migration, and the size of
the generation interval. Migration depends on the state of economic activity in
this country, relative to that of the main areas accepting British emigrants, and
on the state of the law relating to immigration from overseas, and on the state of
our economy in relation to that of countries sending us immigrants.

The generation interval is determined by the age of marriage and the age at
which children are born within marriage. A society where the mean age at
marriage is 23 and the mean age of the mother at the birth of her children is 25,
reproduces itself four times in a century: a population where the mean age of
the mother at all births is 20 would reproduce itself five times. These are
extremes, but clearly recent trends towards earlier marriage and greater
"bunching" of all births in the early years of marriage lead by themselves to a
somewhat larger rate of increase of the population, even if marital fertility
remains constant or falls.

Control over population size and composition (assuming this is what we want
to achieve) would then need to extend to migration in both directions, take into
account the mortality of the older generation and the age and sex composition

of migration, the age at marriage and the pattern of births within marriage. But however flexible as well as precise such a system (leaving aside the question of enforcement), there is no guarantee that the resultant growth rate will in fact be either stable or relevant to the needs of a future generation.

THE AREAS OF MANAGEMENT—SPATIAL DISTRIBUTION

This uncertainty, however, does not mean that there is no aspect of population dynamics which is within the control of the makers of social policy. There are quite wide areas where scientific management of some areas of demographic change seems highly desirable, and it is proposed to discuss these here fairly briefly.

First, we take the question of population distribution. This is quite fundamental to the kind of problem before this conference.

Crowding manifestations are, in fact, confined to relatively small parts of the British Isles: London and the six other conurbations between them account for a third of the population and almost all the feeling of being too close to each other from which some people suffer. This is not to say that crowds occur only inside these cities: they also occur when people from them try to go out into the countryside or at some favourite holiday resorts. More than half the population of the U.K. lives in the south-eastern corner of the British Isles. In contrast there are wide open spaces, not only on the Celtic fringes, but in Northern England, in the South-West, and even within 40 miles of London.

One need not envisage a state of affairs where the whole population is evenly distributed on the whole land surface. Our society is gregarious: most people prefer fairly large urban agglomerations to village life, let alone isolation. Therefore the main aim of British population management has been to decant people from the few congested urban centres to new urban concentrations at distances of from 20 to 100 miles from the old cores. This policy was once associated with garden cities, became the New Towns Act of 1946, and has now extended to expanded towns and new cities. By 1969, a million people were living in the designated new towns, and a further 200,000 people had been added to expanded towns. The schemes now under construction, including the new city of Milton Keynes and a large expansion at Peterborough, will mean that by the mid-seventies about two million people mostly from London, Birmingham and Glasgow will be living in a planned new environment—with relatively little loss of good agricultural land.

But in addition to the New Towns, there has been a much larger and unplanned movement of population away from the old urban centres into smaller towns in and beyond the urban Green Belts. From London alone, some 90,000 people a year move outwards. The same kind of movement is taking place round Birmingham, Manchester and other large cities. Negatively, it could be stopped by withholding planning permissions; positively, it can be encouraged by freeing "white land" for development. Urban uses still account for only 12% of the land surface of the country: if the present process continues, another 2% may have to be converted to residential and industrial use before the end of the century.

In addition to these official policies and the spontaneous movements associated with them, it has also been the aim of successive governments to ensure that the century-old "drift to the South" was halted. Because the population which remained or settled in the South-East was younger, more highly educated, and capable of earning higher incomes, there was also a qualitative change. Growth rates were higher, and there came about an increasing social polarization which had undesirable results in the areas which were declining. Therefore steps were taken to promote industrial growth in the stagnant areas, to renew the social infra-structure, and to improve the environment. These steps have been partially successful, especially as the high cost of congestion and labour shortage in the Midlands and the South-East made these areas less attractive to entrepreneurs, and in recent years there has been a tendency for productive capacity to grow faster in the North and West. The net migratory movements have been almost arrested, except in Scotland.

These population management techniques have not hitherto been conspicuously successful, at any rate in modern democratic societies, but British experience seems to suggest that a mixture of negative planning controls and positive fiscal and social incentives, together with some simple propagandist techniques, can go quite a long way. Without resorting to the direction of labour it is possible to re-distribute population away from congested urban areas and to deter further potential immigrants. But it is not an unlimited process, and experience has yet to show how much further it can go.

METHODS OF MANAGEMENT OF REPRODUCTIVE BEHAVIOUR

In recent years, propagandist bodies have urged on the British government its duty to begin a system of population control, or at least to initiate "a population policy". Apart from a small lunatic fringe, this call seems to have been nothing more than a demand that the government should encourage local authorities to set up Family Planning Clinics. This is in fact the policy of the present Minister of Health and Social Security, and quite a few local authorities have responded to this need. This, however, does not mean that everyone finds it easy to obtain birth control appliances easily and cheaply. The Family Planning Association and the local authority clinics between them reach only a fairly small percentage of the total population "at risk", i.e. women of child-bearing age.

Fortunately this does not mean that the other 90% of the population do not practise birth control. On the contrary, as a recent survey undertaken by the Population Investigation Committee has shown (Langford, 1969), 90% of all British couples do practise birth control, and of those who do not, few if any fail to do so because they are ignorant or because they have no access to appliances. In fact, birth control in Britain has been almost total for many years. In the 1930s, long before there was a government or local authority policy, birth control, by a variety of means, some now discredited, reduced births to below replacement level. It is therefore nonsense to say that Britain has as many births as she has because people are unable or unwilling to limit their families. The vast majority do so. Since the mean age at marriage is now in the early twenties, and since almost all marriages remain unbroken by death until the end of the child-bearing age, the average family size should be of the order of eight or ten children without birth control. The actual completed family size is in fact only a little over two children.

Of all children born, 85% are first, second or third children, only 7% of all children are fifth or higher order births. If one adds the childless couples, one finds in fact that over two thirds of all parents stop at two children or earlier. This is not to say that birth control is perfect in these families, or that a third child is not "a mistake" as these things are sometimes called. What it does mean is that for many parents a third child is not such a disaster that they resort to stricter measures of birth control, or abortion, to prevent its appearance. But for each family there is a threshold, and the nearer this approaches, the more drastic the attempts to limit conception or birth. Only a very small minority, mostly of people with strong religious convictions, or of a rare extreme of fecklessness, will go on having children to the limit of their biological capacity.

Given this almost total knowledge of fertility control, measures to reduce fertility still further are difficult to find—without resorting to actual penalties for large families. It is commonly believed that official policies encourage births, because of maternity allowances, family allowances, the national health service, free education, housing subsidies and other *bêtes noirs* which are anathema to the liberal economist. There is, in fact, no evidence at all that people have children to collect family allowances, or extra points on the housing list. There are quite sufficient penalties attached to having a family of three or four children without any further discrimination on the part of the state. In our age, large families, apart from being the butt of popular jokes, find it impossible to obtain adequate housing unless they belong to the upper 5% income groups. Local authorities do in the end provide homes, but these tend to be very limited in space. Despite family allowances, the Government Social Survey's *Family Expenditure Surveys* shows that people with more than three children can spend less on food *per capita* than smaller families, less on clothes, entertainment, travel and durable consumer goods. These are truisms, which ought not to require statistical proof, but unfortunately there are many who believe that to bear children is to acquire in some mysterious way a higher standard of living. The opposite is true, and child poverty, affecting perhaps 25% of all children, is now a widespread phenomenon.

There is, therefore, in an advanced and competitive society, a premium on smaller families. Children of smaller families can be shown to get on better in life; only children, best of all. "Giving the children a start in life" is a national ambition. As housing becomes ever more difficult, as it is often necessary for mothers to work to make ends meet, the pressures against having children mount.

The results are already clear. Since 1964, the birth rate has been dropping steadily. An entirely new phenomenon has been observed in the national statistics. Until 1966, births, and especially first births (which are 40% of all births) were directly correlated with marriages in the previous year. (A third of all pregnancies was pre-marital or extra-marital, the rest followed marriage very quickly.) This relation has now been broken. The young obviously practise birth control much earlier, and therefore choose the birth of their first child consciously in the light of their earnings and savings.

It is difficult, then, to know what the advocates of population control want the government to do. Withdraw family allowances after the second child? Make third children pay school fees? Withhold taxation relief? Pillory parents of large families? Refuse them housing? It is doubtful whether any of these things would have any effect. In the thirties people restricted their families even in the absence of any governmental pressures. In the post war era, most countries in the world saw a long term upswing in fertility, and only a handful of these had pro-natalist or even welfare policies. The real value of family allowances and especially taxation reliefs has been eroded over the years, but the speed of that erosion does not correlate with movements of the birth-rate.

Abortion Law Reform is of course one step in the direction of making population control easier. This has been with us for a year, yet it is very unlikely that the event will show on the map of fertility curves. The decline set in before the Act. Illegitimacy is a substantial part of total fertility (approaching 10%) and if the widespread use of the pill, plus freer abortion, reduces this incidence, something will have been gained—though not much overall loss of fertility. This we shall not know for a year or two. The short answer on this score, therefore, must be that although the government can do much to ease social problems resulting from families larger than parents can feed, such socially necessary measures are very unlikely to be reflected in a smaller population. Inasmuch as larger and poorer and more ignorant families also have higher infant mortality, the effects of a social policy of facilitating birth control and improving family health may well be to keep a larger proportion of babies born in poorer families alive. (A marginal effect, but so are all the measures we have discussed.)

We turn now to the question of encouraging larger families. This was a vital question 30 years ago; it was connected with Eleanor Rathbone (1927) and the movement for Family Endowment. The declining fertility especially of the intelligentsia led to a demand, on the part of the Eugenics movement, for the special discrimination for certain classes still in evidence, as a comic historical relic, in the shape of £50 child allowances for university teachers. Those fossilized in their academic grades of ten years ago, and still having dependent children, draw these allowances to this day. On a much larger scale, the welfare state did what it could, ostensibly for all classes, but more particularly for the articulate middle classes. A professional man paying standard rate income tax, or even surtax, on a large slice of his income, can still attract tax allowances of much greater value than the poor man's family allowances. The longer his children stay in full time education, the more assiduous he is in ensuring that they receive all the medical and dental attention they need, the more they use facilities like libraries, national parks, university grants and other forms of free provision, the easier, relatively, his burdens become. Yet it is quite impossible to conceive of people in this position desiring children for the sake of the benefits they will receive from the state. As Professor Titmuss (1958) has long shown, this sort of thing is a form of social injustice. But if it were stopped, and the middle classes were discriminated against, it is still unlikely that it would affect their views of a proper family size negatively, just as there is no evidence that the existence of these benefits encouraged them. In America the middle classes have also produced more children since the war, without a welfare state.

On this score, then, we are on equally uncertain ground. It is highly likely that within very few years the birth-rate will have dropped once again below replacement rate. The present size of a completed family of 2.15 children after 15 years is not in the long run enough to replace the parent generation. (These are technicalities: one can get a net reproduction rate of less than one and the population can still go on growing.) There are difficulties ahead. There is now a serious unbalance of the sexes, about 5% more boys than girls in the younger age group, so that they could not all marry even if all girls were willing to do so. There is still a certain amount of involuntary, as well as voluntary sterility, and of course, a certain almost unavoidable wastage between birth and marriage (congenital defects, accidents). When this failure to replace ourselves reaches clearer proportions, the movement against population will no doubt be reversed very quickly, and we shall get a new wave of pro-populationist hysteria. This will come all the more quickly if the fertility of white Britons falls more rapidly than that of the immigrants, who usually belong to socio-economic groups which, whether black or white, have higher fertility. As the age structure of the whites becomes less favourable, and the young immigrants continue to reproduce, the cry will go up that we are being "swamped" by the fertility of immigrants, a belief being assiduously fostered by unscrupulous politicians. At this stage the demand will go up that the government should encourage reproduction. But this (even if it is heeded) will be as unsuccessful as the reverse movement. Parents will produce extra children (something for which they clearly have basic biological and social urges) if and when they can do so without impairing their own and their children's standards of living drastically. If they cannot obtain or pay for a house if they have children, they will have none. Of course a government can help there, by building more and larger houses, and increasing subsidies, but this is not the whole story. Real earnings must go on rising, and the security of long term income must improve.

CONCLUSION

I therefore conclude that population management is a highly inexact science. Even supposing that we could prove that one level of population size or growth rate is in some way "optimal" for any given date ahead, we have no means of ensuring that such a target would be reached. Short of totalitarian levels of controls of immigration and emigration, and movements within the country, and extreme bribes or deterrents for parents, nothing can alter the collective effect of individual views on the prospects of the family. Policies now widely agreed as an integral part of our social structure, relating to welfare, health, education and housing, are neutral in relation to population size: they can keep a given number of people healthier and perhaps happier than they would otherwise be, but an increase in the level cannot produce more children, and a decrease cannot diminish births. (It has to be remembered in any case that higher benefits for some people mean higher taxes on others; so if there is an income effect, it probably cancels out.)

Only in the field of territorial distribution of the population within the country is there any sign that the government and local authorities can plan with some success. Following the Barlow Report, the Abercrombie Plan, the Reith New Towns Report, and a mass of post-war legislation and administrative action, Greater London is now rapidly losing population. It is likely that there will be no more than just over seven million people in the capital by the early eighties, or nearly two million less than there would have been had London retained its natural increase, and perhaps three or four million less had there not been policies to redistribute industry and offices, and fairly tough administration of the Green Belt. For the first time in its history London has ceased to grow rapidly (G.L.C., 1969a).

It should be clearly understood, however, that this survey of population control aims and possibilities can only be applied to an advanced industrial country with a low rate of natural increase and a high level of individual control over births and deaths. In a country with a natural increase rate of over 2%, where deaths have been sharply reduced but there is little control over fertility, and where *per capita* incomes are stagnating at somewhere less than $500, it can be demonstrated much more easily that such growth rates are directly unfavourable to economic growth and that there is a threat of a very adverse movement in the death-rate in the foreseeable future unless something is done to reduce births. Calcutta cannot be compared to London. Crowd effects are different at a low level of technology. Equally, control measures, from sheer propaganda to financial inducement to sterilization, can operate more easily in such an environment. Few British fathers would submit to sterilization for the sake of a colour television set: some more South Asians can be bribed, perhaps, with a transistor radio. But even there the effects are not all one way, and modern economists are not all agreed that more means worse, or that high population growth rates always prevent economic growth.

REFERENCES

Cole, G. D. H. (1947). "The Intelligent Man's Guide to the Post-war World", p. 429. Gollancz, London.

Economic Trends (1969). The Measurement of Self-sufficiency in Food and Agricultural Products, No. 190.

G.L.C. (1969a). Greater London Development Plan. Report of Studies, Ch. 2, 11.

G.L.C. (1969b). Report on Part III of the Greater London Transportation Study. "Movement in London", pp. 23-25, 41-44, 85-88.

Kahn, H. (1969). Impact of the Friendly Computer.
The Times, London. 9 November 1969.

Langford, C. (Jan. 1969). Birth Control Practice in Britain.
Family Planning 17(4).

National Plan (1965). H.M.S.O., London.

Ohlin, G. (1967). "Population Control and Economic Development", Ch. IV, O.E.C.D., Paris.

Rathbone, E. (1927). "The Ethics and Economics of Family Endowment". London

Reddaway, W. B. (1939). "The Economics of a Declining Population". Allen & Unwin, London.

Titmuss, R. M. (1958). "The Welfare State". Allen & Unwin, London.

CHAPTER 9

The Legislation Barrier

A. L. N. D. HOUGHTON

House of Commons

My terms of reference are these: supposing we accept (a) the absolute necessity for population limitation and (b) the responsibility of government for the necessary action; and say what, then, are the barriers of politics and Parliament?

The short answer is barriers of conventional thought on moral issues; religious beliefs; personal convictions; prejudice; fear of social consequences; fear of political consequences, not to mention the impedimenta of Parliamentary procedure; all of which hold governments at bay, exert disproportionate influence in a marginal political situation, and by Parliamentary resistance and obstruction delay action on matters of conscience for a decade or more. These barriers would reinforce the bigger barrier of substantial doubt and disbelief about the need for government action.

Population control means birth control for the common good. Few people in this country have thought of it that way. The population explosion is generally believed to be in India, not here. Population increase in Britain is thought of as something to be provided for, not something to be stopped. The positive aims and benefits of family limitation would therefore need to be well defined and vigorously put across to become accepted in a democratic society as a desirable objective of social and economic policy. Whether to solve or avert manifest evils of over-population or to improve the quality of living in a fuller sense, they would have to carry conviction.

Party programmes offering economic and social programmes for better living, better housing, schools, hospitals, roads, education and social services never mention population control as a means of attaining these desirable aims. No equation between population increase and a higher standard of living is ever offered for public examination. Warnings from the demographers about the rising ratio of dependent old and young go largely unheeded. The underlying philosophy of the political approach is that the duty of the State is to make itself rich enough to provide a good life for the population presented to them by the mothers of the country. That is what economic growth is believed to be about.

No other domestic purpose has been included in any party political programme in this country so far. Birth control and family limitation has remained in the sphere of personal morals or of individual decision, assisted in some cases by medical opinion or the advice of social workers.

The fact is that public and religious attitudes towards the various forms of family limitation, such as contraception, sterilization and abortion, keep us in a state of perpetual social and moral confusion. The formation of a secular Society for the Protection of Unborn Children (SPUC) to campaign for the human right of the fetus to live is an example of extreme reaction to the first relaxation of our abortion law for 100 years.

As I must keep to the supposition of "absolute necessity for population limitation" I will not enlarge on the powerful case behind it. No matter how powerful the case, the barriers are up and have always been up. It is therefore necessary to consider the strategy of the politics of legislation on population control in an atmosphere continuously and highly charged with emotional and religious conflict where party differences cease to exist and fears of public disapproval are never far from a politician's mind.

Birth control for the good of all has hitherto been less acceptable than family planning for personal happiness and welfare. And the struggle to get that has been long and hard. The prevailing doctrine is that "It is no business of the State to tell us how many children we shall have". The United Nations has in fact said the same thing. Late in 1967, 30 countries declared that "any choice or decision with regard to the size of the family must irrevocably rest with the family itself, and cannot be made by anyone else" (U Thant, 1968).

While this may logically come within a Declaration of Human Rights, it cannot easily be reconciled with the assumption of wider and heavier responsibility by communities everywhere for child and family welfare.

The economics of family size are no longer the sole responsibility of the parents. Family size *is* the business of the State: it is joint responsibility and mutual benefit can come from it.

An essential condition of any population policy is that this doctrine should be fully accepted. It never has been and is not fully accepted today. Consider the history of the matter.

The Royal Commission on Population (1949) (which must have been appointed in a fit of absent-mindedness) recommended as long ago as 1949 that our numbers should be stabilized; that the government should make some official body . . . responsible for a continuous watch over population movements and their bearing on national policies; that it is impossible for policy to be "neutral" on this matter since over a wide range of affairs policy and administration have a continuous influence on family size; and that "control of men and women over the numbers of their children is one of the first conditions of their own and the community's welfare". All this was ignored by government. Nothing was done.

Those members of that Royal Commission who have survived the ensuing 20 years and have seen the population increase by seven million are doubtless gratified that some of their recommendations were given partial legislative approval in the Family Planning Act, 1967.

The inevitable link between population control and birth control in the work of the Royal Commission may have discouraged public and Parliamentary discussion. Or it may be that we had to wait for a younger generation with a different outlook. Or perhaps the subtle technique of the "hidden persuaders" has helped a little.

When birth control became "family planning" it became more respectable. It also disposed of any hint of population control or even (except very indirectly) the limitation of the size of the family. The purpose of family planning, *inter alia*, is to avoid "unwanted pregnancies", not to save the community from unwanted people. The emphasis was upon freedom of choice. A year ago I ventured to express a contrary opinion. Speaking at the Sociological Research Foundation, I said: "Just as marriage and divorce is not a purely personal and private matter, just as abortion isn't either, so the procreation of children is not a purely private matter. The more we do jointly with the State—or the community—the greater our social obligations".

These and other even more controversial comments (which for the sake of peace I will not repeat) brought a swift reaction. The then Minister of Social Security issued a disclaimer on behalf of the government ("in the government's view the size of the family is a private matter"). The Prime Minister, faced with a critical Early Day Motion (1968) on the Order Paper of the House of Commons, sponsored by Labour Catholic M.Ps., and the threatened resignation of two of them from the Parliamentary Labour Party (of which I am Chairman), gave the assurance that "as head of the government, I confirm . . . that those views of Douglas Houghton to which you took objection do not in any sense represent the views or policy of Her Majesty's Government. Nor are they in any way Party policy" (Wilson, 1968). With that comfort the resignations were withdrawn though the political reverberations of that speech continued for a long time.

The truth is that political parties and governments find these matters extremely distasteful. They fight shy of them. They arouse emotions, deep personal convictions and religious differences. They are embarrassing; they are bad for party unity; they are (supposedly) vote losers.

The Labour Party has debated birth control twice in 40 years: 1927 and 1940; the Conservative Party not at all.

Mr. John Wheatley (1924), Minister of Health in the first Labour Government, rejected a resolution of the Labour Women's Conference in 1924, demanding that Welfare Centres should be permitted to give birth control advice to married women who desired it on the ground that "permission of Parliament was required, that public money was involved, that the government had no mandate and that religious feeling would be outraged". Birth controllers heard similar reasons for doing nothing from subsequent Ministers time and time again.

The House of Lords proved then (as it has done since) to be the more enlightened Chamber of the two: on 28th April 1926 it called upon the government "to remove all obstacles to the introduction of birth control advice in Maternity and Child Welfare Centres". Effect was given to this Motion 41 years later by the Family Planning Act, 1967.

After mounting pressure, chiefly from local maternity and welfare authorities, the Minister of Health in the second Labour Government (Mr. Arthur Greenwood) issued the historic circular (M.O.H., 1931a), permitting Maternity and Child Welfare Centres to give contraceptive advice "in cases where a further pregnancy would be detrimental to health", but in no other cases. No general power was given to set up birth control clinics, but clinics for nursing and expectant mothers and those suffering from gynaecological conditions were allowed to offer help where a further pregnancy would be harmful to health.

Subsequently, a further circular was issued to curb the more enthusiastic health authorities. This underlined that birth control advice must be "strictly incidental to the purpose for which the Centre is established" and "should not be regarded as falling within the scope of the normal duties of medical officers of a Local Authority" (M.O.H., 1931b).

That is how matters stood 33 years later when the Minister of Health (Mr. Kenneth Robinson), in the Labour Government of 1964, came to apply his progressive mind to the subject. He was advised that legislation would be required to extend the permissive powers of local health authorities beyond those laid down in the Ministry Memorandum of 1930. Moreover, he soon learned that merely to re-issue that Memorandum in rather more enthusiastic and encouraging language than Mr. Arthur Greenwood had used 34 years previously raised questions of political expediency in the cliff-hanging uncertainties of the Parliament of 1964.

It is to the credit of Mr. Robinson's firmness of purpose that the Ministry Memorandum was eventually re-issued in February 1966, and that the extension of local authority powers to enable birth control advice to be given on other than medical grounds was included in a draft government Bill which was forestalled by Mr. Edwin Brooks (Labour M.P. for Bebington) in his Family Planning Bill (now an Act) in 1967*.

Mr. Robinson's initiative is being strenuously reinforced by the present Secretary of State for the Social Services, Mr. Crossman. He is criticizing local authorities for inaction. The present squeeze on local government expenditure is the excuse given by local authorities for doing nothing. Others are plainly

---

* I think it was a pity it was done this way. It would have been better if the government had shown the resolve to do it themselves and so give this quite historic measure their full authority and backing.

obstructive. The Act, however, gives the Minister the power to lay upon any local authority a statutory *duty* to provide the permitted services.

For full measure we can contemplate the abortion "backlash", which alas is in full spate as I write. The shame of Britain being "the abortion capital of the world" is proclaimed abroad by some who should know better, while the depths of the evil of abortion "on demand" (and by foreign girls too) are plumbed by journalists, columnists and M.Ps. who know that one death from abortion is more newsworthy than thousands on the roads.

The barriers to political and Parliamentary action are made more difficult to overcome because up till now no government in Britain has adopted or pursued a population policy. What has been done has been for human and social benefit, to relieve women from the burden of frequent and unwanted pregnancies, and children from neglect and poverty. No discouragement has been imposed by the State on large families, nor has positive encouragement been given to keep them small. In family allowances and tax reliefs for children, in social benefits and social provision generally, the State has aimed at preventing poverty in large families, not at penalizing them. Our society is deeply committed to the welfare state and is therefore confronted with the dilemma of having to endow what it wants to avoid. The improvident behaviour of parents must not be visited upon the children. We are all agreed on that, or nearly all.

In Britain the desire to spare the parents of large families any feeling of social irresponsibility or personal incompetence, and the children of any feeling of inferiority, does inhibit public discussion, especially now it can get mixed up with racialism. The case for birth control has to be put on the highest level of public understanding and enlightenment. My enormous post-bag last year revealed how sensitive people are to any "slur" on the large family: mothers proud of the success of their children at school and university; fathers proud of the bravery of their sons in war. It was disturbing to see how some people took my remarks personally to heart, and how insulting they felt it was to hear of the "social irresponsibility" of large families. Many feel that far from imposing a burden on the community or adding to undesirable population pressures, they are making a significant contribution to the good of the nation. Some critics went further: they suggested that population control was Hitlerism!

These attitudes cannot be entirely discounted. People do not readily put their personal happiness, family pride and joys and deepest emotions into commission for the benefit of the State.

As the Prime Minister said in his reply to Sir David Renton, M.P., in correspondence on this question—"I am very conscious that, as you recognize yourself, influencing family sizes is a very delicate matter for any government; nor would it be easy to achieve any marked effect. Moreover, the trend towards earlier marriage, and the increasing number of people who get married and have children, are also important factors in population growth; and these are, of course, even less open to influence by the government" (Wilson, 1967).

While there can be no doubt that family limitation is gaining acceptance for the attainment of personal happiness through wise parenthood, any widening of this purpose to include population control would require considerable political skill and courage.

It may help to assess just how much from a brief outline of what the "necessary action" by government would probably be.

The aim of any population policy would be to induce parents to bring the national interest (as presented to them and as they understood it to be) into their decisions on family planning. These inducements would be partly positive and practical and partly indirect and economic.

Clearly the first requirement would be to will the means to the end. People cannot practise what they do not know, or know imperfectly, or cannot afford. We should therefore need a National Family Planning Service, run in conjunction with the Health Services. This would popularize birth control and all forms of contraceptive techniques and appliances by giving the fullest information about them and making them freely available.

The full authority and approval of the State would carry with it inclusion of all means of contraception within the National Health Service as the Royal Commission on Population recommended they should be 20 years ago.

This would be the keystone of the whole policy. The "absolute necessity" for population limitation would, we hope, drown the scorn about "sex on the Health Service" and charges of encouraging sin on the State among unmarried women.

The place of voluntary sterilization in the policy would probably become important. This again would be part of the Health Service.

The Abortion Act, 1967, could probably be left as it is for a longer period of trial. To extend the liberalized abortion laws from personal health and family welfare to be one of the means of securing population limitation would be extremely controversial.

This "package" on the physical side of the policy would call for a radical change in political attitudes.

The principal difficulty would be the need for *government* to sponsor this policy. Obviously no population policy could be carried through solely by private propaganda and pressure groups. It would have to be formulated and strongly backed by government. Government neutrality on these moral issues of sex, birth control and family limitation would come to an end, as the Royal Commission said it should 20 years ago. Legislation would have to be government legislation and not pushed aside, as these thorny subjects at present are, to the chance and hazards of Private Members' Bills. This would put heavy strain upon some of its supporters, both outside and inside Parliament. Indeed, such a policy as this would cut across the political parties. It would be a political nettle the like of which no government had grasped for years, and might lead to a political upheaval comparable with the crises over Irish Home Rule and Tariff Reform. These issues not only divided parties but split them.

Much would depend on how the government set about it. Party politics might be taken out of the controversy (as in the Common Market) by agreement between the two Front Benches, leaving dissenting M.Ps. to follow their own conscience. This course, if possible at all, would not weaken but strengthen the government backing of the policy. Its aim would be to avoid a *party* political conflict.

It is doubtful, however, whether any government would get advance support from its party conference. Parties seeking unity and enthusiasm for battle do not go in for birth control. The initiative would have to come from a government convinced of the urgency of the population explosion in Britain and of the threat it contained to living standards, amenities and the contentment of the people. The only comparable event in recent times was Baldwin's conversion to a tariff policy in 1929, and the Conservative Government's decision to apply for entry into the Common Market in 1960.

Even if the political difficulties could be smoothed over the barriers of Parliamentary procedure remain.

Parliamentary procedure was designed to safeguard the rights of minorities. Governments cannot govern without the Whips, and Whips cannot get conscientious objectors into the Lobby. No population policy requiring legislation could be got through Parliament in face of substantial opposition and obstruction unless it had enough supporters to force procedural motions through the House of Commons and keep to a timetable. (Even then the House of Lords could, under present powers, delay the passing of a Bill for a year.)

Given the "absolute necessity" for population limitation—upon which not enough people or politicians are yet convinced—then any government so convinced and carrying a substantial body of Parliamentary and public opinion could get the necessary legislation through.

It could be done. It will be done one day. There is no time to lose in preparation.

It is conceivable, however, that both politics and Parliament could be spared the worse agonies of a holy war, at least for the present.

"Politics" it is often said "is the art of the possible". Art it certainly is. No bull in Whitehall ever goes at a gate if there is a way through the fence.

The question is how to find a way round the barriers. There is no way round some of them but not all of them are deeply entrenched.

It may be that for the present the population controllers should go along with the family planners. Self-interest can be the ally of population control, at least up to a point. That point may not be far off: it appears to have been reached in the United States. Have we passed it here?

In the United States President Nixon has taken up the cause of birth control for the United States citizens. "But", says Peter J. Smith (in *New Society,* 24th July 1969), "the problem isn't lack of birth control: it's excess desire for children". He says: "The main reason for the growth of population in the United States is not any real or imagined inadequacy in birth control and family planning services, but is, quite simply, that on average American parents *want* more than the average maximum number required to stabilize the population. This changes the whole complexion of the problem".

It may do so here, though a Gallup Poll taken in July 1968 suggests that while 41% of Americans think four or more children is the ideal number, the percentage in Britain who think likewise is only 23 (*New York Times,* 13th November 1968).

Professor Kingsley Davis, director of international population and urban research at the University of California in Berkeley, is reported (*Times,* 13th November 1967) to have said that "reliance on family planning may in fact be a basis for dangerous postponement of effective steps to curtail population increase".

"Why not go along for a while with family planning as an initial approach to the problem of population control?", he writes in *Science.* "The answer is that any policy on which millions of dollars are being spent should be designed to achieve the goal it purports to achieve".

We have as yet no policy on that scale of expenditure. In Britain there is a long way to go yet to make family planning more effective. In the N.H.S. we have an agency the Americans have not for doing this. To provide the knowledge and the means free of cost, or at a moderate charge (probably unavoidable so long as other Health charges remain) would make a great deal of difference. A change in the attitude of the Vatican towards birth control by "artificial" means would also be a welcome aid to this policy.

Finally, there are the indirect or negative inducements to family limitation. So far we have none here. In India, where population control is now taken very seriously indeed, the government of Madhya Pradesh State is reported (*Times,* 31st July 1969) to have decided to refuse medical facilities free or at reduced rates to any government employee who has more than three children. In Britain, family allowances, social benefits and tax reliefs all favour the larger family.

One Consumer Group has calculated the immediate cost to the State of every newborn child to be £177 apart from the longer term cost of child care, health and education (Corby Consumer Group, 1969). A man, wife and three children, earning £16 a week, receives a net increase in income of over £3 a week from social benefits, direct and indirect. At £20 a week the same family is better off by over £2 a week. Only beyond £30 a week does that family suffer any net loss of income by taxation and other compulsory levies: up to that point taxes and contributions are more than made good by social benefits.

There is, therefore, some room for curtailing the net bonus to the larger families on average or above average incomes. (This was done indirectly and on a modest basis by leaving family allowances unchanged for 11 years before 1968, and then confining the full benefit of the increase to the poorer families by a "clawback" from the standard rate taxpayers through the tax system.)

Professor Kingsley Davis suggests a variety of measures "to lead people to postpone or avoid marriage, and at the same time to institute conditions which motivate those who do marry to keep their families small". For instance, paying people to permit themselves to be sterilized; the charging of a substantial fee for a marriage licence; a "child tax"; cease taxing single persons more than married ones; stop giving parents special tax exemptions; reduce paid maternity leave; stop the points system for council houses based on family size; and stop educational grants for wives and children of students. To cure women of "their idealized view of marriage and motherhood due to the scarcity of alternative roles or of combining them with family roles", Professor Davis suggests that it might "change this situation if women could be required to work outside the home or be compelled by circumstances to do so" (*Times,* 13th November 1967).

These suggestions offer a wide choice of political and Parliamentary barriers. They are his suggestions and not mine. It may be, however, that the real barriers are in neither politics nor Parliament, but in attitudes towards women and their place in the home and in society. Brigid Brophy has a view on this (*Listener,* 24th July 1969) which provides a background commentary to the whole discussion:

"Women have been, as a class, reared to believe the world owes them prestige and, via a husband, a living, simply in return for their having babies. Tell them having babies is now anti-social, and at the same time fail, as we are failing, to educate them . . . to either support or express themselves as persons . . . and you have a disaffected, demoted bourgeoisie on your hands, divested at one sudden go of its status and its private incomes . . ."

REFERENCES

Corby Consumer Group (1969). *Abortion Law Reform Association Newsletter,* 23.

Early Day Motion (1968). House of Commons. Session 1967/8, 3rd July 1968. No. 373.

M.O.H. (1931a). Ministry of Health Memo. 153/MCW. March 1931.

M.O.H. (1931b). Ministry of Health Circular 1208. July 1931.

Royal Commission on Population (1949). Report. H.M.S.O.

Thant, U. (1968). International Planned Parenthood Federation. *News,* February 1968.

Wheatley, J. (1924). *New Generation.* June 1924.
Wilson, H. (1967). Letter to Sir David Renton—"The Population Problem". Published by D. Renton, London.
Wilson, H. (1968). Letter to Labour Party Members of Parliament (unpublished).

Discussion

D. R. COPE: I would like to comment on an assumption made explicitly by the first speaker from the floor this morning, and implicitly by some of the speakers from the platform. This is the assertion, to my mind somewhat condescending, that ordinary people—the man in the street—are not aware of the problems of population pressure. We heard yesterday and this morning of these problems—urban blight, pressure on education and the social services, the effect of the motor car, pollution and so on. Mr. Houghton has said that ordinary people do not think much further than the week ahead, but aren't these problems the very things which dominate their thoughts during that week. Whether or not we accept there is a "population problem" we have to recognize that people are concerned over this matter.

G. RATTRAY TAYLOR: Earlier speakers have discussed the economics of maintaining the population without regard to the wider social context in which all such operations take place. I would like to offer a thought which may help to lead the discussion from these narrow considerations to broader ones.

I want to draw attention to the role of mobility in increasing the effective size of a population. When a gas is contained in a chamber the pressure is raised either by introducing more molecules or by heating, i.e. increasing the mobility of the molecules already there. Similarly, if a given population becomes more mobile, so other people interact more often, the absolute numbers must be reduced if we wish to preserve the *status quo*. It follows that it is not satisfactory to define an optimum population simply in terms of the number of individuals in the territory. Equally, since man's mobility is in fact rising and will probably continue to do so, it is arguable that an optimum population will, in fact, be a steadily declining one. This has economic implications.

The discussion seems to me to be avoiding the thorny problem of actually defining an optimum population for this country. We have asked: how many people will there be, how can we support them and what are the consequences? But we have not asked what are the social consequences of a population of 58 million or is it too many?

We are now three-quarters way through the conference and seem to be making little progress towards arriving at any understanding of the nature of an optimum population for this country, which I take to be the object of the exercise. In particular, we have given no consideration to the question of "quality of life". The phrase has been used by several speakers, but no attempt to quantify it, or even to say whether a larger or a smaller population would improve the quality of life.

M. SIMMS: Dr. Eversley, you said that as we become more affluent we become more "space-intensive". Consequently, as population increases we have to train ourselves to become less "space-intensive" or there won't be enough space to go round.

Would this not mark a very serious deterioration in the conditions of a civilized existence?

Would it not be more rational to aim at fewer people and more space rather than the other way round?

Would you not agree that even carefully planned new towns and regional redistribution would provide only a temporary mitigation of an intractable problem that will need to be honestly faced at some stage well before population pressures become completely intolerable?

D. EVERSLEY: I think there is enough space to go round if we use what we have more rationally. This means first of all reducing the extent of the concentration of population in the south-east of the British Isles. We can all have enough room to live in, and for recreation, if we build up new settlements in a pleasant environment away from the conurbations which now hold too large a proportion of the total.

Secondly, we must make more open space available to all. Much of it at present is in very restricted private use. There is enough coast and countryside for all.

Thirdly, we must accept some restriction on the use of our most space-intensive possession: the motor car.

A. G. COCK: I suggest that Dr. Eversley is suffering from a "Malthusians under the bed" syndrome; he seems to imagine that most or all biologists espouse extreme "political Malthusian" views. His attempt to minimize, or deny altogether, the parallels between animal and human populations is one symptom of this syndrome.

Some of the discussion of the distinction between "unplanned" and "unwanted" children seemed to miss the crucial point. Few, if any, would deny that some "unplanned" pregnancies give rise to children who, sooner or later, are "wanted". Family planning is therefore not the same thing as population control. But it is equally not irrelevant to population control, as Dr. Eversley has argued. This would be true only if *all* unplanned pregnancies gave rise to *wanted* children; no one has produced evidence or arguments to support this.

K. MELLANBY: We are supposed to be discussing optimum populations, but these are difficult to define. Professor Southwood has admirably described the way natural animal populations are controlled, and it is clear that if man does not control his rate of increase, these factors, all very unpleasant, will affect human populations also. Our knowledge of optimum animal populations does not help very much. Conservationists can define the optimum population for animals like the Red Deer. This gives the highest productivity of the species for a given area, and is sustained by the correct level of culling. We could thus have an optimum human population, provided that cannibalism were an acceptable method of control! Otherwise, without effective methods of birth control, we shall increase and inevitably suffer the fate of other animal species.

P. R. EHRLICH: It is a common error to think of overpopulation as being a matter of brute population density—that is the number of people per square mile. But the best definition I have heard of overpopulation is the situation where human numbers are pressing on human values.

By any standard you wish to select Britain is grossly overpopulated. People have been reticent to express their opinion on what an optimal population for Britain would be, but I won't be reticent about it. I am certain that it would be well under 20 million people. This is based on our calculations at Stanford of upper limits on the world optimum which turns out to be, from almost every point of view, under one billion people. It's very important to recognize that although family planning is a social good, since no sane person wants unwanted children born, family planning is not population control. The idea of "every child a wanted child" is all too often translated into "we're going to breed like rabbits but we're going to plan and space the children very carefully". If there were no more births of unwanted children in the world from now on, we would still have a very serious problem of population growth—people just want too many children.

I can't think of any scientific technological advance possible in the next couple of decades that will contribute to a general technological solution to the population-resources-environment crisis. Indeed about the only thing that would do any good would be to repeal the laws of thermodynamics. Perhaps we should work very hard on Congress and Parliament to do that!

CHAPTER 10

How Much Pressure on the Individual?

M. SIMMS AND J. MEDAWAR

INTRODUCTION

This paper starts by assuming that the population of this island must be controlled if a civilized way of life is to be possible in the next century.

Maynard Keynes asked: "is not a country over populated when its standards are lower than they would be if its numbers were less"? Such standards are material but also moral, political and aesthetic and no advanced society can now evade the urgent need to find an answer to Keynes's question and consequently to the question which is the subject of this paper.

PAST OPINIONS

Before discussing the size of the problem and ways of tackling it without interfering with the liberty of the individual, it is interesting to remember how strongly opposed to birth control the Establishment was only thirty years ago—and understandably, because people then were wringing their hands over the problems of too *few* births and the so-called *twilight of parenthood*. When Mr. David Logan, a father of ten, spoke in 1935 to parliament of birth control as "one of the curses of the age", "fit for the gutter" and as "the knowledge of the prostitute" (Logan, 1935), no outraged replies were recorded. In 1939 Norman Birkett reported as Chairman of the Government's inquiry into abortion (Birkett, 1939), that birth control ought not to be made universally available, as this would "affect adversely the continuity of the state" and would "tend to lower the traditional and accepted standards of sexual morality" and might often be "a source of temptation". The Church of England gave its blessing to contraception, when responsibly used in marriage, only 11 years ago (Anon., 1958).

PRESENT OPINIONS

Today, opinions have changed to the point where the question is not whether we should regulate births, but how we should do it while preserving the liberty of the individual. How much self-sacrifice will an individual make in order to preserve the essentials of civilized living—decent housing, education, clean air, quiet countryside and unpolluted rivers and seas? The question cannot be answered in the abstract: the degree of self discipline tolerated in the wider interests of society depends on how clearly a danger is perceived, and on the development of the individual; for some, a glow of righteousness may compensate for foregoing a third and wanted child, but for others the glow is insufficient.

In Japan the pressure of births in the late forties was acute enough to permit the introduction of state-supported legal abortion and birth control; and there the birth rate was halved in ten years. Even so, if present rates are maintained, a child who joins the present hundred million on the Japanese Islands will have to share them with another hundred million by the time he has reached four score and ten. As India's economy is threatened by the rising tide of births, increasingly radical measures are accepted to stem the flood; soon legalized abortion will join the national birth control and sterilization programme; people will sacrifice some freedom in a national emergency in order to prevent the destruction of all freedom—but first they must be convinced that the sacrifice is necessary.

NEW PROBLEMS AND OLD IDEAS

In this country today, the majority of children now survive to have children of their own. The injunction in Genesis was to "be fruitful, multiply and *replenish* the earth": but when the earth is not emptying but filling in proportion of two births to every death, blind or careless replenishment is a fatal prescription. When infant and maternal mortality were high, society valued women's reproductive function highly and encouraged the qualities which help it and are associated with motherhood—patience, conservatism, self-sacrifice and fatalism; but even in our own relatively advanced society, where women have fairly equal rights, the notion of the "intrinsic virtue" of childbirth dies slowly. Only four months ago, a judge told a pregnant woman convicted of stealing and soliciting for the sixth time: "I am going to give you a chance. You are expecting a baby. You have faced up to that pregnancy when you could have had it terminated on the National Health. I think that merits some respect." But the report on the case made it clear that the woman could not look after her existing children without stealing. Yet the judge respected her for increasing her family, and his views reflect those of a society that does not yet accept rational criteria for choosing to have children. We may feel sympathy for the woman, but not respect for the judge.

After centuries in which the survival of race apparently depended upon uncontrolled fertility the earlier lesson has not only to be unlearnt, but put into reverse. This lesson is especially hard for women to learn. The good, fertile mother who often literally sacrifices herself for her children has been put on a pedestal and the qualities which put her there, though not always attractive by themselves, were formerly at least functional in serving the biological requirements of the species.

In this country the situation appears not to be the same as in so many others; here, in spite of occasional die-hard opposition, the problem is not how much coercion people will stand to persuade them not to want too many children; it is how to help them carry out their own intentions. The Quarterly Returns (1968) estimate that completed family size will average 2.5 or a little less; illegitimate births are expected to remain at about 8% and gain from migration to contribute little of itself to population change in England and Wales in the longer term. The problem at present is therefore largely technical and not political.

REASONS FOR FAILURE

If the Registrar General's figures correctly interpret people's intentions, why is it necessary to ask questions about how much pressure can be put on the individual? If most individuals are convinced, why are they not guided by their convictions? When more children are born than were planned the causes vary from human weakness and dislike of method to lack of knowledge and lack of opportunity.

THE UNPLANNED

Many married couples have more children than they want. Even in Aberdeen, which has one of the most advanced Local Health Authority birth control services in the country, Sir Dougald Baird (1969) found that over a quarter of the children were "unplanned and mostly unwanted".

According to Thompson and Illsley (1969), large unplanned families are drawn primarily from three major overlapping categories of women—those who marry before they are twenty, those who conceive before marriage and those who marry a semi-skilled or unskilled manual worker. In family planning, social convention counts for more than intelligence and emulation has an important effect on whether or not it is used. Thompson and Illsley also found that after five years of marriage, 10% of their sample already had more children "than they felt able to manage without excessive strain". Nearly two-thirds of first and second pregnancies were unintended, four-fifths of third pregnancies and all fourth or later pregnancies occurring in the first five years. Professor Norman Morris (1968) found from research at Charing Cross Hospital that only a quarter to one-third of all babies were planned; and in a study in London and in Hertfordshire, Fraser and Watson (1968) found too that about half the pregnancies were unplanned. It may be true that many unplanned babies turn into wanted children under the alchemy of the maternal instinct, but this is no argument for society to approve of behaviour which puts a child into an overcrowded world with this sort of risk.

THE ILLEGITIMATE

About a hundred and fifty thousand unmarried women become pregnant in this country each year. Half of them marry before the birth of their child. It is reasonable to suppose that a majority of these pregnancies are unwanted at conception, and if a conservative estimate of one in three were actually wanted, one hundred thousand children are born unwanted in this category alone. The Pregnancy Advisory Service (Anon., 1969a) in Birmingham recently reported that 40% of the girls who came asking for their pregnancy to be terminated had never used contraception and 60% had not used it on the occasion when they became pregnant. If the birth of the unwanted hundred thousand babies were prevented, with about half of the hundred and twenty thousand third children born each year, most of the fifty thousand fourth and virtually all the fifty thousand fifth and subsequent children, the present annual total of some eight hundred thousand births would fall below six hundred thousand and we should no longer feel anxious about the prospect of overcrowding in the British Isles. Our present 16.9 crude birth-rate would also be down to one of the lowest in the world.

POWER FOR LOCAL HEALTH AUTHORITIES

Generally speaking, opinion is now in favour of making birth control services available to all who need them. The question is not whether or not to provide them but by whom they should be provided and in what way. It is now two years since the Acts were passed which empowered the two hundred and fifty or so Local Health Authorities to make family planning services available for all, either by setting up their own services or by using the Family Planning Association as their agent. So far, 39 are offering a complete service, 36 of them by using the FPA, and 129 are giving a part service, also through the FPA. Coercion is conspicuously absent both from the Acts and from the Family Planning Association's policy, which is permissive in allowing freedom of conscience within their 950 clinics to those who do not want to help the unmarried mother with her problems.

ACTION

Aberdeen has adopted an enlightened programme to make birth control services fully available, and the methods by which a drop in the birth of unwanted babies has been managed need worry no one; the citizens of Aberdeen remain free to choose the size of their family for themselves. The difference beween Aberdeen and other towns in this respect is that the choice is offered, and the local climate of public health opinion reinforces any wish not to become accidentally pregnant and makes it easy to take the necessary action. The Medical Officer of Health, Dr. Ian McQueen (1969), now enlists the health visitors alongside the doctors and nurses in the Health Service; birth control is a normal part of the health education programme for health visitors and is carried by them into the houses of the people whom they serve.

Within three years of starting this service, the illegitimate birth rate has been brought below the average for Scotland, even in the Registrar General's lowest social groups. It is curious to find this model of how the service should be run flourishing in Scotland, where the Act passed on July 26th 1968 to enable birth control services to be provided by all Local Authorities was nullified by a Circular in the autumn of 1968 preventing them from doing so on grounds of financial stringency. The paradox illustrates the way in which decisions are made largely according to character: one man sees only the initial cost in the current financial year; another sees further to the long-term benefits and dividends in human welfare and saving of public money.

DOMICILIARY SERVICES

The same saving results from a domiciliary service which takes birth control into the homes of people too worn out, often by child-bearing, to find the energy needed to find someone to look after their children whilst they visit a clinic. Such schemes have been pioneered in Newcastle, York, Southampton and London. They have been described in detail and the results sent by the Family Planning Association to every County Medical Officer of Health—but there has been no enthusiastic adoption of this pattern. The tragedy is that the web of cause and effect is not displayed for all to see: budgets are departmentally designed to meet established needs and to show that public money is not mis-spent—and not to proclaim that £1 spent on birth control by the General Purposes Committee would show a saving of £10 in the Child Care Department.

Much more must be done, and can now be done without pressure on the individual. Every Local Health Authority should follow the main outlines of the service provided in Aberdeen, either themselves or in co-operation with the FPA, adding full domiciliary services to help "problem" families and, with appropriate tact, through Health Visitors, should extend them to make sure that families with three or more children are not inadvertently added to through want of information. This could remove unwanted pressures from the mother, the family and society.

TRAINING AND EDUCATION

The FPA, as the largest provider of birth control services in the country, is now helped by a government grant for training; it is greatly increasing the programmes which trained a thousand doctors and nurses last year and is extending training to the social services and to social workers from home and overseas. But though it sees about half a million patients a year, the Association's resources are limited and far more needs to be done on a national scale to manage the problem of the unwanted pregnancy.

Steps have already been taken by the Government to provide sex education under the guidance of the new Health Education Council; this should sponsor films and leaflets and advertise them in libraries, employment offices, post offices, and hospitals, and on radio and television.

For hundreds of thousands of years women have been praised for their fertility: there is now no time left for an equally long period in which to teach the need for only wanted children to be born, so the message must be immediate, strong, clear and sustained.

HOSPITALS AND JOURNALISTS

Several additional forward steps could also be taken, still without causing any loss of individual liberty. The teaching hospitals must start to introduce training in contraception into their normal medical syllabus and routinely provide it for all lying-in patients. A genetic counselling service should be available in hospitals to help parents avoid the risk of giving birth to an abnormal child, if they have the slightest reason to suspect that they may be at risk.

The Genetic Counselling Unit at the Great Ormond Street Hospital has already shown that a high proportion of couples advised by the Unit decided against having more children even when there was only a minimal chance of a particular inherited defect (Anon., 1968).

Then the Editors of those women's magazines which still spread a perhaps unconscious message that women are only fulfilled by maternity—and that the best sort of maternity is prolific—should be invited to an official briefing on the issues at stake and on their responsibilities towards them. When the public world is alarming, noisy and competitive, and standards are changing faster than in any period of history the temptation is, of course, powerful to retreat into a private world with enough children to make a microcosm; for many this may be ideal and possible—but to present it as a panacea, as is often deliberately done, is dangerous and indefensible. In America commercial pressures are exerted to keep women at home and reproducing; here the same pressures are not yet highly developed but they exist. The women's magazines and television could also do much to change the present attitude to childless couples—that they are "abnormal" if they choose not to have children. A survey in *New Society* in March this year reported that some of the 320 infertile couples interviewed felt themselves "social outcasts"—an entirely misfitting verdict in the present situation (Anon., 1969b).

ABORTION

Until birth control is fully effective, the need for abortion will remain. To meet the need efficiently and safely abortion law reformers believe that abortion units should now be established in every Regional Hospital Board at present providing an inadequate and below average National Health abortion service (Simms, 1968). These units should co-operate closely with local maternity and birth control services, and conduct much-needed research into the problem of the unwanted pregnancy, to find out why otherwise intelligent and well-educated girls so often fail to use contraceptives. In the first year after the passing of the Abortion Act 40,000 women have been able to have their pregnancies terminated in decent conditions, and the deaths from legal abortions have fallen to a figure below that for maternal mortality. Too many women, however, still turn to criminal abortionists, from human weakness, from tradition or because of the attitude of some doctors—or of inadequate abortion facilities. In Newcastle, which according to the Chief Medical Officer of the Department of Health provides a model abortion service, 675 NHS abortions are performed per million population. In Birmingham, Liverpool and Sheffield, the number is below 300 (Anon., 1969c). Once the idea of a rational population policy is accepted in principle, it becomes absurd that a woman who does not want a baby should be obliged for any reason to have it.

CONCLUSIONS

Unwanted births can probably be reduced by all these methods, gradually and undramatically, without any noticeable increase in pressure on the individual, but they will be reduced only if all the methods are followed, consistently and persistently as an agreed national policy, and only if the assumption is correct that population growth is largely due to the births that couples would have preferred to avoid. If the assumption is wrong and people do actually want more children than the number required to stabilize the population, we are back to asking how much pressure an individual will tolerate on his private life for the benefit of what the government believes is in the public interest.

When the question has been asked in recent debates, the general opinion has been unequivocally and unsurprisingly against any form of direct government compulsion. Yet what Professor Titmuss once called "inadvertently pro-natalist policies" still persist and do leave some room for discouragement of large families by fiscal means.

At the moment, in this country, no simple answer exists to the question "how much pressure?"; but clearly, the pressure least likely to succeed is that exercised by a government on an electorate not fully aware of the need for social responsibility in this sphere.

On July 18th President Nixon asked Congress to establish a Commission to consider the effects of both population growth and shifts in population, and drew attention to the alarming figures which backed his request.

The setting up of a Commission cannot produce an immediate solution, but it might, as Theodore Fox wrote in 1967, "produce a policy more rational than the one now holding the field—a collection of assumptions made by people living, biologically, in the past".

What is needed is not compulsion, because compulsion would not work, nor a grandiose scheme, because conditions may change, but a decision about the direction we want to take and a good attempt to go there. We do not need to know everything a Commission can tell us before we do anything: and, as we have tried to show in this paper, plenty of useful things can be done at once which, far from increasing pressure on individuals, would relieve them, their families and the country of the strains which this Symposium is trying to understand and remove.

REFERENCES

Anon. (1958). The family in contemporary society.

Anon. (1968). Rep. Lambeth Conf., S.P.C.K., pp. 142-171.

Anon. (1969a). *Medical Tribune,* 29 August 1968. First progress report, Birmingham Pregnancy Advisory Service, p. 8.

Anon. (1969b). *New Society,* No. 337, 13 March 1969.

Anon. (1969c). *Sunday Times,* 6 July 1969, p. 13.

Baird, D. (1969). "Social Research and Obstetric Practice". Pemberton for Rationalist Press Association, Question 2, p. 9.

Birkett, N. (1939). Report of interdepartmental committee on abortion. Ministry of Health and Home Office, H.M.S.O.

Fox, T. (1967). Noah's new flood or the multiplication of man. *Family Planning* 15, 91-99.

Fraser, A. C. and Watson, P. S. (1968). Family planning—a myth? *Family Planning* 17, 72-73.

Logan, D. (1935). House of Commons, *Hansard* 304, cols. 1134-1135.

McQueen, I. A. G. (1969). An integrated local authority planning service. *Family Planning* 18, 31-34.

Morris, N. (1968). Family planning in Britain. *Family Planning* 17, 31-34.

Quarterly Returns (1968). G.R.O. No. 48, 31 December 1968, pp. 56-58.

Simms, M. (1968). The need for abortion units. *Abortion Law Reform Assoc. Newsletter* 21, 1-2.

Thompson, B. and Illsley, R. (1969). Family growth in Aberdeen. *Jour. biosoc. Sci.* 1.

CHAPTER 11

Not by Bread Alone:
Anthropological Perspectives on Optimum Population

M. M. R. FREEMAN

Memorial University of Newfoundland

Anthropology is increasingly concerned with complex and modern, or modernizing, societies, though the great majority of substantive writings in the anthropological literature are involved with technologically and economically simpler societies.

Regrettably, population is one topic that has received scant, and for the most part uncritical treatment by anthropologists. However, as many of the societies that anthropologists traditionally favour studying are becoming affected by often abrupt culture change, correlates and consequences of changing population size and structure are increasingly demanding investigation.

The demographic changes that occur when traditional, non-industrialized societies become increasingly urbanized and modernized are well known. Initially, mortality rate falls, but birth-rate continues unaffected and high, so that a population explosion takes place. In time the rate of population growth may decrease, through reduced birth-rate, but with increasing life expectancy population growth nevertheless continues. Various explanations are available to account for the declining birth-rate that occurs during the so-called "demographic transition"; such factors as increasing literacy, new-found knowledge of birth control, greater participation of women in urban economic pursuits, a decreasing dependency on family support and security and so on. Sometimes the implication is that before such involvements with forces of modernization, traditional peoples had large families because they lacked knowledge of how to prevent conception or birth, or other means of reducing fertility. Furthermore it is assumed in this line of argument that once modernization introduces the required knowledge, people will willingly limit their procreative propensities. Unfortunately for everyone, such conclusions are quite false.

Virtually every traditional society about which we have knowledge possesses definite norms with respect to family size, and several methods and social arrangements for limiting fertility are known and practised in nearly all such societies. There appears to be very little evidence to suggest that religious or social pressures against birth control are effective in any societies once individuals have decided to practise fertility control, but the fact remains that for the most part among traditional peoples great value is placed on high fertility. For this reason more than any other it is evident that population control, as distinct from family planning, is very difficult to effect in such recently modernizing and burgeoning societies, and that the widely publicized family planning campaigns do not in themselves lead to fertility decline. Davis (1967) goes so far as to argue that efforts to propagandize and further family planning campaigns confuse the real issues and frustrate attempts to deal effectively with the matter of population control. Family planning does, among its other shortcomings, stress the medical scientist and technology, thereby minimizing, if not denying, the crucial fact that decisions affecting procreation and child-rearing are social happenings. Glass (1960) warns that acceptance of new demographic modes will involve developing new incentives that require to be integrated into the existing social framework, and Spengler (1966) concludes that demographic characteristics of a society correlate with the society's system of rewards and sanctions. Rewards, costs and sanctions can be economic or social (through, e.g. loss or gain in status, prestige or influence).

Many studies have attempted to correlate fertility levels with economic factors, such that an increase in the cost of raising children, compared to the use of that same capital to achieve other goals, will depress fertility, whereas an increasing value placed on children will increase fertility. Modernization and concomitant urbanization lower fertility because the cost of children in an urban setting is usually greater than in a rural economy. However, in the 18th and 19th centuries huge population growth occurred in Okajama (Japan) during a period in which the economy of the province changed from small-scale agriculture to commercial and pre-modern manufacture (Hanley, 1968), and both Ireland (McKeown and Brown, 1955) and late 19th-century Hungary (Demeny, 1968) offer good examples of voluntary control of marital fertility without modernization of the economic infrastructure. In the Hungarian example the evidence suggests in part an economic motive for lowered fertility, more especially the goal of land-owning in the face of an otherwise increasing population. Land-owning does, however, include non-economic parameters, especially if the culture places high value on land-owning by affording status to land-owners. There may also be strictly demographic reasons for such reduced fertility, as there was in fact among Polish peasants at that time. Stys (1957) found that the average completed family size among Polish peasant women born in the latter half of the 19th century was proportional to their farm size. Thus among landless peasants the average number of births per mother was 3.9, whereas on farms greater than seven hectares area the average number of births was 9.1. Although the author concludes that a high economic level increases fertility, the explanation lies mostly in the variation of mothers age at marriage, a potent means of influencing fertility (Cole, 1954).

Whatever the non-economic reasons are in the cases cited above, an attitude study conducted among contemporary American hill farmers in the Appalachians indicated a positive correlation between improved economic status and the goal of increased fertility. Thus 1.5 children is the average desired by "not-well-off" respondents, 2.79 for "average" and 4.02 for "well-off" (DeJong, 1965).

The apparent anomalies in the evidence as to how modernization and urbanization influence fertility have led some to question whether urbanization can be regarded as a determinant of fertility level. The resolution of this problem may lie in the discovery that firstly, in low fertility regions (such as eastern Europe and America) certain inter-related variables contribute to high fertility until threshold levels of social and economic improvement are passed, after which time fertility levels decline (Spengler, 1966), and secondly that urbanization does not by itself lead to greater economic well-being for the migrants to the cities.

Recent studies have indicated the likely resultants of modernization and urbanization that are potential intermediate variables effecting fertility decline; foremost among these variables is probably a decreasing dependence on kin for economic security within the urban-modern setting (Freedman, 1963; Heer, 1966). Large families may therefore reflect a conscious expression of anxiety about future security. One study has quantified this relationship: allowing that each married couple wishes to be 95% certain of having at least one son survive till the father's 65th year, and allowing that a perfect method of birth control is available, then the Gross Reproductive Rate will fall from 5.2 when life expectancy is 20 years, to 0.95 when expectancy rises to 74 years (Heer and Smith, 1968).

Given the high birth-rate among most traditional societies, population control has more often involved reduction in fertility levels than an increase in mortality. In passing we might note that territorial expansion following population increase may involve warfare, but that mortality resulting from warfare has only exceptionally been a deliberate instrument of population control (Livingstone, 1967).

The more important methods of depressing fertility include contraception, abortion, infanticide*, celibacy and postponement of marriage; certain cultural values may justify these normative practices, e.g. high value on pre-marital chastity, rules governing inheritance and succession, etc. Sometimes practices effecting lower fertility became normative under ecologic conditions where such restrictive policies were adaptive, yet persist even when conditions change and the society is threatened by serious depopulation. Examples of this include the

---

* Infanticide more correctly affects the *effective fertility* of a population, which is the measure of births occurring after exclusion of foetal and infant deaths. The term fertility will be used here to include effective fertility.

high incidence of self-induced abortion on the Micronesian Island of Yap, and infanticide among the Tapirapé Indians of Brazil, where in both cases depopulation threatens the very existence of the society (Vayda and Rappaport, 1963).

It appears probable that infanticide has been one of the more widespread and important means of reducing fertility and altering the composition of human populations since the Pleistocene, and for most hunter-gatherer societies (encompassing more than 90% of the total number of human beings who have ever lived) incidence of infanticide probably ranges from 15 to 50% of live births (Birdsell, 1968). Infanticide was institutionalized in Britain and several European countries during the 19th century, and certainly in cities the figure of 15% seems not unrealistic (Langer, 1963).

Under primitive conditions, especially among non-nomadic peoples, it is questionable whether induced abortion represented a greater health risk than normal childbirth, and this may account for the use of the practice in about 99% of all societies known to anthropologists. Today abortion is the most common single method of birth control in use (Hardin, 1969).

Social arrangements that result in lowered fertility are also practised in almost all societies. These restrictions range from allowing only the eldest son and one daughter to marry, as among the Nambudiri Brahmins of southern India (Yalman, 1963) to the requirement that young men undergo a long and arduous initiation period before and during which time they cannot marry. Among certain Australian groups for example, this initiation period occupies the time of a man's peak sexual potency, and also results in the older men, some of whom may have passed their sexual prime, having exclusive access to the younger and more fecund women. Further, in the early years of marriage, the younger man often has to marry an older woman, who may have passed the climacteric. However, it would be wrong to infer that this is a conscious, or even effective, means of achieving reduced population fertility. The significance of these social arrangements concerns the maintenance of social control by the older males, and it has been argued (Rose, 1968) that the resulting polygynous households under the headship of an experienced older man is an adaptive arrangement that facilitates child-rearing and enhances survivorship of the progeny. Indeed, infanticide is prevalent in this society and it is therefore increasingly important to ensure the viability of those infants that are allowed to survive.

Population sizes and population densities vary considerably according to habitat, historical and cultural exigencies. Some Australian hunter-gatherer societies live at the fantastic sparsity of one person per 100 square miles, whereas some north Nigerian hill farmers maintain populations at densities of 1200 persons per square mile, and populations of greater density are recorded for some horticultural-fishing societies in Micronesia. Modern urban populations are found at an even higher order of magnitude.

Societies at both extremes of density control fertility levels, though for different reasons: hunter-gatherers control fertility to facilitate mobility, and some agricultural and island populations for reasons of space limitation.

I have given mobility and space, rather than food supply, as reasons for limiting fertility, because of the classic but misleading over-emphasis existing in both older anthropological writings and popular writ that traditional, pre-industrial, and especially pre-agricultural, societies were constantly under the threat of starvation, or at least uncertainty and anxiety about food supply. This view has recently been challenged (Douglas, 1966; Binford, 1968; Sahlins, 1968) and evidence exists in many ethnographic accounts to suggest that in fact hunter-gatherers spend very little time on food-getting activities, and that further, for most of these societies starvation or prolonged food shortage is a very unlikely event. If such societies express concern over food supplies, it is most likely because of a threatened or imagined shortage of *preferred* foods, not the threat of outright starvation. Hunter-gatherers with relatively simple technologies have an impressive knowledge of environmental resources and the perspicacity to realize the latent potential whenever conditions demand. It needs stressing that though hunter-gatherers are generally believed to occupy marginal areas, marginality is with respect to agricultural practice and not survival.

The Bushmen of the Kalahari Desert illustrate these points well. Though to agricultural peoples, including ourselves, the Kalahari is a forbidding place, no less than 85 species of edible food plant are to be found there, including 29 species of edible fruits, berries and melons and 30 species of edible roots and bulbs. No less than 223 species of animal are known to, and classified by, the Bushmen, with at least 54 of these species considered edible. However, 60–80% of the Bushman diet by weight is obtained from vegetable foods gathered during a few hours' activity every third or fourth day throughout the year, with major dependence on but one main food, the mongongo nut *(Ricinodendron rautanenii).* The daily diet of around 300 mongongo nuts yields about 1260 kcal and 56 g of protein, and furthermore is readily available near at hand for 10 months of the year. During the end of the dry season, in September and October, daily walks of 10 to 15 miles may be undertaken to gather the desired mongongo nut, even though there are several other sources of food available. The conclusion one anthropologist has drawn from this is that food is both plentiful and constant, though the distance one may have to travel to maintain this constancy of input may vary seasonally (Lee, 1968). Similar non-arduous living has been noted for other hunter-gatherer societies (references in Binford, *op. cit.*) who are generally, if erroneously, held to be most precariously placed with regard to subsistence.

Hunter-gatherers therefore place high value on mobility, not merely to ensure physical survival, but importantly to maximize certain culturally-defined goals with respect to the kind of life they wish to enjoy. Where the desired goal concerns diet, it may reflect more concern with obtaining certain preferred foods than with ensuring a minimal caloric intake. Indeed, the evidence available to anthropologists suggests that human populations, in common with non-human populations, tend to "stabilize" themselves at levels that may be far below the maximum possible for the biological carrying capacity of the habitat, and figures of 20–30% utilization of environmental food resources are suggested (Lee and DeVore, 1968). As Douglas (*op. cit.*) has persuasively argued, ceiling on population may not be imposed by food supply, but by certain culture-specific scarce resources, which may often include access to limited social advantages.

It is evident that voluntary or inherent controls on fertility must precede Malthusian checks near the point of population-resources equilibrium because otherwise selection pressure would continually be exerted on human populations to innovate in food capture methods once the point of diminishing returns was reached, with a hastening of ecologic collapse as a result.

Earlier I mentioned space and settled agriculturalists, where apart from the evident economic need for a given-sized land-holding; the social effects of crowding are also important. Too great a crowding of people and their domestic stock may lead to interpersonal conflicts, and a recent study of a New Guinea agricultural people has admirably demonstrated how density-dependent conflict initiates a whole ecologic and ritual cycle involving large-scale livestock reduction and distribution of protein, enforced conservation of certain wild mammals, and warfare and land fallowing and redistribution (Rappaport, 1968).

The various biological consequences of high population density are probably less important as direct determinants of human population fertility than are resultant socio-cultural factors. For example, though a high density of hosts may favour the spread of certain diseases, infant mortality rates of 230–240/1000 occurred in both urban and rural populations in pre-industrial England (Wrigley, 1968) and despite very low population size and density, infant mortality rates of 600/1000 are postulated for some traditional Australian societies (Rose, 1968). Insofar as infant mortality rate and population density are related, it appears more likely that the number of children per household, rather than the number of households per unit area, is the important density-dependent variable (McKeown and Brown, 1955; Knodel, 1968).

This emphasis on socio-cultural determinants is not to deny altogether the biologic consequences of high population density on fertility rates. One pertinent medical study has indicated that less than optimal environmental conditions during pregnancy result in greater foetal loss and lowered viability of the ensuing progeny. The conclusion in this study (Stott, 1962) was that there is a genetic provision to ensure production of inferior quality offspring during times of stress; the correlated increased incidence of congenital defects, premature births, lowered viability and a skewed male:female birth ratio (in favour of males) would all be important depressors of fertility.

This explanation is in accord with the zoologically attractive genetic-polymorphism-behavioural hypothesis of Chitty (Krebs, 1964), which appears more generally applicable to mammalian populations in nature than the earlier adreno-pituitary exhaustion hypothesis (Christian, 1950). Too great an emphasis on phenotypic-physiological controls in human biology tends to deny man's characteristically high degree of cortical control over behaviour. On the other hand, genetic controls, adaptive in an evolutionary rather than an ecologic sense, appear to me to be far more likely, and perhaps necessary, as ultimate causes because of the persistence in man of powerful forces of both psychological denial (Hardin, 1968) and physiological adaptation, as evidenced by high fertility in spite of malnutrition persisting in many less-developed regions of the world.

The concept of optimum population has been variously described, depending on the nature of the goals that the population seeks to maximize (references in Spengler, 1967). Anthropologically, the concept refers to a human group within the size range required for the suitable expression of a normative pattern of social organization and for the adequate realization of certain internalized cultural goals; such a population will normally become stabilized below the biological carrying capacity of the environment.

Human groups in which traditional value systems remain operative almost invariably maintain their population on a homeostatic plateau by institutionalized negative feedback practices. These checks on positive feedback (birth-rate), ensure not only limitation of population size but, importantly, that the composition of the population conforms to the demographic model demanded by the culture. Thus, for example, if prolonged lactation does not allow the degree of child-spacing needed to allow the mother to adequately fulfil her domestic role, taboos on sexual intercourse during lactation, abortion, adoption or infanticide may necessarily be strategies utilized to achieve the required result. This emphasis on quality, or composition, of population is probably ecologically important also, and elsewhere (Freeman, in press) I have suggested that a demographic shift from a youthful to a mature population may increase stability under certain ecologic conditions.

In adopting such a cybernetic model of society it is important to understand the nature of the controls imposed on positive feedback, for in human populations, contra infra-human populations, individuals may choose to cheat against, or reject, normative values or behaviour, at least to the point where the integrity of the system is threatened. It is also pertinent to note that the desire to maintain absolute constancy in a system is pathological, and therefore dangerous, and consequently excessive restraints can themselves produce instability (Hardin, 1963). Inappropriate negative feedback is exemplified by abortion practices in Scandinavia, where legal abortion has been relatively accessible since the 1930's. However, despite the availability, economy and safety of legal abortion, illegal abortion remains on a high level, and increasing numbers of Scandinavian women travel to Poland to obtain legal abortions there. It appears that individuals do not want the State managing their pregnancies for them, and will take alternative action to retain an acceptable level of personal control.

Ecologists and engineers are well aware that the stability of a system can be increased by providing alternate pathways for energy and information flow, divers routes for escape and choice. Freedom, when coupled with responsibility, enhances stability. Even the most traditionally organized societies appear to offer alternatives to some institutionalized restraints; among the Pelly Bay Eskimos, for example, female infanticide appears as an almost invariable demographic norm, yet naming, adoption, espousal, birth order, or even the mood of the father at the time of birth sometimes allowed female infants to survive (Balikci, 1967).

In conclusion then, what do these summary statements and observations concerning other societies have to contribute to the demographic and ecologic problems of Britain entering the 21st century?

Firstly, it would seem that high density of population need not be pathological, and that high density is unlikely *per se* to result in involuntary (physiological) fertility control. Any reduction in birth-rate that may occur will result from voluntary (cultural) limitation, which will be the conscious expression of changed societal goals, or changed strategies adopted by society to achieve those goals.

Secondly, that the concept of optimum population as here defined depends on various ecologic variables which include cultural values defined by society itself. Thus for substantially reduced or zero population growth to occur, high value must be accorded low fertility, and rewards and sanctions applied by society to those who respectively conform to or transgress norms reflecting those values. To be effective these norms require to be internalized by members of society, therefore every pedagogic and persuasive means available should be employed without delay. These norms, being cultural-ecologic in nature, embrace more than purely demographic matters, and consequently a high degree of integrated planning and co-ordination of effort will be necessary to effect any population policy aimed at reduction of birth-rate. If the goal sought is considered desirable, and as it undoubtedly concerns the quality of life available it must be so considered, then social and legislative reform must be resolutely enacted. In the same way that society accepts the need to impose restrictions on some classes of people, e.g. criminals, the mentally unstable, dangerous drivers, excessively successful capitalists, etc., the time has probably arrived when excessive reproduction must be regarded as antisocial, threatening behaviour, and for the common good requires common sense control.

Thirdly, given the choice, it is apparent that societies reduce fertility by selecting means that involve the least institutional reform and the least human cost. It is unrealistic, therefore, to promote such causes as celibacy, delayed marriages with chastity outside of marriage, or abstinence inside of marriage as means of achieving reduced fertility. It would be more expeditious to alter existing fiscal arrangements, so that, e.g. illegitimate or supernumerary offspring are heavily taxed, and tax exemptions apply to single persons or couples with one or no children (unless adopted), and higher pensions are paid to senior citizens without supportive children. At the present moment most advanced nations encourage high fertility through their tax structures and family allowance and welfare systems.

Finally, the patchwork of knowledge we do have about social-psychological parameters of human reproduction is woefully inadequate, more especially as it affects our own society. What are the incentives today for marriage at a particular age, or for having a first child now and not some years later, for having a second child then or not at all, for having a small family or a large family? Must the desire for large families include biological reproduction, or could it be satisfied by adoption as evidently it does in many societies? Answers to these and similar questions are not merely a prerequisite for humane and effective legislation, they are a probable pre-condition for effecting the desired reform of such emotion-charged institutions as motherhood and the family.

If people are the nation's greatest asset, then we are remarkably lax in our efforts to husband rationally and indeed realize this wealth, for the time is fast approaching when the freedom to breed must be constrained by global policies, and as one demographer has pointedly remarked . . . "we know more about what people expect, want and do with respect to planting wheat or purchasing T.V. sets than with respect to having babies" (Stycos, 1963).

REFERENCES

Balikci, A. (1967). Female infanticide on the Arctic coast. *Man* 2, 615-625.
Binford, L. R. (1968). Post-Pleistocene adaptations. *In* "New Perspectives in Archaeology" (S. R. and L. R. Binford, eds.), pp. 313-341. Aldine, Chicago.
Birdsell, J. B. (1968). Some predictions for the Pleistocene based on equilibrium systems among recent hunter-gatherers. *In* "Man the Hunter" (R. B. Lee and I. DeVore, eds.), pp. 229-240. Aldine, Chicago.
Christian, J. J. (1950). The adrenal-pituitary system and population cycles in mammals. *J. Mammal.* 31, 247-259.
Cole, L. C. (1954). The population consequences of life history phenomena. *Q. Rev. Biol.* 29, 103-137.
Davis, K. (1967). Population policy: will current programs succeed? *Science, N.Y.* 158, 730-739.
DeJong, G. (1965). Religious fundamentalism, socio-economic status, and fertility attitudes in the southern Appalachians. *Demography* 2, 540-548.

Demeny, P. (1968). Early fertility decline in Austria-Hungary: a lesson in demographic transition. *Proc. Am. Acad. Arts* **97**, 502-522.

Douglas, M. (1966). Population control in primitive groups. *Brit. J. Sociol.* **17**, 263-273.

Freedman, R. (1963). Norms for family size in underdeveloped areas. *Proc. R. Soc. B* **159**, 220-245.

Freeman, M. M. R. (in press). Ethos, economics and prestige: a re-examination of Netsilik Eskimo infanticide. *Proc. 38 int. congr. Americanists.*

Glass, D. V. (1960). Population growth, fertility, and population policy. *Adv. Sci., Lond.,* November 1960, 1-11.

Hanley, S. B. (1968). Population trends and economic development in Tokugawa, Japan. *Proc. Am. Acad. Arts* **97**, 622-635.

Hardin, G. (1963). The cybernetics of competition: a biologist's view of society. *Perspec. Biol.* **7**, 58-84.

Hardin, G. (1968). The tragedy of the commons. *Science, N.Y.* **162**, 1243-1248.

Hardin, G. (1969). *In* "Population, Evolution and Birth Control" (G. Hardin, ed.), pp. 278-282. W. H. Freeman, San Francisco.

Heer, D. M. (1966). Economic development and fertility. *Demography* **3**, 423-444.

Heer, D. M. and Smith, D. O. (1968). Mortality level, desired family size, and population increase. *Demography* **5**, 104-121.

Knodel, J. (1968). Infant mortality and fertility in three Bavarian villages: an analysis of family histories from the 19th century. *Popul. stud.* **22**, 297-318.

Krebs, C. J. (1964). The lemming cycle at Baker Lake, Northwest Territories, during 1959-62. *Tech. Pap. Arctic. Inst. N. Amer.* **15**, 1-104.

Langer, W. L. (1963). Europe's initial population explosion. *Amer. Hist. Rev.* **69**, 1-17.

Lee, R. B. (1968). What hunters do for a living, or, How to make out on scarce resources. *In* "Man the Hunter" (R. B. Lee and I. DeVore, eds.), pp. 30-48. Aldine, Chicago.

Lee, R. B. and DeVore, I. (1968). Problems in the study of hunters and gatherers. *In* "Man the Hunter" (R. B. Lee and I. DeVore, eds.), pp. 3-12. Aldine, Chicago.

Livingstone, F. B. (1967). The effects of warfare on the biology of the human species. *Nat. Hist.* **76**, 61-65.

McKeown, T. and Brown, R. G. (1955). Medical evidence related to English population changes in the eighteenth century. *Popul. stud.* **9**, 119-141.

Rappaport, R. A. (1968). "Pigs for the Ancestors". Yale University Press, New Haven.

Rose, F. G. G. (1968). Australian marriage, land-owning groups, and initiations. *In* "Man the Hunter" (R. B. Lee and I. DeVore, eds.), pp. 200-208. Aldine, Chicago.

Sahlins, M. D. (1968). Notes on the original affluent society. *In* "Man the Hunter" (R. B. Lee and I. DeVore, eds.), pp. 85-89. Aldine, Chicago.

Spengler, J. J. (1966). Values and fertility analysis. *Demography* **3**, 109-130.

Spengler, J. J. (1967). Population optima. *In* "The 99th Hour" (D. O. Price, ed.), pp. 29-50. University of North Carolina Press, Chapel Hill.

Stott, D. H. (1962). Cultural and natural checks on population growth. *In* "Culture and the Evolution of Man" (M. F. Ashley-Montagu, ed.), pp. 355-376. Oxford University Press, New York.

Stycos, J. M. (1963). Obstacles to programs of population control—facts and fancies. *Marr. fam. liv.* **25**, 5-13.

Stys, W. (1957). The influence of economic conditions on the fertility of peasant women. *Popul. stud.* **11**, 136-148.

Vayda, A. P. and Rappaport, R. A. (1963). Island cultures. *In* "Man's Place in the Island Ecosystem" (F. R. Fosberg, ed.), pp. 133-142. Bishops Museum Press, Honolulu.

Wrigley, E. A. (1968). Mortality in pre-industrial England: the example of Colyton, Devon, over three centuries. *Daedalus* **97**, 546-580.

Yalman, N. (1963). On the purity of women in the castes of Ceylon and Malabar. *J. R. Anthrop. Inst.* **93**, 25-58.

CHAPTER 12

Population Control or Hobson's Choice

P. R. EHRLICH

Stanford University

There is a growing consensus of opinion that the fate of Western Civilization will be sealed by events of the next decade or so; this makes writing about the effects of world conditions on Britain in the year 2000 quite a challenging assignment. The first question which must be considered is whether the situation at the turn of the century can be predicted by extrapolation of trends now obvious, or whether major discontinuities will occur that will make such projections rubbish. Judging from events of the first two-thirds of the century, discontinuities will be the rule, not the exception. Indeed, many of the trends developing today seem to lead directly to such discontinuities. It would be extremely foolhardy, therefore, to expect accuracy in predicting 30 years into the future; it would be equally foolhardy, however, not to take a critical look at the major possibilities. The first four possibilities below assume, among other things, that there will be no effective world-wide population control. If there is not, Britain will be in the position of the patrons of Mr. Hobson's famous stable, who had to accept whichever horse was standing nearest the door. There will be little opportunity for some 60 million island people to select a future. It will be a question of taking what you get—Hobson's Choice.

THERMONUCLEAR WAR

There is a tendency for laymen and scientists to suppress thought or discussion of the possibility that a thermonuclear war might intervene in the "orderly" march of world events (Frank, 1967). For instance, even a supposedly systematic projection such as Kahn and Wiener's *The Year 2000* (1967) tends to discount the possibility. This is in part a tribute to the authors' faith in the efficacy of nuclear deterrence, a faith that is not surprising as Kahn was one of the major architects of deterrence theory. Unfortunately, deterrence theory depends on demonstrably false assumptions about human behaviour (Green, 1966), non-existent systems analysis, and inapplicable games theory.

In spite of the psychological need to discount the potential for thermonuclear war, such a conflict is clearly possible before the year 2000, and if one should occur before then it would be the major determinant of world conditions at the end of the century. At the moment the probabilities of general war seem to be rapidly increasing, not just because of ABMs, Middle Eastern tensions, and the Sino-Soviet confrontation, but because of more subtle world-wide developments. There is, indeed, every reason to believe that every person added to the world population adds ever so slightly to the odds favouring Armageddon. Systematic studies done by my colleague, Professor Robert North of Stanford's Department of Political Science, have added to the mass of anecdotal evidence that over-population is a factor leading to war. Professor Georg Borgstrom of Michigan State University has recently argued (1969) that the continuing growth of competition for water is a source of international tensions, involving the basins of the Mekong, Indus, Jordan, Nile, Euphrates-Tigris, Amur, Danube, and other rivers. Needless to say, demand for water is just one of the sources of conflict which can be traced in large part to population growth. Land shortage alone may be a major factor, as it was in the recent war between El Salvador and Honduras. Another factor, which is bound to escalate in importance over the next decade, is competition for fisheries. Unquestionably, generalized competition (in the biological sense*) will continue to increase as the population of the world increases. Access to petroleum, copper, wheat, beef and many other commodities will become critical problems for nations without ample domestic supplies. The over-developed and generally resource-poor countries such as the United States, Great Britain, Western Europe and Japan will find it increasingly difficult to maintain the favourable trade positions so necessary for their continued affluence, especially when they will be unable to offer food in exchange for the goods they need. People of the under-developed countries are acutely aware, for instance, that the prime commodity of all, protein, flows not from the well-fed to the hungry nations, but vice versa. As Borgstrom says (1969, p. 248), "One-third of the world's population can simply not expect that it will be allowed to continue to gulp down two-thirds of the world's food . . ."

When Sol M. Linowitz, United States Ambassador to the Organization of American States, returned in early 1969 he warned of coming "Communist" revolutions in Latin America. It does not take much of a crystal ball to see them coming. In most Latin American countries populations are doubling every 20–25 years, heralding an inevitable and continuing decline in standards of living. And this decline will occur where people have, as Adlai Stevenson put it, "rising expectations". It seems unlikely that governments favourable to the commercial interests of the United States and other developed countries can be maintained in power much longer. Some big question marks, from the point of view of the

---

* Biologists say that two organisms are in competition when they both are utilizing a resource which is not abundant enough fully to satisfy both, or where the presence of one organism impedes the access of the other to the resource.

probabilities of world war, are what the reaction of the developed countries, especially the U.S.A. and the U.S.S.R., will be to events in the under-developed countries, and the degree to which China might choose to involve herself in these affairs.

The future behaviour of China is a major source of uncertainty as far as population-related war pressures are concerned. The possibility of a United States-Soviet confrontation seems largely limited to Eastern Europe and the Middle East, but an expanding China, desperately seeking food, resources, and lebensraum on the Asiatic continent and in Africa, shows vast potential for triggering disaster. Her record to date has been analysed in detail by North (personal communication) and has been relatively more violent than previously thought. The Far Eastern situation is complicated by the high probability of Japan turning aggressively toward the Asiatic continent. Japan is desperately dependent on imports and fisheries for the maintenance of her population. She imports food equivalent to the agricultural products which she grows. Japan's fisheries supply fully one and a half times the protein produced by her farms (Borgstrom, 1967). With a population growing fast enough to double every 63 years, and with the prospects of decreased yields from the sea (and possibly decreased availability of food imports), Japan will have to find a safety valve somewhere, even if her population growth is slowed.

A final potential population-related source of international tensions must be mentioned. It is clear that man's polluting activities, especially those of the developed countries, are going to have increasingly profound effects on the lives of all humans. One needs only to think of the chlorinated-hydrocarbon eco-catastrophe now in progress and the great Rhine fish-kill of June 1969 to see the trend. But most severe are the possible consequences of pollution-caused weather modifications. As dust, CO_2, contrails, and other pollutants change the climate of the Earth and gradually begin to make our planet uninhabitable, some nations will feel the pinch first, and will call for drastic action. One might guess that less affected nations will be reluctant to do much, and another major area of international conflict will develop.

So, unpleasant as the prospect may seem, there are many reasons, both in conventional politics and on the population-food-environment front, for considering a thermonuclear war as possibly being the major determinant of Britain's A.D. 2000 environment. If it is, almost any rational analysis makes it seem likely that little of interest to the Briton of 1969 would remain. Immediate effects, of course, would vary with the size, nature, and timing of the attack. How many megatons targeted on the United Kingdom? Are they detonated at ground level or above (an important variable affecting the amount of fall-out and the size of fire storms and conflagrations)? Are they aimed at military facilities or population centres or both? Is the attack carried out before or after the harvest is gathered? These and many other questions would have to be answered before any semi-precise estimate of total damage could be made. In general, however, in any situation (barring a possible, carefully limited air-burst strike against military facilities) the prognosis for the survival of British civilization as we know it is negative.

Any attack involving population centres, especially London and the Midlands, would strike a lethal blow to the British nation. And from heavy levels of death and injury from blast, fire, and fall-out, the economy would be utterly wrecked. The simultaneous destruction of a large portion of the transport system and power net, the decapitation of industry and finance, and the total demolition of key industries would make recovery all but impossible. Britain would seem especially vulnerable to damage which would cause the kind of downward economic spiral described by Stonier (1963) in his consideration of the possible effects of thermonuclear war in the United States. In addition, recovery from the gross ecological, psychological and medical effects of an attack would undoubtedly be hampered by the small size of Britain. No substantial hinterland would be available from which relief could come. The dissipation of world trade which would inevitably accompany a general war would make economic or other help from overseas problematical. Presumably most nations, at least in the northern hemisphere, would be in need of help, not potential aid donors.

In the unlikely event of a major thermonuclear war *not* involving Britain the outlook still would be grim. Britain's viability would depend on the kinds of factors enumerated above. Should, for instance, huge amounts of smoke and debris be added to the already overburdened atmosphere, then cooling comparable to that accompanying the 1815 eruption of Tomboro (in what is now Indonesia) could occur, destroying, at least temporarily, England's agricultural production. If trade were heavily disrupted, the United Kingdom might well face starvation. If sufficient dust were added to the atmosphere, a vicious cycle of cooling could set in, leading to greater snow corridors, increase of the Earth's albedo, further cooling, and so on. If enough of the North Atlantic were to freeze over, the Gulf Stream could be deflected (Humphreys, 1940; Stonier, 1963), altering the climate of England and Europe more or less permanently. There is considerable current controversy over the causation of ice ages, but the consensus seems to be that one may be brought on quite precipitously.

Similarly, increased silting of the North Sea and chemical run-off from ruined cities (assuming the European continent was hit) might seriously damage crucial fisheries, and fishing in general might suffer from a lack of fuel oil. And, of course, there would be the general health hazards of increased environmental radiation, to say nothing of the plagues which would almost certainly develop in a war-ravaged world, even if biological warfare were not used.

In short, world population growth is almost certainly contributing to the chances of a thermonuclear war. In the absence of population control it may be the "Hobson's Choice" that England ultimately confronts; and her chances of surviving it, as something resembling the nation she is today, are slim.

WORLD-WIDE PLAGUE

At the present time the world has the largest, densest population of human beings that it has ever seen. And every year an additional 70 million souls are being added to the approximately 3.6 billion already present. In addition to the densest population, it is also the weakest. Some 1–2 billion people are now under-nourished or malnourished and their situation seems likely to deteriorate. Add to this our great capacity for transporting sick people rapidly around the world, and you have the potential for an epidemic unparalleled in human history. Even without further environmental deterioration the health hazard is great; a mutant flu virus could readily decimate mankind. Furthermore, there is a grave threat of accidental escape (or deliberate use) of biological warfare agents. Superviruses, constructed "on order", give even poor nations the possibility of creating doomsday weapons. There are already rumours, for instance, of a pneumonic form of rabies, which, if it were transmissible before symptoms appeared, could wipe out most of mankind. And, if the world faces the kind of breakdown anticipated in the next section, many of mankind's ancient scourges, plague, typhus, cholera, malaria, and so forth, may again become preponderant.

Because of Britain's insular position and relatively high quality of medical care (in infant mortality, a good indication of the quality of such care, the United Kingdom in 1966 ranked number 10 in the world, the U.S.A. number 15), she would be in a better position than most countries to ward off infection. But, again, her dependence on trade makes her position vulnerable. If we can infer from the history of past catastrophes (Langer, 1958; Stonier, 1963; Frank, 1967), it seems likely that world trade would suffer serious derangement, and that Britain, for purposes of quarantine, would stringently have to limit access to English ports of those ships still operating.

Should a major epidemic hit England, its effects would be likely to change British attitudes and behaviour for centuries, even if the other disasters dealt with in this paper are avoided. Such relatively minor events as the Irish potato famine have had long-lasting consequences for the societies involved. A plague killing perhaps one-half or more of the population could easily cause the collapse of British society. Disruption of food supplies, riots (especially among those attempting to flee from affected areas), breakdown of garbage collection, disruption of water supplies, cessation of fire-fighting and police protection, and so forth would probably create horrors beyond even those experienced in England during the Black Death of the Fourteenth Century (to say nothing of the London blitz!). If nothing else, the degree of change in the life of the average citizen would be much greater now than then. But the overall consequences of a world plague for the England of the year 2000 would depend on the state of so many variables that any kind of detailed prediction would be reckless. About the most that can be said is that, if Mr. Hobson's horse is plague, the results may be less severe than in the case of thermonuclear war, but they hardly present a pleasing prospect.

ECO-CATASTROPHE

A final type of gross discontinuity in projections of the world future must be mentioned—eco-catastrophe. An eco-catastrophe is a widespread, strongly deleterious change in the human environment. Signs of past, rather minor eco-catastrophes are easily seen in such places as the Tigris and Euphrates valleys, the Sahara desert, and Angkor Wat. Today we seem to be witnessing the start of a global eco-catastrophe caused by the action of chlorinated hydrocarbons released into the environment. The nature and current extent of this disaster is so well publicized (summary in Ehrlich and Ehrlich, 1970) that I need not deal further with it here. The chlorinated hydrocarbon situation *could* lead to the loss of virtually all food from the sea, and a great reduction in the amount which may be obtained from terrestrial agriculture. It also may lead to greatly reduced life expectancies world-wide. Hopefully, however, the manufacture and dissemination of these compounds will be halted before it is too late (unless, of course, we have unknowingly passed the point of no return already).

If population is controlled, it should be possible to stop air pollution before the entire planet becomes uninhabitable. Pollution increases gradually, and is more or less reversible, although its reversal may mean great expense and hardship. The greatest danger of a generalized eco-catastrophe originating in air pollution lies in the possibility of dramatic changes in the weather. There are, for instance, several ways in which a new ice age could be rapidly generated—one of which already has been mentioned in connection with thermonuclear war. Even in the absence of such a war the veil of pollution which now encircles the Earth might create sufficient cooling to start the downward spiral. On the other hand there are those (Wilson, 1964; Hollin, 1965; Haas, 1968) who feel that ice ages may start with the Antarctic ice cap slipping rapidly outward. The increase of the albedo resulting from a large increment in the area occupied by ice creates the necessary cooling effect. Most Britons, however, would be spared the after-effects of an ice age brought on in such a manner, since its initiation would create great tidal waves which would sweep over much of the British Isles.

On the other hand, an overall warming trend created by increased carbon dioxide in the atmosphere might cause the planetary "heat engine" to turn over more rapidly, perhaps producing dramatic cooling in England or changing her weather for the worse in some other way. Another possibility is that the course of the jet streams will be altered, perhaps indirectly as a result of contrails of high-flying jet aircraft. The contrails form the nuclei of cirrus clouds which, in ways not fully understood, deflect jet streams. And, of course, there are always the possibilities of dramatic changes wrought by the contrails of high-flying supersonic transports (SSTs). The SST, even without considering its ecological effects, must surely be viewed as a major competitor for the prize of "most ridiculous non-military technological development of all time". But when possible ecological problems related to its contrails and exhausts are considered, it has the potential for becoming a major threat to humanity. The exact meteorological consequences for the weather of SST effluents deposited above the tropopause do not seem to be predictable at this time; we shall have to wait for this most interesting experiment to be run.

The climate of the Earth is, of course, changing gradually all of the time, and man already has had considerable influence on it, especially through deforestation and the creation of deserts. In the last century, for instance, man has increased the amount of the Earth's land surface that is desert or wasteland from less than 10% to about 25% (Doane, 1957). Further acceleration of change, no matter what the direction, cannot but adversely affect the carrying capacity of the planet, at least in the short run. The reason for this is simple: agriculture is extremely dependent on climate and agricultural practices are slow to change. Any substantial reduction in the amount of available food will be bad for Britain, dependent as she is on imported food. Should, for instance, changes in the course of the jet stream create an "instant desert" in the mid-west of the United States and freeze the plains of Canada, the United Kingdom will be in deep trouble. For, instead of drawing on these two countries for food, she would find herself in competition with them for sustenance.

It seems quite likely that one of the horses close to the door of Mr. Hobson's stable is named "Eco-catastrophe", but his breed is uncertain. As the human population grows, so do man's polluting activities, and so (at least so far) does his dependence on ecologically ignorant agricultural practices. Without population control, or even with it (since at least several decades will pass before it could be effective), mankind will have to face a series of difficult-to-grasp but very potent threats to the life-support systems of the planet.

CURRENT TRENDS CONTINUE—THE DOWNWARD SPIRAL

What if there are no drastic discontinuities between now and the year 2000? What kind of year will Englishmen face then? Assuming current trends continue, some reasonably certain statements can be made. All resource-poor countries, those whose standard of living depends heavily on imports, will suffer declines in their standard of living. The United States and Great Britain both will suffer, the latter more severely because of its less favourable resource position. As the population of the world grows, it will be impossible for England to maintain her present level of imports. The proportion of the world's people who are hungry will escalate rapidly, and the flow of protein from under-developed countries (UDCs) to developed countries (DCs) will slow or cease. Political turmoil will be the rule over much of the world, and the starving UDCs will be attempting to get food in exchange for their hard resources. Under these circumstances, England may find it extremely difficult to import the materials that her industrial plant requires. A partial list of these resources which must be obtained from outside the British Isles includes petroleum, iron, chromium, copper, tin, lead, manganese, molybdenum, mercury, magnesium, tungsten, vanadium and zinc (United Nations, 1967). It is interesting to note that projections of United States cumulative demand (1960–2000) indicate that the United States alone *plans* to use virtually all of the non-Communist world's reserves of some of these minerals—especially tungsten and copper—and far more than her "fair share" of most of the rest (Landsberg *et al,* 1963). Furthermore, both phosphate rock and potash, critical to British agricultural production, must be imported. According to the 1966 U.N. figures, Britain produces only 49% of the wheat she consumes, 71% of the other cereals, 97% of the potatoes, 37% of the sugars, 13% of the pulses, nuts, and seeds, and 65% of the meat. It would appear that even if the fertilizers were available to keep production up, a Britain unable to obtain imports of food would be in deep trouble.

Britain, then, by the turn of the century, probably will be extremely hard-pressed to feed her population. A general decline of world fisheries, from over-exploitation and pollution and increased competition from other nations (especially Russia and Japan), will have greatly reduced the amount of food which Britain can extract from the sea. Expansion of her terrestrial agriculture is virtually impossible. That lesson was learned during the First and Second World Wars when the government had to stop the ploughing of marginal land and over-grazing, in order to prevent massive soil erosion (Borgstrom, 1969).

Even in the absence of clear-cut eco-catastrophe, Britain probably will suffer heavily, both directly and indirectly, from world ecological conditions by the year 2000. Global air pollution will affect the health of all citizens, regardless of whether they live in the industrial Midlands or the mountains of Scotland. Chlorinated hydrocarbon loads will likely be increasing the death rates from various nervous disorders, hypertension, cirrhosis of the liver, hepatic cancer, and so on. Death rates from emphysema, bronchitis, and other respiratory diseases will have sky-rocketed. As diseases such as plague, cholera, and various "flu's" create vast epidemics, Britain will find it more and more difficult to isolate and protect her increasingly malnourished population.

Finally, there will be the psychological trauma for the British population engendered by decades of economic decay and loss of world influence. If current trends continue, by the year 2000 the United Kingdom will simply be a small group of impoverished islands, inhabited by some 70 million hungry people, of little or no concern to the other 5–7 billion people of a sick world. No—if the horse that Britain gets from Mr. Hobson's stable is named "Downward Spiral" the British will have little to cheer about. But neither will anyone else.

CURRENT TRENDS DRAMATICALLY CHANGED

Is there any way that Britain can avoid Mr. Hobson's choice of one of those four nags, "Thermonuclear War", "Worldwide Plague", "Eco-catastrophe" or "Downward Spiral"? Can Hobson's stable be by-passed completely? There is a possibility, but it would involve a series of changes in human attitudes and behaviour that must be labelled Utopian. An obvious first step is to recognize the relationship between science and war. As the French scientists, Fetizon and Magat (1968) put it: "We must either eliminate science or eliminate war. We cannot have both." The super-powers must face the utter bankruptcy of the theory of nuclear deterrence (Green, 1966) and start replacing the gross risks of continuing the arms race with the lesser (but still perhaps serious) risks of disarmament. Such a move is essential, not just to avoid the ultimate disaster of a thermonuclear war, but also to free the resources needed for an attempt to avoid a "crash" in the human population—an end to civilization as we know it through a combination of famine, plague, and eco-catastrophe. The need for such a change has been clearly recognized on both sides of the Iron Curtain—it has been articulated recently by Academician Sakharov (1968) and Lord Snow (1969). Both feel that expenditures of the order of 20% of the gross national product of the rich countries will be necessary for the next decade or so if the growing UDC-DC gap is to be closed, and such figures are probably unrealistically low if the entire problem of arresting environmental deterioration is to be tackled. A basic problem, then, is a refocusing of the developed world's energies from unrealistic and eventually lethal arms races to an attempt to preserve civilization. This seems like a well-nigh hopeless task, but perhaps with the help of growing knowledge about human conflict and its resolution (*see* Frank, 1967, for summary) we might have a chance.

If the resources became available and the people of the DCs decided seriously to try to avoid the approaching disaster, what then? Population control in both DCs and UDCs is a *sine qua non* of success. It is not, of course, a panacea for all human problems, but, if achieved, would at least give mankind the opportunity of trying to solve the others. It is abundantly clear, for instance, that mankind will have great difficulty providing an adequate diet for 3.5 billion people by the year 2000, and that providing a proper diet for 7.0 billion by that time is out of the question (President's Science Advisory Committee, 1967; Paddock and Paddock, 1967; Borgstrom, 1969; Ehrlich and Holdren, 1969; Ehrlich and Ehrlich, 1970). Only the most determined disregard for biology, physics, human behaviour and economics permits any other conclusion (e.g. Clark, 1958). If we are lucky and if we initiate population control measures immediately, we might hope for some amelioration of the world food situation shortly before the turn of the century (there is a built-in time lag of decades before any programme of birth control can show results).

One factor working in mankind's favour is that population control should be easier to achieve in the developed countries, where, in at least one sense, population growth poses the greatest threat. These countries are the major wasters of protein and non-renewable resources. They are the source of the most threatening environmental decay. If the money to try and save civilization becomes available a great deal of it will be spent in the developed countries, helping to cure their over-development, clean up the environment, train ecologically knowledgeable agricultural technicians, plan population control programmes and train personnel to carry them out, and so forth. The problems of how to help the UDCs achieve population control and a reasonable level of agricultural development are especially complex and will require the co-ordinated efforts of a trained manpower pool which does not exist at present. This whole nexus of problems is dealt with in detail elsewhere (Ehrlich and Ehrlich, 1970).

The question always arises as to whether population control can be achieved by voluntary action. If by "voluntary action" is meant the standard family planning approach of "every child a wanted child", the answer is clearly no. The idea that the population problem can be solved by eliminating unwanted births has been thoroughly discredited (Davis, 1967). It is clear that governments, including eventually a world body, must undertake the task of regulating the population size just as they now attempt to regulate economies. There are many different ways in which this might be attempted beyond providing family planning programmes which include access to abortion and voluntary steriliza-tion. For instance, any policies which affect marriage ages, employment opportunities for women outside the home, and economic advantages or disadvantages for large families are likely to influence reproductive behaviour. Tax systems which favour single people and small families, preferably without penalizing the poor, and bonuses and lotteries for late marriage, delayed childbirth or childlessness are among the economic possibilities. Encouragement of adoption and stringent measures against illegitimate pregnancy, such as compulsory abortion and/or placement for adoption could be relatively direct policies against births. Provision of outside employment for women may be particularly helpful, and giving such assistance as paid maternity leave (perhaps limited to two babies) and day care would still probably encourage outside work more than it encouraged maternity.

Social climates also can be influenced by governments. Disapproval of more than two children per couple can be fostered, as can alternate life styles, such as easily dissoluble marriages for the childless. At present there is strong social pressure in many countries on people both to marry and to have children. This pressure could be reversed, and status become attached to the free and single individual and to childless couples.

Sex education, which includes instruction in birth control and moral stress on the social responsibilities involved in reproduction, certainly should be a part of government policy. These measures do not involve compulsion; they do involve governmental manipulation. But such manipulation by government and industry is already accepted as an integral part of our lives, and indeed seems to increase along with the population. Those who have a vested interest in promoting "family planning" (often combined with an acceptance of the most outlandish fantasies of agriculturists and a total ignorance of ecology), tend to discount the value of other approaches (e.g. Berelson, 1969). Perhaps they are right, but I believe, in view of the patent failure of family planning, that various population control programmes must be tried immediately, while simultaneously research into the possibilities of compulsory family size regulation goes ahead at top speed. For, if the world continues to listen to the siren song of the myopic optimists, it will wake up one day to find out that *compulsory* birth control offers the only hope of survival. Not all compulsory methods are necessarily horrifying. Indeed, Ketchel (1968) has argued cogently that a mass fertility reducing agent, administered to everyone, would be the most democratic and humane method of controlling the population.

There is little doubt in my mind that, given the necessary changes in human attitude, a successful attempt could be made to pull us through what is clearly the most dramatic crisis *Homo sapiens* has ever faced. Certainly there will be an escalation in suffering before an amelioration is achieved. As Professor Borgstrom (1969) has said, "There are not many oases left in a vast, almost world-wide network of slums." Even with the most dramatic programmes, the general deterioration of the planet and of the human condition cannot be halted instantly. But, if the effort is made, it is possible that by the early part of the 21st century the *quality* of the average human life could far surpass that of today.

I would be less than honest if I expressed the conviction that such a change will occur. If I were a gambler, I would take even money that England will not exist in the year 2000, and give 10 to 1 that the life of the average Briton would be of distinctly lower quality than it is today. I am afraid that they and all the peoples of the world are going to end up, figuratively, at Mr. Hobson's stable.

REFERENCES

Berelson, B. (1969). Beyond family planning. *Science, N.Y.* **163**, 7 February, 533–543.

Borgstrom, G. (1967). "The Hungry Planet", rev. ed. Collier Books, New York.

Borgstrom, G. (1969). "Too Many". Macmillan, New York.

Clark, C. (1958). World population. *Nature, Lond.* 181, 1235–1236.

Davis, K. (1967). Population policy: Will current programs succeed? *Science, N.Y.* 158, 10 November, 730-739.

Doane, R. R. (1957). "World Balance Sheet". Harper, New York.

Ehrlich, P. R. and Holdren, J. Population and panaceas. *Bioscience* (in press).

Ehrlich, P. R. and Ehrlich, A. H. "Population, Food, and Environment." Freeman (in press).

Fetizon, M. and Magat, M. (1968). "The Toxic Arsenal". *In* "Unless Peace Comes" (Nigel Calder, ed.), p. 146. Viking Compass, New York.

Frank, J. D. (1967). "Sanity and Survival". Vintage, New York.

Green, P. (1966). "Deadly Logic". Schoken, New York.

Haas, E. (1968). Common opponent sought . . . and found? *Bull. Atomic Scient.* November, 8–11.

Hollin, J. T. (1965). Wilson's theory of ice ages. *Nature, Lond.* 208 (5005), 12–16.

Humphreys, W. T. (1940). "Physics of the Air". McGraw-Hill Book Company, New York.

Kahn, H. and Weiner, A. J. (1967). "The Year 2000". Macmillan, New York.

Ketchel, M. M. (1968). Fertility control agents as a possible solution to the world population problem. *Perspect. Biol. Med.* 687–703.

Landsberg, H. H., Fischman, L. L. and Fisher, J. L. (1963). "Resources in America's Future. Patterns of Requirements and Availabilities 1960–2000". Johns Hopkins Press, Baltimore.

Langer, W. L. (1958). The next assignment. *Am. Hist. Rev.* 63, 283-304.

Paddock, W. and Paddock, P. (1967). "Famine—1975". Little, Brown and Co., Boston.

President's Science Advisory Committee. (1967). Panel on World Food Problem, *World Food Problem.* Washington, D.C.

Sakharov, A. D. (1968). "Progress, Coexistence, and Intellectual Freedom". New York Times Book, New York.

Snow, C. P. (1969). "The State of Siege". Charles Scribner's Sons, New York.

Stonier, T. (1963). "Nuclear Disaster". Meridian, Cleveland.

United Nations (1967). *International Trade Statistics Yearbook.* New York.

Wilson, A. T. (1964). Origin of ice ages: an ice shelf theory for Pleistocene glaciation. *Nature, Lond.* 201 (4915), 147–149.

Discussion

D. BURLESON: Dr. Freeman, I want to take issue with the use of the term "institutionalization of infanticide in Britain". I think that this is an incorrect use of the term in its sociological or anthropological sense. Apparently there was a wide degree of *tolerance* of infanticide in Great Britain during the period under discussion, but it was never made a part of the "institutionalized" social fabric in any way comparable to the way infanticide has been practised in primitive societies and in parts of Asia.

M. M. R. FREEMAN: The term institutionalized refers more to the *de facto* demise of children in foundling hospitals than any *de jure* homicidal process. Malthus went so far as to observe that a proliferation of orphanages and foundling hospitals would serve as a major check on rapid population increases in contemporary Europe. Langer's paper, to which I refer, mentions other ways in which risk of infanticide was increased by the child-care practices of the day.

In reply to a question involving the procreative desires of men, whereas women are the object of clinical programmes.

M. M. R. FREEMAN: Perhaps realistic government demographic policies will require more female representation on the executive of political bodies. In several less developed countries, education of the men may be far more important than focusing the propaganda at women, many of whom are only too aware of the connection between large families, poverty and poor health. In Puerto Rico, for example, men appear to have purely egoistic reasons for starting large families immediately after marriage, so that programmes aimed at the wives are an utter waste of time and money (J. M. Stycos in "Health, Culture and Community", Russel Sage Foundation, New York, 1955).

T. R. E. SOUTHWOOD: Dr. Freeman, is it likely that reduced nutrition will produce infertility in man?

M. M. R. FREEMAN: The evidence suggests that man has powers of ecophenotypic adaptation such that fertility remains high even with falling and inadequate food supply—hence the existence of a population problem in the world today. The levels of nutritional stress required to depress permanently man's fertility are so extreme (e.g. concentration camp conditions) that we can extract no comfort from the existence of such involuntary checks on population growth.

K. MELLANBY: In my paper I said that I thought that pollution, in Britain, need not be a limiting factor affecting population growth in the next 30 years. I said that if we used our existing knowledge, even with an increased population,

Britain might be cleaner in the year 2000 than it is today. However, if we do not use this knowledge, and if population is not controlled, I agree that pollution will eventually be disastrous, but this can be put off for some considerable time.

Professor Ehrlich has painted a very different picture. I disagree entirely with his statement about the dangers from organochlorine pesticides, which he has equated as a potential danger of the same magnitude as a nuclear war. Organochlorines have indeed done harm to some forms of wildlife, particularly to vertebrate predators, and residues are widespread. I agree that if organochlorines were used more widely and without proper controls they could do serious ecological damage. However, I am convinced that long before the year 2000 we shall have phased out these insecticides, and replaced them with less persistent chemicals and with non-chemical methods of pest control.

P. R. EHRLICH: I hope that Dr. Mellanby is right about the organochlorines going out of use, although we see no real sign of that in the United States at the moment. DDT is now the most ubiquitous synthetic molecule in the world, and it seems likely that its concentration in oceanic food chains will continue to increase over the next decade or so even if we cease its use immediately—a great deal of it is still lying around on the land. It could easily change the balance of the marine phytoplankton community in such a way as to greatly reduce or even eliminate our fisheries productivity. From all the latest estimates we seem doomed to a *per capita* decrease in our fisheries productivity over the next few decades anyway as we move from the present 60 million metric tons a year catch toward the theoretical limit of sustainable catch in the vicinity of 100 million metric tons. Since the oceans provide an extremely important component of the world's diet—about 20% of its animal protein—we are tinkering with a colossal disaster by continuing our use of organochlorines.

We of course have very suspicious signs that the heavy chlorinated hydrocarbon load isn't doing individual human beings much good either. There is some indication from experimental work in animals that DDT will produce liver tumors, and that it will also induce the production of certain liver enzymes. There is one study of a sample of human autopsies which shows a high correlation of DDT load with death from portal cirrhosis of the liver, liver cancer, softening of the brain, and hypertension. American biologists are virtually unanimous in their condemnation of the continuing heavy use of organochlorines.

C. JEFFREY: I wonder if we have in fact, as Professor Southwood implied, increased the carrying capacity of our environment. Is it not rather that the changes wrought by man have merely increased the proportion of the world's biomass that is human flesh, without causing any increase in the biomass as a whole?

I feel Dr. Eversley's comparison of the population densities of Britain and Hong Kong is somewhat misleading, unless we understand fully what comprises the space occupied by a human being. This is made up of two components, a small direct area on which he physically lives, and a much larger indirect area being his share of the area taken up by the production of the food, goods and services he utilizes and affected by the activities he indulges in. Since only the much smaller direct space is strictly locality-dependent, it is obviously a fallacy to assume that pressure upon the environment is dependent only upon the local population density; it is largely independent of the distribution of population. Much of the population pressure on our environment exerted by the population of Hong Kong, for example, clearly falls on areas outside the territories of Hong Kong itself.

In a constant system we cannot maximize simultaneously for two variables, and even in a growing system it proves difficult to improve the environment while numbers continue to rise. If there are a million people in this country with housing so sub-standard as to be deemed virtually "homeless", then one contributory factor for this is surely that over the last five years we have had about 5,000,000 more young couples seeking accommodation than there would have been had our population been stable and not increasing at a rate of about 1000 per day. And, of course, the system cannot continue to grow indefinitely. For all practical purposes we have to accept that we cannot create matter, nor destroy it. We can merely alter its state, and what we can do with our technology is really very limited. The pollution problem is a good instance of this, as it is one frequently cited as being soluble technologically. But one cannot get rid of a waste product, one can merely convert it into something less inimical. But the inimicability of a substance is, unfortunately, concentration-dependent. One household in a country with its nearest neighbour 10 miles downstream can without stricture dump all its waste and sewage into the river; by the time it becomes his neighbour's drinking water the stream will have purified itself. Replace the two neighbours by two settlements of 500 people and the situation is changed; the sewage must be processed to inorganic wastes before it can be released. When the settlements become towns of 50,000 even this is not enough, for the inorganic wastes themselves would overburden the river's ecosystem and by eutrophication destroy it. The processed sewage would have to be piped directly to the sea, there merely to add to the pollution of the waters of the continental shelf. To conclude, the greater our population pressure becomes, the less becomes our freedom to choose. We must decide which we value most, our numbers, our affluence or our freedom. Technology cannot make the choice for us, nor can it enable us to avoid making it.

R. BARRASS: I hold the opinion that this country is already over-populated. None of our speakers has had, as a brief, the task of presenting the case that the present population is at, above or below an optimal level. We would need more research, perhaps, before the case could be presented. Is this country over-populated? Clearly many people are unable to support or look after themselves or their family but is this number a greater or smaller percentage than in the past? Is the present great need for welfare an indication that we have too many people already? We may find indications of over-population by looking at changes in both the environment and in the people.

Professor Eversley distinguishes man from animals on the grounds of man's ability to learn from experience. Man's actions often suggest that human populations do not learn from experience. Many regions of the world are no longer cultivated because of misuse and yet in other regions we still misuse the land. Professor Eversley sees in overspill and dispersion a relief of population problems in this country but to me these are both forms of erosion of the ecosystem, and in this sense they represent irreversible forms of pollution.

As a biologist I should like to see the survival of other living organisms than man himself and organisms needed for the food of man. We can attempt to do this by designating green belts, nature reserves and national parks, but experience indicates that these can only be maintained until there arises some other superficially greater economic need. Biologists should do more to emphasize the importance of their science and to teach non-biologists, concerned with population problems, the importance of the ecosystem.

E. BROOKS: I speak from some personal experience of the politics of family planning in Britain. After half a century of dedicated—and frequently courageous—voluntary effort by the pioneers, it would be tempting to see the unopposed passage of the 1967 Family Planning Act as proof of their victory and vindication.

But such optimisms, and complacency, would be premature. Financial restrictions, indifference and concealed hostility are still present, and it is sufficient to recall that Scotland has still not been included by the Government within the provisions of the legislation. Unrelenting pressure upon the authorities to implement the Act is vital, particularly if headway is to be made in providing a comprehensive service. In particular we need a broader and more flexible concept of a family planning service. We need to provide domiciliary help, linked closely with the work of maternity hospitals. Women at risk will not necessarily attend F.P.A. clinics, however many are opened. But by the very nature of their predicament, they are likely to be regular visitors to the ante-natal and post-natal clinics of hospitals, and here there is much scope for fresh initiative. Such developments will not take place without conscious effort and planning, and the next year or so will provide an excellent opportunity to press such new ideas.

For example we are about to see far-reaching changes in the personal social services of local authorities in the light of the Seebohm Report. Incidentally, family planning does not gain even a mention in the index of that Report, although it is obvious that many of the other problems encountered by families arise from the uncontrolled fertility from which, in a real sense, they suffer.

Then, too, we shall shortly see the reorganization of local government following the Maud Report. In conjunction with fresh thinking about the future of the National Health Service tri-partite structure—on which public discussion will be fostered by the Ministry's Green Paper—this is a critical moment in the evolution of our health and welfare services. This is the time to stake the claim of family planning as an integral part of such services, and unless we succeed in this aim within the coming months, a golden opportunity may have been lost for ever.

I recognize, of course, that family planning is not the same thing as population control. The relationship is one of complexity, and I accept that the technical knowledge which facilitates the spacing of a family is not the same thing as the social motivation which persuades—or instructs—those families to restrict their numbers. Yet without a comprehensive family planning service, it is plain that many people will be born who would not otherwise have added to the pressure of numbers.

To those of us who view with some anxiety the swelling pressure of numbers in Britain, it therefore seems plain that voluntary family planning *and restriction* is a desirable objective. I hold to this view in the face of those arguments which seem to suggest that geographical maldistribution rather than absolute numbers is our major problem.

In 1940 The Barlow Report identified the costs incurred by the congestion in the south-eastern parts of Britain, and much of post-war regional policy has been designed to redress that imbalance between the fortunate and unfortunate areas which was leading to large-scale net migration to the south-east. Yet as the South-East Study of five years ago pointed out—and the picture is still substantially the same today—a massive extra concentration of population is pouring into this congested region. It is pouring in via the net reproduction rate, rather than inward migration, but the costs of congestion within this widespread urban region are no less worrying than they were 30 years ago.

The population of London may be falling; but to draw comfort from this decanting of people to the periphery seems to me mistaken. What we are seeing is basically a redistribution of people within a single Metropolitan Region, rather than a net outflow to Highland Britain. And on top of this the already highly populated south-eastern quadrant of our country is accumulating the substantial surplus of births over deaths. To regard all this as an Act of God, and one which cannot be affected by legislation, financial pressures or public education, seems a confession of weakness.

But I am also concerned about the underprivileged, the socially inadequate and mentally handicapped. For these people the treadmill of motherhood is a social evil. If only to help such people as these, I would urge most strongly that we need Government initiative in the field of population restriction. It is for these families that a domiciliary service of contraceptive advice can provide a therapy from which both they and the country as a whole would rapidly benefit.

MRS. M. OGDEN: I speak from the standpoint (1) of a biology teacher and mother of two children, (2) that the population of Great Britain should be less rather than more, and (3) that our basic population problem is excessive desire for children as well as the birth of unwanted children.

Though I recognize our own obligation to stop at two children, our selfish desire for a third will probably be too strong. I will give three reasons why we want a third child, and for each suggest some legislative reforms which might lessen this desire.

Firstly both my husband and I are "only" children. We have the sole responsibility for two sets of grandparents. We would not like one of our children to face this, therefore, having a third is an insurance for our old age. *Legislation:* Much more humane provision for the aged in society. Many more private unit flatlets grouped near communal facilities for main meals, nursing care and social facilities.

Secondly, both our children are girls. Many friends with one of each sex are happy to stop at two; with two boys they are often too exhausted to contemplate another; with two girls they usually want to have another go! *Legislation:* By the year 2000 there could perhaps be free sex typing of the second child by the technique of partial ectogenesis, but there are ethical and personal objections to such interference and it would probably be too expensive for universal use. Any legislation which improved the status of woman would help parents to feel as fulfilled by having girls as by having boys. Parents would be able to follow a daughter's career with the same interest as that of a son.

Thirdly, under current tax systems it is ridiculous for me to go back to work part-time until our youngest daughter is aged five and at school. So for the next three and a half years the "plant" is, so to speak, lying idle. I might just as well use it to have another child, though this is merely prolonging the day. *Legislation:* Most of the seven suggestions I give will improve the status of women. But I would first like to query whether men in fact want this?

1. Improve the tax and legal status of women; tax all women as single persons.
2. To encourage women to feel that working is normal all women should pay full National Insurance from the age of 18-65.
3. To enable women to pay insurance they must be given a maternity grant for a maximum of 10 years leave.
4. After our 10 years of paid maternity leave we would be expected to return to work either full or part-time.
5. As these married women would be expected to work it would be necessary to find suitable employment near to their homes.
6. Greatly improved provisions would be needed for school-age children between 4 and 6 p.m. and during school holidays.

7. During the period when children were too young for school it should be possible for a married woman to work part-time. If I were encouraged to employ a nanny and char this might get them and myself back to work and away from maternal broodyness.

J. PARSONS: I want to make the point that population is a *political* question and the optimum question should be decided through public debate. We have no experts to optimize our governmental processes—or the educational system—we have to do the best we can by means of *ad hoc* measures and successive approximations—it is *unreasonable* to expect biologists to provide the answer to this very delicate question, we, as a society, must decide for ourselves.

Perhaps biologists, or committees of biologists, sociologists, economists, and other experts could help and advise but the question is political—it must be tossed into the political arena and decided there.

At the moment secret committees are sitting in this country to decide what its "carrying capacity" is—of course they aren't called "secret" committees, they are called "confidential". In one respect I welcome this activity at a high level—interdepartmental committees—and the fact that the government is sufficiently concerned to do something about it. In another respect I resent it—this should be a *public* debate, not one conducted in secret, *I* want to be consulted, we should *all* be consulted and this is why I am arguing that the optimization of population should be decided by political means and not left to "experts". We should all be involved in the great debate about how many people can dwell in safety, comfort and freedom in this land of ours.

D. BURLESON: First, I would like to ask, "How many politicians are there here?" I think that we are making a mistake in constantly referring to politicians as actors in government. Much of our discussion has equated politics with the legislative tasks. Government includes a large number of other institutional approaches and bodies, beyond the administrative, judicial and legislative. Education is one of these—and we have used the word education rather loosely here today.

We have a huge education problem ahead of us and in this I share the impatience of Mr. Brooks. We have the task of preparing hundreds of thousands of teachers around the world to work with ecological and cultural materials. I have listened with great interest to all the papers presented—and much of the time I was deeply impressed at how well the various participants did excellent jobs within their own fields. Practically no one ventured beyond his own field. You in Britain seem to do an excellent job of specializing. We in America perhaps are sometimes too reckless at speculating or asserting things beyond our competency. Nevertheless, I think that this conference has made it clear that we have to get beyond our own fields. During the past six months I have been using the term *cultural ecology* to describe the kind of learning that I believe all of us need. You from the biological sciences need to learn more about the cultural spheres of knowledge, just as we in the social sciences need desperately to learn some good ecology to put man correctly into his natural (and now predominantly man-made) environment.

Life in the 20th century is becoming more and more a race between numbers and the quality of life. Participants and those about to become participants in this vital revolution require an education that includes a consideration of population problems.

The development of population education does not require the introduction of new courses into already overloaded curricula. Rather, incorporation of population education materials into a variety of fields such as civics, geography, history, sociology, mathematics, hygiene, psychology and home economics seems preferable. This technique minimizes the jarring reaction which usually results when teachers are handed new, unfamiliar material. Moderate substitution leaves the teacher's primary material practically the same.

S. G. LAWRENCE: I consider that the tendency of many contributions to this debate has been to present the optimum population as the highest figure we can reach without actually running into trouble and I should therefore like to draw attention to Lady Medawar's quotation from Maynard Keynes: "Is not a country overpopulated when its standards are lower than they would be if its numbers were less". However, in view of what Professor Ehrlich has just told us in his paper about the dangers to which Britain is exposed it may be that the smaller our population the less we should suffer if some of the dire possibilities he mentioned actually came to pass.

P. R. EHRLICH: I do not think that whatever action is taken in England will have any direct effect on the world crisis, although of course there are many things that the English could do to improve their chances of getting through the next few decades without the destruction of their society. However, there is a great deal that England can do indirectly by serving as a model. Many of the underdeveloped countries which were once British colonies still look to England, overtly or covertly, to set standards. For instance, if England should have the good sense to declare that she is overpopulated and take steps to control her population, that would undoubtedly make it much easier for certain governments in the underdeveloped countries to take similar steps. The same thing goes for banning certain insecticides, requiring certain kinds of environmental clean-up, and so forth.

M. M. R. FREEMAN: As this symposium nears its end, I am a little disquieted with the impression that divergent and perhaps irreconcilable points of view typify the alarmist biologists on the one hand, and the confident *laissez-faire* social scientists on the other. This is the more disturbing as I feel that opinions expressed in public by social scientists may carry more weight than biologists' opinions when discussion involves the human population dilemma.

Though invited here as a social scientist, I find myself unequivocally with the biologists at this time, though I am somewhat heartened by Professor Eversley's thoroughgoing analysis and his conclusion that rational management can ensure a continuation of the good life. However, I remain with the biologists because I think there is no certainty that the present decline in birth-rate will continue (indeed birth-rate is now rising in the United States) and my suspicion is that as living standards rise here, so will birth-rate *unless something is done about it*. Further, I anticipate a time in the immediate future when a preponderance of people will be an acute embarrassment to planners, for there just will not be enough jobs available, when post-industrial times are fully upon us.

I must stress the fact that in developed countries, where mortality rates are low, it takes only a very small increase in average family size to effect sustained and rapid growth of population. For example in the United States the difference between having two children per family and three is the difference between a stable population and one that doubles in about 43 years. Earlier in this symposium we were told that the three-child family is near the norm in Britain. The mind boggles at the prospect of twice as many people, twice as many cars on the roads, intense competition for resources, the need for strict controls. Stewart Udall has warned that though one can double-deck roads, and even cities, it is impossible to double-deck parks. Denials of one sort or another will be increasingly demanded with increasing population, and I suspect the privileged nations will feel the lowered quality of life more than the less privileged, and will be less able to adjust to the concomitant trauma.

No one at this symposium has yet proposed an optimum figure, and that is fortunate because on several grounds I believe that number has been exceeded; by ignoring such a painful statistic, participants are saved from having to contemplate or suggest ways of *reducing* population size, or controlling its further growth very stringently. I will suppose, for the sake of argument, that the present population of Britain is optimal and that it should remain stable so that the present quality can be maintained, though hopefully improved, but in any case stabilized, so that future gross deterioration of the environment is prevented.

In a developed country such as Britain, population stability is a definitely realizable goal. Furthermore, the means to achieve this goal are neither alien, excessively repugnant or politically unacceptable at this time, nor I believe are they excessively difficult or costly to effect. Further, as peoples' aspirations, achievements and ethical standards rise, the task of stabilizing population should become easier rather than harder. The goal is to produce an average of 2.0 children per family; some may have three children or even more, for others may choose to have none or just one.

Insofar as family size is determined by a conscious desire to have children, it becomes important to understand what needs a child fulfils in his parents, and to provide, wherever possible, institutional alternatives to satisfying or obviating those felt needs.

It is pertinent to note that social scientists believe that what type of behaviour is repeated and what is not repeated turns not so much on values and internal states (which change slowly), but whether particular kinds are consistently and continuously rewarded or not. In this view then, the rewards and sanctions that a society offers can be important means of fertility control.

As a start, society should take the pressure off young people to marry early and start families early; this can be effected by legislative reforms suggested in my paper and mentioned also in Dr. Ehrlich's paper. In summary, certain prerequisites must be met:

1. An increase in general awareness of the issues at stake, and the urgency in obtaining almost total compliance with the demographic goal being sought.

2. The need to variously decrease the dependence that adults place on childbearing as a means of self-validation or otherwise attaining or satisfying certain perceived psychological or social ends.

3. Continued need to expand the efficiency, availability and awareness of the full range of family planning measures and services available so that individuals and families can conform to the reproductive norm they choose to achieve within the limits allowed consonant with national goals.

4. An increase in national concern for the value of every child born, reflected in the best medical care, educational and occupational opportunities in each individual case.

This last is very important. It is not unreasonable to suppose that in return for requiring that parents produce fewer children, the system rewards them for compliance in the manner promised, viz. increased quality of life. This means jobs and training facilities, decent housing and so on, provided irrespective of geographical location, ethnic or social background or recency of arrival: there can be no question of maintaining a dual standard or undue privilege. From what anthropologists know of plural, multi-ethnic societies, it seems not unlikely that a group that feels threatened, culturally, if not socially, politically or economically, might revert to excessive childbearing as a deliberate means of averting what may be perceived by them as unfortunate consequences of their minority status.

If the necessary legislative reforms suggested in my paper appear unpalatable, let me return briefly to the reactions registered yesterday to remarks made by Professor Eversley, who quite correctly pointed out that we live in a finite world and we have to pay, in one way or another, for what we wish to get out of it. I saw no error in this logic; however, several people reacted strongly in favour of Sir David Renton when he suggested that to balance the equation by lowering living standards was quite unacceptable. Although most will agree with Sir David here, I must nevertheless stress the obvious, and say that what was rejected was not Professor Eversley's economic model, but one of several possibile solutions to the problem it posed. The model is not invalid, so it remains to find other solutions to the problem of maximizing returns within the constraints imposed by a finite system. The only way to rationalize the problem is by introducing controls: there are no other means, no simple panaceas; restraints are required. Population size and growth is dependent on the three variables: birth, death and migration. Migration begs the question (as we are dealing with a global problem), so control can only be exerted through increasing deaths or reducing births. There is absolutely no other way.

By way of encouragement let me remind you that Britain has already accepted a modal family of moderate size, a large degree of government control over the economy and various social processes, and liberal, and realistic, laws involving a full range of birth control practices. On the assumption that people wish to at least maintain the generally existing standard and pattern of living, and the further assumption that this is to be achieved within a democratically organized society that permits parenthood to all qualified couples, politicians and society at large must work towards two clear objectives:

1. To creat a society in which no unwanted child is born (for social rather than demographic reasons, see (4), p. 172) in which the decision to produce (*contra* conceive) a child, is made solely by the potential parents, and
2. To create a society in which decisions about childbearing are made in a social context that defines the three-child family as large.

POSTSCRIPT: G. P. HAWTHORN

"Because the occasion was a notable non-meeting between social scientists and biologists," wrote one commentator (*New Society* 2, October 1969, p. 504), "the publication of their papers in one book will be an important step towards future confrontations." Since a reading of the papers and the discussions on them (as always and perhaps inevitably at conferences, more statements than true exchanges) might confirm this judgement, and since confrontations rather than genuine discussions are undesirable, it is worth recording a few impressions after the event.

Social scientists do tend to concentrate on the social and economic environment in their arguments at the expense of the natural one. It was perfectly clear from the Symposium that any complacency about the future of the latter is unfounded. These different professional foci are an important cause of non-communication, since one environment is not fixed whereas the other is.

Against this, it is not analytically very useful to elicit distinctions between what is happening elsewhere, for instance in the United States and in Britain. One explanation for the greater despoilation and danger in America is that that is a society in which state control for the public good is not a familiar and accepted principle. This is quite separate from anything to do with population growth. Similarly, analogies from primitive societies in which the causal links between environment, population size and growth and the quality of social life are so much more direct are not especially illuminating, except as bases for constructing simplified models which will enable one to see what sorts of questions need to be asked. There are far closer connections between non-human population dynamics and those of primitive societies than there are between either of these and the social systems of complex societies.

It would, I think, be very interesting to have an analysis of the psychological mechanisms whereby slight shifts in the rate and direction of population growth seem to arouse extraordinarily intense reactions of fear and alarm. British population trends in the space of 20 years have alternately produced despondency about national decline and extinction and alarm about crowding and environmental decay quite disproportionate to their actual tendencies. [Economists were concerned at the falling birth-rates between the wars (Eversley, p. 105), biologists at the rising birth-rates since. Editor.]

Lastly, and against what may perhaps be construed as the lingering complacency of the last four paragraphs, there must be a more thorough discussion of the hiatus between the prevalent concerns of politicians in power, to make sure that things do not fall about their ears in their term of office, and the concerns of the informed population that goals and techniques for social and environmental management over much longer periods be formulated and implemented by such politicians. Paradoxically, the greater reliance by politicians on academic or quasi-academic advisers, who frequently conclude with customary professional caution that not enough is known, is a greater excuse than ever for inaction. My own, relative, complacency was moved enough by the Symposium to make me sure that the case for inaction is very much not proven.

Author Index

Numbers with an asterisk refer to pages in the References at the end of each chapter

Subject Index

A

Abortion, 53, 84, 90, 113, 118, 119, 121, 131, 132, 136, 137, 141, 145
Adoption, 67, 84, 142, 145-46
Advanced societies, 131-32
Africa, 40
Age,
    distribution, 5
    structure, 13, 46, 114
    at marriage, 7, 8, 10, 11, 109-12, 140, 160
Aged, care of, 168
Ageing effect, 5
Aggregate wealth, 10
Aggregation, xi, xxiii
Agricultural Act 1947, 18
Agricultural efficiency, 16, 27, 40, 41, 157
Albedo, 154, 156
Allbutt, Dr. H., 50
America, 40, 45, 48, 59, 78, 123-24, 136-37, 151, 153, 157, 158, 169
Animal produce, 15, 22, 36, 41
Asia, 41, 153
Atomic power, 44
Australia, 142, 144
Average family size, 7-13, 78, 80, 81, 99, 112, 114, 117, 119, 125, 133-34, 139, 140, 161, 171

B

Barlow Report, 167
Batteries (of animals), 22, 36, 41
Biological warfare, 155
Biomass, 95-96
Birth control, 9, 49-52, 67, 83-84, 99, 111-13, 118, 120-22, 124, 129, 131-34, 136-37, 141, 160-61, 167

Birth rate, xv, xvi, 4, 6, 46, 49-50, 54, 81, 89, 90, 95, 96, 100, 103, 107, 113-14, 117-19, 139, 141, 146
Birth ratio, 1, 4, 144, 174
Black Death, xi, 40
Bushmen, 143

C

Carbon dioxide, 156
Cannibalism, 91, 92, 129
Carrying capacity (of land), 15-42, 145, 157, 164, 169
Celibacy, 141, 148
Census, 3, 7, 8
Cervical smear, 56
Change, rate of, 6
Chemical run-off, 154
Child-bearing age, 7
Child labour, 10
Child spacing, 145
Children in care, 65
Chlorinated hydrocarbons, 156, 158, 163
Colonization (by man), 1
Corsica, 63
Commonwealth, 13
Communication, 64
Communication, 152, 158
Components of change, 3-5
Congenital defects, 55, 57, 92, 136
Conservation, 67, 74
Contraception, 9, 49-52, 67, 83-84, 99, 111-13, 118, 120-22, 124, 129, 131-34, 136-37, 141, 160-61, 167
Contrails, 157
Convergence, 13
Cost of children, 140
Crime, 65
Cronism, 91-93
Crop areas, 17, 26, 34, 35, 39, 47
Crop yields, 15, 22, 26-29, 32